Improving Maternal and Reproductive Health in South Asia

A WORLD BANK STUDY

Improving Maternal and Reproductive Health in South Asia

Drivers and Enablers

Sameh El-Saharty, Sadia Chowdhury, Naoko Ohno, and Intissar Sarker

1 2 3 4 19 18 17 16

ISBN (paper): 978-1-4648-0963-7
ISBN (electronic): 978-1-4648-0964-4
DOI: 10.1596/978-1-4648-0963-7

Cover illustration: © World Bank. Permission required for reuse.
Cover design: Debra Naylor, Naylor Designs

Library of Congress Cataloging-in-Publication Data has been requested.

Contents

http://dx.doi.org/10.1596/978-1-4648-0963-7

http://dx.doi.org/10.1596/978-1-4648-0963-7

Boxes

Figures

http://dx.doi.org/10.1596/978-1-4648-0963-7

Tables

http://dx.doi.org/10.1596/978-1-4648-0963-7

Foreword

Maternal death is much more than a personal crisis. It disrupts the health and well-being of surviving children, it often leads to family breakdown, and it amounts to a loss of economic opportunities. The consequences are interlinked and extensive, affecting multiple generations and triggering cycles of hardship in the communities where the death takes place.

In September 2000, the United Nations adopted the Millennium Development Goals (MDGs), setting out a series of time-bound targets with a deadline of 2015. A three-quarters reduction in the 1990 maternal mortality ratio, along with the achievement of universal access to reproductive health, were the two targets under MDG 5: Improve Maternal Health. Maternal survival has significantly improved since then. Globally, maternal deaths dropped by 45 percent between 1990 and 2013.

Among all world regions, South Asia has achieved the greatest progress, with the maternal mortality ratio falling by 65 percent during this period. The region has also benefited from robust economic growth, averaging 6 percent a year, which has contributed to impressive advancements in human development. Such achievement raises important questions. What made South Asia stand out? Was it just higher living standards, or were health policies and interventions central, too? And what would be needed to sustain the progress? These questions provided the impetus for this study.

Improving Maternal and Reproductive Health in South Asia: Drivers and Enablers identifies the interventions and factors that contributed to reducing the maternal mortality ratio and improving maternal and reproductive health outcomes in South Asia. Drivers are interventions at the health sector and program levels, as well as behavioral change interventions at the household level. Enablers are policies, strategies, and actions outside the health sector at the contextual, multisectoral, and community levels. The analysis in the study is based on a structured literature review of the interventions in South Asian countries, as well as the relevant international experience.

The findings in the study indicate that the most effective interventions to prevent maternal mortality are those that address the intra-partum stage—the point where most maternal deaths occur. These interventions include improving skilled birth attendance coverage, increasing institutional delivery rates, and scaling up access to emergency obstetric care. There is also evidence that investing in family planning helps, for the simple reason that it reduces the number of pregnancies. Other interventions have varying degrees of effectiveness.

Beyond concrete interventions, the level of household income, women's education, and completion of secondary education by girls are strongly correlated with improved maternal and reproductive health outcomes. And for given income and education levels, there is evidence that health-financing schemes—both demand and supply side—and conditional cash transfer programs increase the uptake of maternal and reproductive health services.

When putting the findings together, there are several major reasons why South Asia achieved so much progress. First was the governments' commitment to family planning and reproductive health, which benefitted from support by several donors. Second, nongovernmental organizations played a key role in experimenting interventions and contributing to their implementation. Third, many of the interventions were implemented simultaneously, with synergy increasing effectiveness.

Contextual factors, though less well-documented, qualify as an important fourth reason. The countries achieving the greatest progress in reducing their maternal mortality ratio, such as Bangladesh, Nepal, and Sri Lanka, have also progressed in an array of economic and social development indicators—beyond those specific to maternal and reproductive health. Poverty fell rapidly during this period, and growing labor force participation by women, together with their increased access to microfinance, may have strengthened their agency.

The evidence on "what works," synthesized in this study, should assist decision makers in adopting, implementing and scaling-up interventions to accelerate progress toward achieving the maternal reproductive health targets of the new Sustainable Development Goals.

Martin G. Rama
Chief Economist
South Asia Region
The World Bank

http://dx.doi.org/10.1596/978-1-4648-0963-7

Acknowledgments

This study was prepared by a team from the Health, Nutrition, and Population (HNP) Global Practice of the World Bank led by Sameh El-Saharty (Program Leader for human development and Lead Health Specialist), Sadia Chowdhury (Public Health Consultant), Naoko Ohno (Health Operations Officer), and Intissar Sarker (Research Analyst, Consultant).

The study was based on a series of country reports, case studies, and knowledge notes prepared by the South Asia Regional Reproductive Health focal points: Sayed Ghulam (Senior Health Specialist, Afghanistan); Bushra Binte Alam (Senior Health Specialist, Bangladesh); Somil Nagpal (Senior Health Specialist, Bhutan, Maldives, and India); Vikram Rajan (Senior Health Specialist, India); Patrick M. Mullen (Senior Health Specialist, India); Albertus Voetberg (then Lead Health Specialist, Nepal); Manav Bhattarai (Health Specialist, Nepal); Inaam ul Haq (Program Leader, Pakistan); Aliya Kashif (Health Specialist, Pakistan); and Kumari Vinodhani Navaratne (then Senior Health Specialist, Sri Lanka) with support from Federica Secci (then Young Professional).

The study benefitted from background technical reports. Laura Frost and Beth Anne Pratt, Global Health Insights, prepared "A Review of the Literature on Factors Contributing to the Reductions of Maternal Mortality in South Asia" and prepared a first draft of the study; a team composed of Mark Elsner, Senior Advisor, and Ram Mashru, Advisory Associate, from Oxford Analytica Research Group prepared "Drivers and Enablers of Maternal Mortality Reduction in India" and "Drivers and Enablers of Maternal Mortality Reduction in Nepal" in addition to contributing to the first draft of the study. Marcia Rock, Public Health Consultant, prepared an early draft of "Multisectoral Interventions to Improve Maternal and Reproductive Health Outcomes." Elizabeth McLeod, Senior Information Officer, Information and Technology Solutions, the World Bank, conducted the database search on maternal and reproductive health and on systematic reviews for the study. A team from the World Bank office in Chennai, composed of Vivek Kulbhushan Sharma (Knowledge Management Officer), Harsh Anuj (Knowledge Management Analyst), and Deivanai Arunachalam (Knowledge Management Analyst), prepared the data and charts for international comparisons as well as the infographics. Emiliana Gunawan, Martha Vargas, and Julie-Anne Graitge provided critical administrative assistance. The report was edited by Rosemarie Esber (Editor, Consultant).

The study was peer reviewed by Michele Gragnolati, Global Solutions Lead, Population and Development; Sameera Al-Tuwaijri, Advisor on Reproductive Health; Rafael Cortez, Senior Economist, from the HNP Global Practice; and Eeshani Kandpal, Research Economist, Development Economics, all of the World Bank. The team was guided by Julie McLaughlin (then Practice Manger, HNP, World Bank) and Rekha Menon (Practice Manager, HNP, World Bank).

The study was reviewed and discussed in a meeting chaired by Martin Rama, Chief Economist, South Asia Region of the World Bank, and useful comments and review were provided by Dhushyanth Raju, Senior Economist, Chief Economist Office, South Asia Region, World Bank. The study was finally published with the support of Abdia Mohamed and Cindy Fisher of the World Bank Formal Publishing Program.

The authors are grateful to the government of the Netherlands for its support through the Bank-Netherlands Partnership Program (BNPP) Trust Fund managed by the World Bank.

About the Authors

Sameh El-Saharty is Program Leader for human development and Lead Health Specialist at the World Bank. He also holds the position of Assistant Professor (*adjunct*) of international health at Georgetown University. Before joining the Bank, he held several positions and provided consultations to the United States Agency for International Development (USAID), the World Health Organization (WHO), the United Nations Population Fund (UNFPA), Pathfinder International Management Sciences for Health, Harvard University, and Clark Atlanta University. He has more than 30 years of experience working as a researcher, technical adviser, and international consultant on public health, health policy and management, health insurance, and health sector reform programs in more than 20 countries in the Middle East and North Africa (MENA), Africa, and South Asia regions, as well as in the United States. He authored, edited, and contributed to more than 30 publications ranging from books, book chapters, journal articles, policy notes, strategy papers, technical and analytical studies, and knowledge briefs. In addition to his work on maternal and reproductive health, his most recent work has focused on noncommunicable diseases (NCDs), health service delivery and implementation, and delivery science. He also functions as the Global Coordinator of NCDs for the World Bank Health, Nutrition and Population Global Practice. He is a member of the Harvard T.H. Chan School of Public Health Dean's Leadership Council and President of the School's Alumni Association, as well as a member of the Technical Advisory Committee of the MENA Health Policy Forum. He is a medical doctor graduated from the School of Medicine of Cairo University and holds a master of public health from the Military Medical Academy in Egypt and a master's degree in international health policy and management from Harvard University.

Sadia Chowdhury is an independent expert on women and children's health and nutrition, and health policy and management. She has more than 30 years of experience in health systems development and strengthening; reproductive, maternal, and child health; and nutrition. On joining the World Bank, she was first part of the South Asia Region, providing expertise and support for health, nutrition, population, and health-systems strengthening programs, projects, and initiatives throughout the region. In particular, she led the development of the World Bank's support for the National Reproductive and Child Health program in India, which enhanced state ownership and accountability for results; the program maintained a strong pro-poor focus and increased capacity to provide a comprehensive range of reproductive and child health services. She then joined the Human Development Vice Presidency as the lead for sexual and reproductive health, including maternal and child health, and she lead and coauthored the "Reproductive Health Action Plan (2010–2015)." She also managed analytical projects that evaluated needs and identified opportunities to build partnerships and drive innovation related to the supply and demand side of health services; researched fertility behavior in high-burden countries and its links with population and poverty; and coordinated initiatives with global partnerships, United Nations agencies, donors, and civil society. Most recently, she helped establish the BRAC Institute of Global Health, under BRAC University in Bangladesh, incorporating the University's James P. Grant School of Public Health and the Department of Midwifery and Nursing. She is a physician, graduating from Dhaka University; she holds a diploma in child health from the same university and a master's degree in international health policy and management from Harvard University.

Naoko Ohno is a Health Operations Officer in the Health Nutrition and Population (HNP) Global Practice of the World Bank. Since 2010, she has been working on the preparation and implementation of HNP projects in Bangladesh, India, Pakistan, and Sri Lanka. Prior to her current position, she worked in the World Bank's East Asia and Pacific Region, contributing to HNP analytical work, particularly for the Pacific Island Countries and Timor-Leste. Prior to joining the World Bank, she held a position at the Japan Bank for International Cooperation (currently JICA), where she worked on basic infrastructure projects in China and the Republic of Korea, which were financed through Japan's official development assistance. She holds a master's of health science in international health system management from the Bloomberg School of Public Health, Johns Hopkins University.

Intissar Sarker is a Research Analyst at the World Bank. Her research is focused on policy and strategy development for sexual, reproductive, maternal, newborn, and child health programs. She has contributed to several studies and knowledge briefs in the South Asia Region. She also has experience working in the Latin America and the Caribbean and Africa Regions. She holds a bachelor's degree in international studies from American University in the United States and a master's in gender, development, and globalization from the London School of Economics and Political Science.

Executive Summary

South Asia is home to 1.6 billion people across eight countries: Afghanistan, Bangladesh, Bhutan, India, Maldives, Nepal, Pakistan, and Sri Lanka. It is the most densely populated region in the world and 42 percent of the developing world's poor inhabit South Asia. Despite significant progress in providing basic education, on average only 62 percent of young women in the South Asia Region (SAR) are literate compared with 77 percent of young men. One-fifth of the population is between the ages of 15 and 24 and 50 percent of young adults are unemployed (World Bank 2014b).

Among all regions worldwide, SAR has made the greatest progress in decreasing maternal mortality rates between 1990 and 2013 by 65 percent with an average annual decline of 4.4 percent. The Maternal Mortality Ratio (MMR) declined from 550 deaths per 100,000 live births in 1990 to 190 in 2013. The use of skilled birth attendants (SBAs) has increased from 36.2 percent in 2000 to 49.8 percent in 2010. The total fertility rate (TFR) declined from 4.2 in 1990 to 2.6 in 2012, and the region is close to reaching replacement fertility. The average contraceptive prevalence rate (CPR) increased from 41.3 percent to 52.3 percent between 1990 and 2010. This progress has been enabled by successful policies and strategies related to maternal and reproductive health (MRH). Advancements were supported by macroeconomic growth, averaging 6 percent a year, which has significantly funded advancements in human development (El-Saharty et al. 2014). Such achievements implore the question, "What are the factors and interventions that led to this relative sharp MMR decline in SAR against what is predicted by standard socioeconomic outcomes?"

The objective of this study is to identify the interventions and factors that contributed to reducing MMR and improving MRH outcomes in SAR. The analysis will be based on a structured literature review of the SAR countries, relevant international experience, and review of the best available evidence from systematic reviews. The target audience is policymakers and managers of MRH programs in the region and elsewhere. The focus of the analysis is mainly on assessing the "effectiveness" of interventions and, to the possible extent, the effectiveness of interventions in improving MRH outcomes on different sub-populations, which reflects the "equity" dimension of the intervention. The evidence was assessed based on the number of systematic reviews, the number of studies, and countries in which an intervention was implemented. However, the quality of the individual studies, including the endogeneity bias and the heterogeneity of effect, were not assessed. The average effect size of an intervention was reported, whenever available, based on meta-analyses performed in the systematic reviews.

Drivers and Enablers for Improving Maternal and Reproductive Health

Improving maternal health outcomes requires strategic efforts that address internal and external forces affecting the health system. The analytical framework for this study integrates several frameworks and focuses on "interventions" that contributed the most to improved MRH outcomes in South Asia. The "drivers" are interventions at the health sector and MRH program levels, as well as behavioral change interventions at the household level. The "enablers" are policies, strategies, and actions outside the health sector, for example, contextual, multisectoral, and community levels. The group nearest to the outcome—the household level in this case—will have the greatest impact on MRH outcomes and the farthest group, the least impact. The framework provides a practical way of examining the above factors and interventions while intrinsically entailing some overlap that we tried to minimize or clarify to the extent possible. However, the variations in the use of terms for the same programs made it difficult to consistently avoid such an overlap.

Drivers

Household Drivers

Women's education and household income are strong predictors and key drivers correlated with maternal mortality reduction and health service use in SAR. Completion of secondary education is a particularly strong predictor of women's use of antenatal care (ANC), SBAs, and facility delivery in SAR. In Bangladesh, for example, improving the education level of women of reproductive age is one of the key contributors to MMR reduction (Das 2008; El Arifeen et al. 2014). Throughout Bangladesh, women with some education were substantially more likely to use ANC and SBAs than women without education (Munsur, Atia, and Kawahara 2010). Improved household economic status has contributed to Bangladesh's success in reducing the MMR, which in part is because wealthier households are willing and able to pay for private sector maternity services (El Arifeen et al. 2014).

The role of husbands in household decision-making is often an important factor in their wives' access to maternal health services. In the SAR countries where interventions have prioritized male participation, men's involvement has improved ANC and postnatal clinic attendance, births attended by SBAs, and interest in family planning and pregnancy outcomes (Hou and Ma 2013). There is some evidence that suggests that male involvement was significantly associated with reduced odds of postpartum depression and with improved use of SBA and postnatal care (Yargawa and Leonardi-Bee 2015).

http://dx.doi.org/10.1596/978-1-4648-0963-7

Access to information is linked with increased MRH service use. SAR countries have conducted community-level and mass media information, education, and communication (IEC)/behavior change communication (BCC) campaigns to increase knowledge, change attitudes, and stimulate demand for MRH services but evidence about their impact is insufficient.

Program Drivers

Programmatic interventions focused on improving SBA coverage, increasing institutional delivery, and scaling up access to emergency obstetric care (EmOC) have all had a direct impact on reducing maternal mortality in the SAR countries. In Sri Lanka, the increase of skilled birth attendance since 1950 was closely linked to reduction of maternal mortality by 50 percent every 8–13 years and the country virtually eliminated maternal deaths from sepsis and hypertension (Pathmanathan et al. 2003). Afghanistan, through the Community Midwife Education (CME) program, increased the use of SBAs, which contributed to 80 percent reduction in the country's MMR (Currie, Azfar, and Fowler 2007; Rasooly et al. 2014). A systematic review of SBA programs found that SBA was associated with significant reduction of maternal mortality (Berhan and Berhan 2014a). The evidence of the impact of SBA on maternal mortality is considered moderate. There is also strong evidence of the effectiveness of institutional delivery on reducing maternal mortality. In Bangladesh, the percentage of women using institutional delivery increased from 5–29 percent between 1996 and 2011, which contributed to the country's maternal morality reduction (Hotchkiss, Godha, and Do 2014). Also, EmOC initiatives were key to reducing maternal mortality. Nepal has made great strides in ensuring training for and coverage of EmOC since 2002 and the met need for EmOC grew by 2–3 percent per year (Bhandari, Gordon, and Shakya 2011). Bangladesh has implemented a comprehensive EmOC program since the 1990s and gained momentum during the 2001. By 2008, the number of facilities able to provide EmOC had expanded and the MMR was reduced by more than 50 percent since 2000 (El Arifeen et al. 2014; WHO 2014). India has prioritized EmOC since 2005 and the MMR has subsequently dropped from 280 in 2005 to 190 per 100,000 births in 2013 (Vora et al. 2009; Maternal Mortality Estimation Inter-Agency Group 2014). A systematic review found that there is strong evidence that EmOC has significantly contributed to maternal mortality reduction (Holmer et al. 2015). Rollout of EmOC, SBAs, institutional delivery, and other maternal health services with the aim of reducing MMR are frequently accompanied by supportive interventions that facilitate access.

Access to safe abortion services and post-abortion care have been correlated with maternal mortality reduction in some countries. Such services can prevent deaths from unsafe abortion and its subsequent complications (Bhandari, Gordon, and Shakya 2011; Padmanaban, Raman, and Mavalankar 2009). In 2002, Nepal legalized abortion and by 2010, more than 400,000 women made use of the service (Samandari et al. 2012). During this period, Nepal also achieved large reductions in maternal mortality (Bhandari, Gordon, and

http://dx.doi.org/10.1596/978-1-4648-0963-7

Shakya 2011; Padmanaban, Raman, and Mavalankar 2009). In India, a 2001–2003 survey found that the number of maternal deaths due to unsafe abortions declined from 11.5 percent in 1985 to 8 percent in 2001 (Registrar General of India and Centre for Global Health Research 2006). In Bangladesh, through its Menstrual Regulation (MR) program, unsafe abortions declined from 15 percent of maternal deaths in the mid-1980s to 1 percent in 2010 (Vlassoff et al. 2012).

Family planning programs, while not directly affecting maternal mortality outcomes at the intra-partum stage, played an important role in the inter-partum stage that contributed to maternal mortality reduction in the SAR countries. One study estimated that fertility decline caused 39 percent of the decline in MMR in Bangladesh, 32 percent in India, and 22 percent in Pakistan (Jain 2011). Interestingly, these are the three countries that are responsible for most of the maternal death decline in SAR between 1990 and 2013. In an analysis of 172 countries, contraceptive use was found to have averted 44 percent of maternal deaths worldwide in 2008 (Ahmed et al. 2012).

SAR countries that have successfully reduced their maternal mortality frequently cite increased access to ANC as an important correlate; however, the evidence of the impact of ANC on reducing maternal mortality is limited. Over the last decades, SAR countries have significantly increased ANC coverage to 73.7 percent in 2011 in Nepal, 95.9 percent in 2006 in Tamil Nadu, India, 68 percent in 2009–2010 in Afghanistan, 93 percent in Sri Lanka, and 71 percent in 2010 in Bangladesh (Hussein et al. 2011; Koblinsky et al. 2008; Padmanaban, Raman, and Mavalankar 2009; Rasooly et al. 2014; Senanayake et al. 2011). Despite the consensus from different studies in favor of ANC, reservations about the extent of its true effectiveness remain unknown (Carroli, Rooney, and Villar 2001).

Health Sector Drivers

Women's access to and use of MRH services depend on broader health system inputs.

Health care financing. The percentage of general government spending on health among SAR countries —as a proportion of total government spending— is below the global average in most instances and out-of-pocket spending is high; however, these were not associated with MMR. Countries in SAR that have attempted to remove user fees for MRH services to reduce the financial barriers to usage have had mixed success improving service uptake (Witter et al. 2000). In Sri Lanka, the removal of financial barriers to health care is noted as a fundamental contributory factor to reducing its MMR (Pathmanathan et al. 2003). A systematic review found that the removal of user fees provided some evidence of an increase in facility delivery (Dzakpasu, Powell-Jackson, and Campbell 2014). SAR countries have used various health financing schemes to increase uptake of MRH services with considerable success, such as the Dr. Muthulakshmi Reddy Memorial Maternity Assistance Scheme in

http://dx.doi.org/10.1596/978-1-4648-0963-7

Tamil Nadu, India; India's *Janani Suraksha Yojana* (JSY); Nepal's Safe Delivery Incentives Program (SDIP); Bangladesh's Demand Side Financing Maternal Health Voucher Scheme; Pakistan's pay for performance (P4P) program; and Afghanistan's "Performance-based partnership" (Bashir et al. 2009; Benderly 2010; Hanson and Powell-Jackson 2010; Nguyen et al. 2012; Padmanaban, Raman, and Mavalankar 2009; Randive, Diwan, and De Costa 2013; Saadat et al. 2014). There is strong evidence of the impact of health financing schemes on the use of MRH services, as concluded by several systematic reviews (Glassman, Duran, and Koblinsky 2013; Gopalan et al. 2014; Murray et al. 2014; Nwolise et al. 2015). Community-based health insurance schemes were implemented in India and were associated with increased use of health services, including those for pregnant women (Aggarwal 2010; Devadasan et al. 2010).

Health service delivery. Many SAR countries have attempted to ensure that MRH is a priority by creating specialized administrative, service delivery, or programmatic streams within government ministries with an emphasis on maternal and/or reproductive health. Though large numbers of nonpublic organizations are involved in health care delivery in SAR, they do not fill the gap left by inadequate government health systems.

Human resources. National and regional Ministries of Health in some SAR countries have succeeded in professionalizing the maternal health workforce and hiring and training increasing numbers of health providers but the evidence of the impact of training of health workers on maternal health is mixed. Still, a number of SAR countries struggle to ensure that investment in human resources translates into usage. To address this challenge, some countries have used semiskilled volunteers and community workers to partially make up for the shortage of skilled health professionals.

Essential drugs and commodities. The supply chain for drugs and other medical commodities, including those for MRH services, is a vital component (Wilson et al. 2012). In 2013, the leading causes of maternal mortality in SAR countries included maternal hemorrhage, hypertension, and sepsis, all conditions treatable with essential obstetric medicines (Kassebaum et al. 2014). SAR countries attempted to prioritize the delivery of key MRH commodities as part of their programmatic interventions such as in Afghanistan (Kim et al. 2013).

Health information systems. A national information system is another critical pillar of the national health system. Many countries do not have a centralized means to register births or deaths. Therefore, MMR is frequently calculated using modeling. A number of SAR countries have attempted to improve their information systems through reproductive, maternal, newborn, and child health (RMNCH) programs such as in Tamil Nadu in India (Padmanaban, Raman, and Mavalankar 2009).

Improving Maternal and Reproductive Health in South Asia
http://dx.doi.org/10.1596/978-1-4648-0963-7

Enablers

Community Enablers

Deploying female community health workers recruited from and working in the community was successful in providing frontline services to the remote and underprivileged in SAR countries. Pakistan's Lady Health Worker (LHW) Program has deployed over 100,000 LHWs, covering 60 percent of the rural population as of 2013, and trained 5,400 community midwives (CMWs) by 2012 (Bhutta et al. 2013; Malik and Kayan 2014; Middleton et al. 2012). Under the Accredited Social Health Activist (ASHA) program, India deployed 820,000 ASHA volunteers by 2013 (Gopalan, Mohanty, and Das 2012). Nepal also deployed 48,000 female community health volunteers (FCHVs) and this was linked to increases in iron supplementation and postpartum vitamin A distribution and breastfeeding and has contributed to maternal mortality reductions (Government of Nepal 2007; Karkee 2011; Schwarz et al. 2014; USAID 2007). SAR countries have also trained and deployed community-based skilled birth attendant (CSBA) but with mixed results.

In SAR countries, community-based interventions have been implemented to mobilize and empower communities to use MRH services and improve their outcomes. In Nepal's Makwanpur District, a women's group intervention was implemented to reduce maternal and neonatal mortality (Condo et al. 2014). A similar program was implemented in the Hala and Matiari subdistricts of Pakistan (Bhutta et al. 2008). Participatory women's groups were also used in Jharkhand and Orissa, India, to improve home-care practices and health-seeking behavior of pregnant and postnatal women (Tripathy et al. 2010). The interventions in Pakistan and India showed a significant effect on neonatal mortality but did not include enough women to sufficiently study the effect on the MMR (Bhutta and Lassi 2010). Several systematic reviews found evidence suggesting that community-level interventions can reduce maternal mortality and that benefits may extend across the continuum of care (Gilmore and McAuliffe 2013; Kidney et al. 2009; Lassi and Bhutta 2015; Piane 2009; Piane et al. 2014). However, most of these interventions were implemented on a small to medium scale and had various definitions of "community-based interventions." A clearer definition and more evidence to assess the impact of scaling up of these interventions are therefore needed (Lassi and Bhutta 2015; Lassi et al. 2013; Marston et al. 2013; Prost et al. 2013).

Multisectoral Enablers

Education, particularly completion of secondary education, is a strong predictor of women's usage of ANC, skilled birth attendance, and facility delivery and has been a key non-health factor in the reduction of maternal mortality in SAR countries. In Nepal, women's education has been cited as a contributing factor to maternal mortality reductions (Barker et al. 2007a; Bhandari, Gordon, and Shakya 2011). In India, the improvement in maternal mortality since 1990 is in part due to the country's progress in overall development, including education (Rai and Tulchinsky 2015). In Bangladesh, the secondary education of mothers has been credited as "the major driver of reductions in fertility and child malnutrition in Bangladesh" (El Arifeen et al. 2014). A higher level of education—secondary or more years of schooling—is linked with an increase in the age at which a woman marries and has children (Caldwell 2005). Female education has been associated with MMR in global-level studies, which have also showed that lower levels of maternal education are associated with higher mortality rates (McAlister and Baskett 2006; Saffron et al. 2011).

Improvements to rural road and communication networks have led to higher demand for and uptake of maternal and general health services in SAR. In Bangladesh, dirt roads, paved roads, and bridges were extensively constructed between 2001 and 2010, greatly improving access to health facilities, and two rural road projects led to a significant increase in demand for health services particularly for women (Bangladesh Institute of Development Studies 2009; El Arifeen et al. 2014; World Bank 2013b). Transportation linkages are crucial to women's ability to access maternal health services and health care more generally throughout SAR (Babinard and Roberts 2006). Between 2000 and 2010, Bangladesh also increased mobile phone subscriptions, with two out of every three households owning a mobile phone (El Arifeen et al. 2014). During this same period, Bangladesh's MMR dropped from 322 to 194 deaths per 100,000 live births, a decline attributed to greatly improved access to maternity services facilitated by changes within the health and non-health sectors, including communications (El Arifeen et al. 2014). Likewise, in Afghanistan and Sri Lanka, improvements in communications infrastructure as well as access to transportation have been linked to maternal mortality reductions (Rasooly et al. 2014).

Water and sanitation are likely enablers of maternal survival in SAR and globally, though data on the linkages between water and sanitation and maternal health and MMR is limited. Between 1990 and 2011, Bangladesh improved access to improved water sources and sanitation facilities, particularly in rural areas (UNESCO 2014; World Bank 2013a). These improvements occurred at the same time that Bangladesh was reducing its MMR, but it is unclear how exactly these water and sanitation initiatives may have contributed to MMR declines. A systematic review called for closer collaboration between the water and sanitation and maternal health sectors and more research on which specific causes of maternal mortality are associated with poor water and sanitation (Benova, Cumming, and Campbell 2014).

Efforts to improve nutrition for women of childbearing age and pregnant women have seen successes and challenges in SAR countries. Between 1998 and 2006, Nepal reduced anemia among women of reproductive age by almost half, as well as improved overall maternal micronutrient status (Bhandari, Gordon, and Shakya 2011). A study in 2011 found that the percentage of anemic mothers could account for 10 percent of the district variation in maternal mortality (Hussein et al. 2011). Bangladesh introduced several national programs aimed at improving maternal, infant, and young child nutrition and managed to reduce the percentage of women with a low body-mass index (El Arifeen et al. 2014; Faguet 2007; Government of the People's Republic of

Bangladesh 2014). Tamil Nadu, India, had a program to support improved nutrition among poor women and, especially, prevent anemia; however, there was almost no reduction in maternal anemia. This suggests that targeted micronutrient support without a concomitant multisectoral effort to improve household food security and nutritional status may not be sufficient (Padmanaban, Raman, and Mavalankar 2009).

Household electricity has been linked to greater knowledge of public health issues and uptake of maternal health and family planning services in SAR countries. A study in India found that approximately 62 percent of primary health centers (PHCs) had a regular supply of electricity and that access to electricity was significantly associated with an increased volume of services (Kumar and Dansereau 2014). In Bangladesh, households with electricity were more likely to use medically trained personnel for delivery, use ANC and postnatal care, and seek treatment for maternal morbidity than nonelectrified households. Similarly, contraceptive use was higher among married women in electrified households (Barkat et al. 2002).

Conditional cash transfer (CCT) programs that provide cash payments conditional on the use of some merit goods, services, or behaviors that are not limited to the health sector can have a strong effect on use of MRH services. In Bangladesh, the Secondary School Assistance Program provided tuition and stipends to girls to attend secondary school and as a result, enrollment tripled between 1991 and 2005 (World Bank 2009). An impact study of the program found that it has led to an increased age of marriage of 1.4–2.3 years (Hong and Sarr 2012). A similar program in Pakistan was evaluated and the girls exposed to the program were more likely to marry 1.2–1.5 years later and have 0.3 fewer children (IEG 2011). Several systematic reviews have shown that CCTs have an impact on the use of maternity services such antenatal visits, skilled attendance at birth, delivery at a health facility, and tetanus toxoid vaccination, but there was little evidence of impact on maternal mortality or morbidity (Glassman, Duran, and Koblinsky 2013; Murray et al. 2014).

Microcredit programs are often multisectoral in nature as they contribute to household income and women's empowerment and have shown positive impact on contraceptive use. Microcredit programs often target women and play a key role in creating economic opportunities and helping women lift their families out of poverty. Studies have found that microcredit in Bangladesh reduces poverty and increases household consumption, spousal communication and bargaining power, decision-making, and mobility and has a significant positive effect on the levels of contraceptive use (Khandker 2005; Pitt, Khandker, and Cartwright 2003; Schuler, Hashemi, and Riley 1997). Though the literature does not establish a direct causal relationship between microcredit and the use of MRH services or maternal mortality reduction, it does suggest four possible pathways: financing care in the event of health emergencies; financing health inputs such as improved nutrition; as a platform for health education; and by increasing social capital through group meetings and mutual support (Schurmann and Johnston 2007).

Contextual Enablers

Contextual factors in countries can enable or limit the overall impact of health systems and program drivers of MRH. Political, economic, demographic, and sociocultural enablers can contribute or impede maternal mortality reductions in SAR countries and elsewhere. Contextual enablers are influenced primarily at high decision-making levels, often beyond the control of women and their families. They vary significantly across and within countries and require sustained attention to improve maternal mortality rates.

Maternal mortality rates in a number of SAR countries are affected by the political context where health systems are operating and where MRH interventions are implemented. In Pakistan, crisis with governance, proper allocation of funds to rural medical facilities, and the lack of strong political will to implement programs have all been cited as barriers to attaining maternal mortality goals (Bhutta et al. 2013; Mahmud et al. 2011; Malik and Kayan 2014). Political prioritization of MRH is a key factor in reducing maternal mortality in SAR countries. Nepal formulated its National Safe Motherhood Plan in 1987, following the Nairobi Conference of Safe Motherhood (Karkee 2011). The program has received substantial support from international development partners and has delivered significant achievements. The MMR fell from 539 deaths per 100,000 live births in 1997 to 281 in 2006.

Reductions in maternal mortality have occurred concomitantly with economic growth in some SAR countries. Bhutan's MMR dropped from 900 deaths per 100,000 live births in 1990 to 120 in 2013, while its economy was growing, driven by hydropower, manufacturing, and domestic services. In Brazil, economic growth has been an enabling factor in the country's progress on maternal mortality by contributing to declining poverty rates and income inequality (Barros et al. 2010; Victora et al. 2011). Countries with low MMR have higher gross domestic product (GDP) per capita (Adam and Franz-Vasdeki 2012).

In many SAR countries, fertility rates were declining while MMRs were also falling. In Afghanistan, decreases in the MMR occurred at the same time as a decline in the TFR, from 6.3 in 2003 to 5.1 in 2010 (Rasooly et al. 2014). The major contributing factors in this reduction were the use of contraceptive methods and age at marriage, both of which were increasing in the same period (Rasooly et al. 2014).

Cultural barriers in SAR impede marginalized women's demand for MRH services and are obstacles to further progress on reducing maternal mortality. In India, for MRH in particular, studies show that the caste system functions as a barrier to usage of reproductive health services and members of low-caste groups have poorer maternal health outcomes (Sanneving et al. 2013). Gender hierarchies persist in many SAR countries, with men often making decisions about the health care of their wives. In Bhutan, there is greater gender equality, which has contributed to improved MRH outcomes and enabled maternal mortality reductions.

http://dx.doi.org/10.1596/978-1-4648-0963-7

What Worked and the Way Forward

This study has shown that MRH outcomes in the SAR are affected by an array of drivers and enablers. The most effective interventions that prevent maternal mortality are those that address the intra-partum stage—the point where most maternal deaths occur—and include improving skilled birth attendance coverage, increasing institutional delivery rates, and scaling up access to EmOC. This accords with the fact that 38 percent of maternal mortality causes are due to maternal hemorrhage, maternal sepsis, maternal hypertensive disorders and obstructed labor and can be mainly addressed by these interventions. There is also adequate evidence that investing in family planning to increase contraceptive use also played a key role during the inter-partum phase by preventing unwanted pregnancies and thus averting the risk of maternal mortality in SAR countries. Two other interventions were correlated with maternal mortality reduction in some SAR countries: increased access to safe abortion and post-abortion services as well as ANC; however, the evidence that supports their effect is limited. Outside the programmatic interventions, the levels of household income and women's education within the household were key drivers of maternal mortality reduction and the increased uptake of MRH services. Related to women's education within the household, completion of secondary education of girls, an education sector intervention, was also strongly correlated with improved MRH outcomes. There is strong evidence that health financing schemes—both demand and supply side—and CCT programs were effective in increasing the uptake of MRH services in SAR countries and other regions. SAR countries have implemented several other interventions such as male engagement in MRH interventions that may have contributed to increased use of MRH services but the evidence of their impact is limited. It is important to note, however, that some of these interventions were not primarily intended to increase uptake of MRH services but had broader objectives such as training of health providers, removal of user fees, and expanding health insurance as well as community-based interventions and microcredit programs. Moving forward, MRH program managers should establish more linkages and harness the benefits of these interventions.

When examining drivers of change, what becomes most apparent is that very few of the factors examined are mutually exclusive. Success often appears to depend less on rolling out discrete "interventions" than on building entire systems for managing both maternal health and health more generally. The story is really one of simultaneous investment in systems, not just interventions (Frost and Pratt 2014). This finding accords with evidence emerging from systematic and narrative reviews of MRH interventions in low- and middle-income countries (LMICs), emphasizing that **"no magic bullet intervention"** exists for the reduction of maternal mortality, that clinical interventions are not sufficient, and that a comprehensive approach dependent on the context and the determinants of MRH in a setting is needed (Nyamtema, Urassa, and van Roosmalen 2011; Pucher, Macdonnell, and Arulkumaran 2013; and Ross et al. 2005). This finding

http://dx.doi.org/10.1596/978-1-4648-0963-7

points the way toward a broader understanding of how to more effectively address and finance MRH programs in the future.

More evidence, however, is needed in several areas. The cases and papers reviewed for this study point to the fact that there is rarely any discussion of true multisectoral interventions but rather discussions about health sector initiatives and initiatives outside the health sector that likely had the add-on benefit of improving MRH outcomes. However, in no instances did the literature suggest true multisectoral action. In addition, the literature on South Asia and worldwide is silent on the nutrition interventions that contribute to improved MRH outcomes. Similarly, there is lack of documentation on the role of the contextual factors as enablers for improving MRH outcomes. The papers reviewed for this study more frequently demonstrate those factors to be "disabling" to MRH outcomes. There is also lack of information on the cost and cost-effectiveness even for the effective interventions but this may be a limitation of this study. Finally, there is a critical gap in the literature regarding the lack of evidence on interventions that reduce inequity in maternal mortality and limited evidence on improved equity in other MRH outcomes. Even when interventions "enable" positive change for maternal health, they rarely do so consistently throughout a country, since rarely do all regions, ethnic groups, and wealth strata benefit equally from the political, economic, and sociocultural factors. A systematic review of effective interventions to reduce inequalities in maternal and child health (MCH) in LMICs did not find any studies looking at equity in maternal mortality. However, there was limited evidence showing that the interventions that were effective in reducing inequity included the improvement of health care delivery by outreach methods, using human resources in local areas or provided at the community level nearest to residents and the provision of financial or knowledge support to demand side (Yuan et al. 2014).

There are several factors that may have made SAR stand out. First, government commitment to family planning and reproductive health was strong. Governments in India, Bangladesh, and Pakistan—the countries that had the highest decline in maternal mortality in SAR—were committed to population control and later to more comprehensive MRH and child health programs, which were supported by several donors. Also, these programs were always a nonpartisan issue and largely politically secular. Second, while the government commitment was necessary, it was not sufficient and the nongovernmental organizations (NGOs) played a key role in complementing the government's commitment to improved MRH outcomes, particularly in the family planning programs and, to a certain extent, later in the MRH programs. Both Bangladesh and Pakistan provide examples on the NGOs' role in service delivery and their role in India has been active in making the public service providers more accountable. Third, SAR implemented many of these interventions simultaneously; thus, there was an increased synergy and effectiveness, which accords with the findings from a systematic review of 54 programs integrating multiple interventions in 23 LMICs, where interventions in SAR had a higher impact on maternal mortality compared to the other LMICs in the study

http://dx.doi.org/10.1596/978-1-4648-0963-7

(Nyamtema et al. 2011). In addition to implementing a comprehensive package of services, SAR has been a center of innovative interventions such as oral rehydration salt therapy, community-based distribution, and microcredit. Fourth, the contextual factors, even though not well documented, may have played a critical role in improving MRH outcomes in SAR. For instance, the countries achieving the most dramatic progress in reducing their MMR, such as Nepal, Bangladesh, and Sri Lanka, have also progressed in an array of economic and social development indicators—beyond those specific to MRH. Some countries, such as Nepal, Bangladesh, and Sri Lanka, have been more successful than others in reducing their MMR. This is partly due to the fact that in all three countries, health and non-health sector factors have played a role in contributing to maternal mortality reduction and improved MRH outcomes (Frost and Pratt 2015). For example, poverty reduction in SAR was 63 percent between 1990 and 2013 and may have played a role particularly in the microfinance programs started in SAR and these have contributed to women's empowerment and increased household income levels among the poor.

As the global community is moving toward implementing the new Sustainable Development Goals (SDGs), securing adequate funding for MRH will become increasingly challenging for several reasons. First, only two of the 169 SDG targets are related to MRH, including reducing the MMR and increasing access to sexual and reproductive health services. Therefore, governments will struggle to mobilize resources among different competing sectors and targets at the national level. Second, most donor countries are facing an uphill challenge to recover from the recent global economic crisis, which will greatly affect the financial and technical resources that they can make available to support the global development agenda. Third, countries in SAR, such as India and Bangladesh, have experienced significant economic growth in recent years. They may therefore soon achieve middle-income status with the risk of losing access to donor grants and concessional financing.

A confluence of interrelated factors requires the judicious use of available and potential financial and technical resources in support of MRH programs. First and foremost, it will require the use of "available" evidence, knowledge, and data about proven interventions to design effective MRH programs at the outset. Given the limited evidence on what mix of interventions works and how they work to improve MRH in LMICS, it is imperative to generate new evidence and knowledge to improve the effectiveness and efficiency of policies, programs, and interventions within real-world settings to improve MRH outcomes in SAR and worldwide. The "Implementation Research and Delivery Science" initiative—supported by the World Health Organization (WHO), U.S. Agency for International Development (USAID), and the World Bank—is a platform that calls for embedding research within the process of implementation that should be led by policymakers or program implementers, address multiple barriers to implementation, engage different stakeholders, use a multidisciplinary approach, and support a culture of continuous learning and adaptation. Because no one intervention alone will increase the effectiveness of MRH programs, it is essential to develop a mix of synergistic interventions in the health and non-health sector to accelerate progress toward achieving the MRH targets of the new global sustainable development agenda.

Improving Maternal and Reproductive Health in South Asia
http://dx.doi.org/10.1596/978-1-4648-0963-7

Abbreviations

ACU	Accelerating Contraceptive Use
AHPSR	Alliance for Health Policy and Systems Research
ANC	antenatal care
ANM	auxiliary nurse midwife
ASHA	accredited social health activist
BCC	behavior change communication
BHU	basic health unit
BINP	Bangladesh Integrated Nutrition Programme
CCT	conditional cash transfer
CHW	community health worker
CME	Community Midwife Education
CMW	community midwife
CPR	contraceptive prevalence rate
CSBA	community-based skilled birth attendant
DfID	U.K. Department for International Development
DGFP	Directorate General of Family Planning
DGHS	Directorate General of Health Services
DHS	Demographic and Health Survey
DLHS	District Level Health Survey
DSF	demand-side financing
EmOC	emergency obstetric care
FCHV	female community health volunteer
FSSP	Female School Stipend Program
GDP	gross domestic product
GK	*Gonoshasthaya Kendra*
GVK-EMRI	GVK-Emergency Management and Research Institute
HEW	health extension worker
HPSP	Health and Population Sector Program
HRH	Human Resources for Health
IEC	information, education, and communication

IHP+	International Health Partnership
JSY	*Janani Suraksha Yojana*
LHW	lady health worker
LMICs	low- and middle-income countries
MAMaZ	Maternal Health Services in Zambia
MCH	maternal and child health
MDG	Millennium Development Goal
MeSH	Medical Subject Headings
MMR	maternal mortality ratio
MNCH	maternal, newborn, and child health
MOHFW	Ministry of Health and Family Welfare
MOHP	Ministry of Health and Population
MR	menstrual regulation
MRH	maternal and reproductive health
NGO	nongovernmental organization
NRHM	National Rural Health Mission
OR	odds ratio
PBF	performance-based financing
PHC	primary health center
PHM	public health midwife
PMNCH	Partnership for Maternal, Newborn, and Child Health
PPH	postpartum hemorrhage
P4P	pay for performance
RBF	results-based financing
RCH	reproductive and child health
RMNCH	reproductive, maternal, newborn, and child health
SAR	South Asia Region
SBA	skilled birth attendant
SDG	Sustainable Development Goal
SDIP	Safe Delivery Incentives Program
TBA	traditional birth attendant
TFR	total fertility rate
UN	United Nations
UNESCO	United Nations Educational, Scientific, and Cultural Organization
UNFPA	United Nations Population Fund
UNICEF	United Nations Children's Fund
USAID	U.S. Agency for International Development
WDI	World Development Indicator
WHO	World Health Organization

CHAPTER 1

Introduction

As the international community celebrates the achievement of many of the 2015 Millennium Development Goals (MDGs), it is launching a new set of Sustainable Development Goal (SDGs). To increase the effectiveness of global development programs, it is critical during this period of transition to examine the overall progress toward the MDGs and analyze the factors that contributed to their achievements to guide the implementation of effective interventions toward achieving the SDGs.

Globally, progress on the health-related MDGs has been mixed. While child mortality, MDG 4, has rapidly reduced, progress has been slow for maternal mortality, MDG 5. Nonetheless, maternal mortality has dropped dramatically since 1990. Worldwide, there were an estimated 289,000 maternal deaths in 2013—a 45 percent reduction from 1990 (WHO, UNICEF, UNFPA, the World Bank, and the UN 2014). Globally, the maternal mortality ratio (MMR) has reduced between 1990 and 2013, from 380 to 210 maternal deaths per 100,000 live births. Despite these impressive improvements, progress has been uneven, and maternal mortality rates remain high in many Low- and Middle-Income Countries (LMICs). Two regions account for the majority of annual maternal deaths—Sub-Saharan Africa accounts for 62 percent (179,000) and South Asia accounts for 24 percent (69,000). Even so, South Asia Region (SAR) has had the world's highest decline in maternal mortality of 65 percent since 1990, ahead of all other regions with an average annual decline of 4.4 percent. The MMR in SAR declined from 550 deaths per 100,000 live births in 1990 to 190 in 2013. This progress has been enabled by successful policies and strategies related to MRH. Advancements were supported by macroeconomic growth, averaging 6 percent a year, which has significantly funded advancements in human development (El-Saharty et al. 2014). However, such an achievement implores the question "What are the factors and interventions that led to this relative sharp MMR decline in SAR against what is predicted by standard socioeconomic outcomes?"

The objective of this study is to answer this question and identify through an analysis "what worked" in terms of factors and interventions that contributed to improving MRH outcomes in SAR based on a structured literature review of the

SAR countries, relevant international experience, and review of the best available evidence from systematic reviews. The target audience is policymakers and managers of MRH programs in SAR and elsewhere.

The Analytical Framework: Drivers and Enablers for Improving Maternal and Reproductive Health Outcomes

Several frameworks have been developed to relate maternal mortality and other MRH outcomes to different causes and factors. The analytical framework used for this study integrates several elements from such frameworks, namely Three Delay Model (Thaddeus and Maine 1994); Ecological Model (McLeroy et al. 1988); five health system control knobs (Roberts et al. 2004); Pathways to Improved Maternal Health Outcomes (Claeson et al. 2001); "UNICEF's Conceptual framework for maternal and neonatal mortality and morbidity"; and "U.K.'s Framework for Results for improving reproductive, maternal and newborn health in the developing world." A detailed description of these frameworks is provided in appendix A.

The causes of maternal mortality may be organized into six concentric spheres that indicate the constraints interacting with girls' and women's lives and health (figure 1.1). The outer sphere represents the country context, which includes

Figure 1.1 Concentric Spheres of Constraints that Cause Maternal Mortality

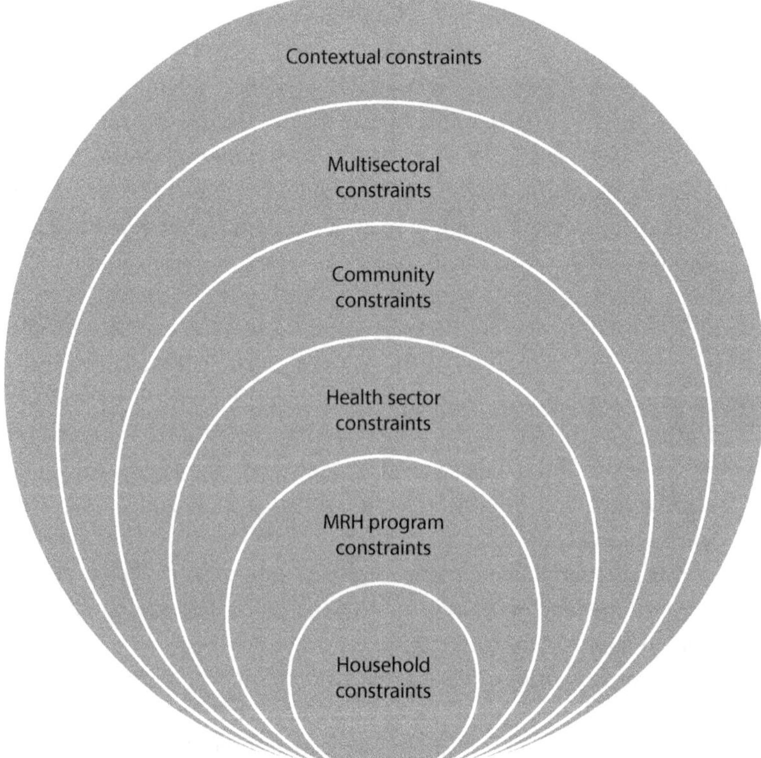

http://dx.doi.org/10.1596/978-1-4648-0963-7

governance, political stability, economic growth, social development, demography, culture, and values. The next is related to the different constraints in the non-health sectors such as infrastructure, education, social protection, and water and sanitation. The next level represents community constraints, including the level of community mobilization, culture, values, and norms in a particular community. The constraints related to the health sector in general follow, such as low public health spending, poor access to health services, shortage of health workers, and interrupted drug supplies. The next sphere is related to the MRH program and its service delivery system—such as low availability and use of family planning services, limited number of Skilled Birth Attendants (SBAs), and poor access to emergency obstetric care (EmOC). The last but most important constraints occur at the household level, such as household knowledge and attitude, income level, and women's education and status.

"Drivers and Enablers for Improving Maternal and Reproductive Health Outcomes" is the integrated analytical framework used in this study. This framework focuses on those factors and interventions, which contributed most to improved MRH outcomes in South Asia.

Using the **"Ishikawa Diagram"** to depict the "cause and effect" of an outcome (Ishikawa 1990), the analysis groups these interventions according to the different spheres outlined in figure 1.1. However, we distinguish between "drivers," which are interventions at the levels of (a) the household, (b) the MRH programs, and (c) the health sector and "enablers," which are those policies, strategies, and actions outside the health sector at the levels of (a) community, (b) multisectoral, and (c) contextual. The level nearest to the MRH outcome—the household level in this case—makes the greatest contribution and the one farthest from the MRH outcome has the least influence or impact (figure 1.2). In conducting the analysis, the following factors were examined:

- **Drivers**
  - Household
    - Household gender dynamics and role of men in decision-making
    - Household knowledge and attitude
    - Women's education and status
    - Household income level
  - Maternal and Reproductive Health Programs[1]
    - Skilled birth attendance
    - Institutional delivery
    - EmOC
    - Access to abortion and post-abortion care
    - Increased contraceptive use
    - ANC
  - Health Sector
    - Health financing: public health finance, health financing schemes
    - Service delivery: Expanding health coverage and access, particularly for maternal health

http://dx.doi.org/10.1596/978-1-4648-0963-7

Figure 1.2 Drivers and Enablers for Improving MRH Outcomes

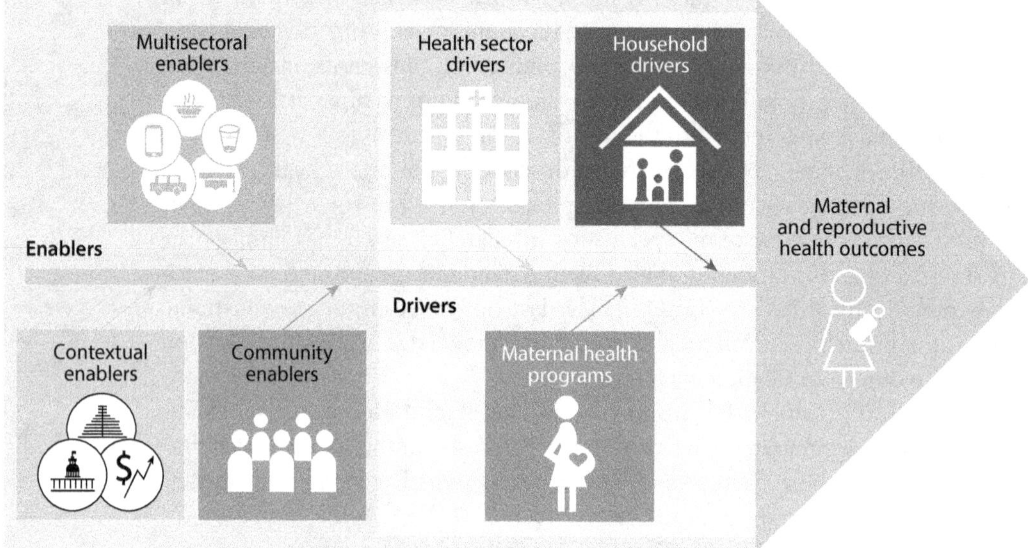

  - Health workforce: Availability of human resources for health
  - Essential drugs and health commodities
  - Health information systems
  - Leadership and governance
- **Enablers**
  - Community
    - Community health workers
    - Community participation and mobilization
    - Engaging community leaders
  - Multisectoral
    - Education
    - Transportation and communication
    - Water and sanitation
    - Nutrition
    - Energy
    - CCTs
    - Microfinance
  - Contextual
    - Political
    - Economic development
    - Demography
    - Sociocultural development

The framework provides a practical way of examining the above factors and interventions while intrinsically entailing some overlap that we tried to minimize

http://dx.doi.org/10.1596/978-1-4648-0963-7

or clarify to the extent possible. For example, the level of "woman's education" as a driver within the household and "girl's education" as a multisectoral enabler appear to be similar. To make the distinction, we refer to the former as the level of education attained by the "mother," which could have been through formal education, literacy programs, or other channels while the latter refers strictly to the formal education sector. Another example is the "availability of health workers" as a health sector driver, which refers to the formal health sector workers, and "community health workers" as a community enabler, which refers to those recruited from the community. However, the variations in the use of terms for the same programs made it difficult to consistently avoid such an overlap.

In summary, the analytical model assumes that improving maternal survival and reproductive health outcomes is influenced by a multitude of forces from within and outside the health system and considers factors at the household and community levels, as well as interventions in other sectors and factors in the enabling environment.

Research Methodology

We applied three research approaches for this study: (a) a structured literature review on maternal mortality in South Asia and in other LMICs, (b) a literature review on selected MRH interventions, and (c) a review of the "systematic reviews." on maternal mortality and MRH.

First, we conducted a literature review to understand the factors that explain the significant reductions in maternal mortality in South Asian countries. What lessons can be learned from a close examination of their progress? What is the context of countries' successes and remaining challenges? How do the experiences of reducing maternal mortality in South Asia compare with those of countries outside the region? This narrative review of the literature examines these questions and identifies the drivers and enablers that explain the progress in reducing maternal mortality in South Asian countries.

This narrative review used a structured literature review strategy. It assessed a subset of articles from a larger literature review on child and maternal mortality. This broader literature review drew from English language articles, reports, and other literature focused on the reduction of maternal and child mortality at the country level in the 139 countries that the World Bank designated in 2015 as LMICs.[2] The cut-off date for all literature included was May 1, 2015. No specific start date was selected to include as broad a time frame as possible. Databases searched were PubMed, World Bank e-library, SSRN, JStor, EconLit, Lilacs, and the Google Scholar search engine. Several search strategies for this broader literature review were employed using key words, combinations, and medical subject headings (MeSH) such as "maternal mortality," "millennium development goal," "on track," "success," "progress," "factors," and the names of each of the 139 LMICs. The search strategy did not include study design filters to capture all information of potential interest in the review. Additional published and grey literature was identified through a Partnership for Maternal, Newborn, and

http://dx.doi.org/10.1596/978-1-4648-0963-7

Child Health (PMNCH) Endnote Web database for the Success Factors study series and a purposeful search of Google and bibliographies of papers retrieved. We reviewed the abstracts and full text of the papers in the broader literature review in two phases and assessed them for inclusion based on six exclusion criteria. The details of this research approach are included in appendix B.

Second, a literature review of the same databases was conducted but using more restricted search strings drawn from a set of published and unpublished country case studies and reports conducted by the World Bank regional reproductive health coordinators. It can be found on the World Bank website (World Bank 2015b). The search words were "skilled birth attendance," "community midwifery training," or "role of men/male in reproductive health." The search focused on South Asia countries and a subset search was done to include each of the 139 LMICs.

Third, we conducted a search of the systematic reviews databases including the Cochrane Library of systematic reviews, Health Evidence, PubMed, Medline, GeoBase, Global Health, and other relevant electronic databases for systematic reviews published between 2005 and 2015 related to interventions identified in the analytical framework and the above reviews that have affected MRH outcomes. The search resulted in 215 papers that were abstracted and reviewed. Papers that did not assess the effect of the intervention on any of the MRH outcomes were excluded and duplicates were removed, which resulted in 43 papers that were included. The full papers were then reviewed and narrated. The list of the systematic reviews included in this study is found in appendix C.

There are several considerations and limitations related to the scope of this study. First, the focus of the analysis is mainly on assessing the "effectiveness" of interventions and, to the extent possible, the effectiveness of interventions in improving MRH outcomes on different subpopulations, which reflects the "equity" dimension of the intervention. Other dimensions such as efficiency, cost-effectiveness, and quality of the interventions were outside the scope of this study. Second, the evidence was assessed based on the number of systematic reviews, the number of studies and countries in which an intervention was implemented. However, the quality of the individual studies including the endogeneity bias and the heterogeneity of effect were not assessed. The average effect size of an intervention was reported, whenever available, based on meta-analyses performed in the systematic reviews. In addition, to the extent that the systematic reviews cover a small set of studies or do not exclude studies that fail to sufficiently control for endogeneity bias or target the population of interest, these limitations will be noted.

Organization of the Report

In addition to this "introduction" chapter, the report has eight other chapters. Chapter 2 provides an overview of the regional trends in MRH. Each of the subsequent 6 chapters (3 through 8) provides an analysis of each of the enabler/driver in the analytical framework and related factors/interventions. Each of these chapters starts with cross-country benchmarking, whenever applicable, then a review of the examples/best practices related to each of the potential factor/intervention that were implemented in SAR with a focus, as much as possible, on the countries that contributed most to the MMR decline, followed by relevant examples from international experience, and finally a review of the systematic reviews that support the evidence of effect/impact of these factors/interventions, whenever applicable. The last chapter provides a discussion and conclusions of the report that attempt to answer the question identified at the outset.

Notes

1. There are other program activities and clinical interventions with various degrees of effectiveness and impact on maternal mortality such as tetanus toxoid immunization, anti-malarial drugs for preventing malaria during pregnancy, antibiotics for preterm rupture of membranes, magnesium sulfate for pre-eclampsia, and active management in third stage of labor, which are beyond the scope of this study.
2. The list of 139 countries can be found at http://data.worldbank.org/about/country-and-lending-groups.

http://dx.doi.org/10.1596/978-1-4648-0963-7

CHAPTER 2

Regional Trends in Maternal and Reproductive Health

Key Messages

- South Asia made the greatest regional progress in decreasing maternal mortality rates between 1990 and 2013.
- Bhutan, Maldives, and Nepal are among the 19 countries worldwide that have reduced maternal deaths by 75 percent or more by 2013, thus achieving MDG 5A.
- India, Bangladesh, and Pakistan had the greatest share of the decline in the number of maternal deaths in the region.
- South Asia lags behind all other regions in skilled birth attendance, except for Sub-Saharan Africa.
- Health care use differs across socioeconomic strata, with much greater use in urban areas compared with rural areas.
- While South Asia is close to reaching replacement fertility levels, and contraceptive prevalence has increased, an unmet need for contraception remains, especially among the adolescent age group.
- The reproductive health needs of youth require targeted interventions and greater resources.

This chapter provides an overview and comparison of the MRH situation in the eight countries of South Asia as well as in relation to other comparable middle- and lower-income countries and regions.

Regional Context

SAR is home to 1.6 billion people across eight countries: Afghanistan, Bangladesh, Bhutan, India, Maldives, Nepal, Pakistan, and Sri Lanka. It is the most densely populated region in the world. The region is diverse and includes fragile, low-income, and middle-income countries with wide variations in populations—from 400,000 inhabitants in the Maldives to more than 1.2 billion in India.

SAR is geographically, ethnically, and culturally distinct and requires country-specific reproductive health (MRH) strategies—and frequently provincial and community-specific strategies—to improve maternal and reproductive health outcomes.

The region has benefited from robust economic growth, averaging 6 percent a year. This growth has contributed to impressive advancements in human development and is projected to increase to 6 percent in 2015 and to 6.4 percent in 2016 (World Bank 2014b). The proportion of the poor in SAR is lower now than at any time since 1981. Despite impressive economic growth in recent years, 42 percent of the developing world's poor inhabit South Asia. The World Bank's most recent poverty estimates indicate that about 500 million people in South Asia survive on less than US$1.25 a day (El-Saharty et al. 2014).

Human development in SAR tends toward lower-middle-income averages but is slightly better than in Sub-Saharan Africa. The SAR has made great strides in improving MRH. Yet, while SAR has made significant progress in providing basic education, the female adult literacy rates in SAR rank last among all regions of the world. Literacy rates among youth are low in all countries except for Maldives and Sri Lanka; South Asia has the largest gender gap in the world. On average only 62 percent of young women are literate compared with 77 percent of young men (El-Saharty et al. 2014). Economic inequality persists in every sector and negatively affects progress in human development and economic prosperity.

The South Asian population is young. One-fifth of the population is between the ages of 15 and 24. India has an estimated 200 million youth. Youth unemployment is an acute problem in SAR. Young adults comprise 50 percent of the unemployed. Formal job growth has not kept pace with economic growth in most countries and schools often do not teach the skills required by employers (World Bank 2015a).

Maternal Mortality

Maternal and infant mortality are sensitive indicators in determining whether the health sector is functioning effectively (Goodburn and Campbell 2001). The costs of maternal mortality are direct, including the cost of health care to the family and the health system, and indirect in the form of lost income and productivity. Progress toward achieving the MDGs is due to successful policies and strategies related to safe motherhood, neonatal health, nutrition, and gender. Overall, SAR has made excellent progress toward achieving MDG 5A of reducing the MMR by three-quarters between 1990 and 2015. The MMR declined from 550 deaths per 100,000 live births in 1990 to 190 in 2013 (Kuruvilla et al. 2014). The target rate was 137.5 by 2015.

South Asia has had the world's sharpest decline in maternal mortality since 1990. Between 1990 and 2013, South Asia experienced a 65 percent decline in maternal mortality with an average annual decline of 4.4 percent (figure 2.1). Other regions also reduced their maternal mortality rates: 56 percent in East Asia

http://dx.doi.org/10.1596/978-1-4648-0963-7

Figure 2.1 MMR Reduction by Region, 1990–2013
Percent

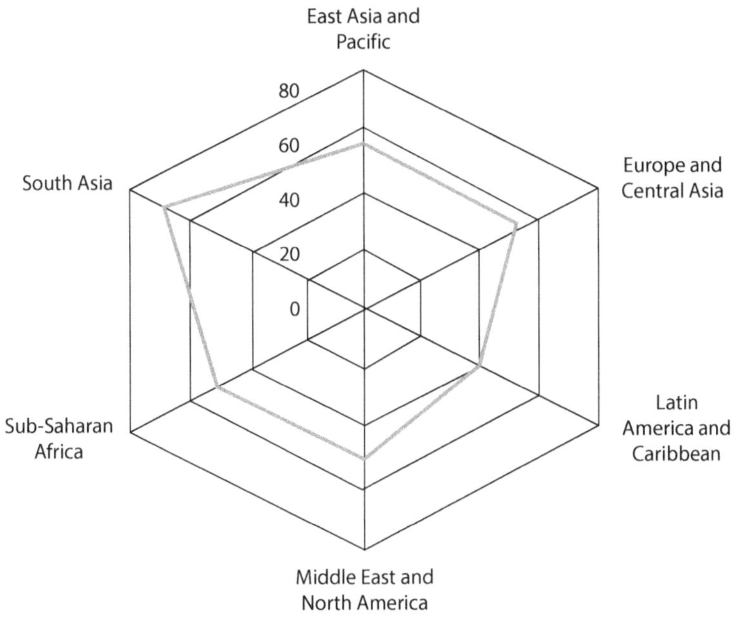

Source: WHO et al. 2014.

and the Pacific; 54 percent in Europe and Central Asia; 51 percent in the Middle East and North Africa; 49 percent in Sub-Saharan Africa; and 40 percent in Latin America and the Caribbean (figure 2.2). However, 24 percent of global maternal deaths in 2013 still occurred in SAR.

South Asia's MMR was 190 deaths per 100,000 live births in 2013 but there is a wide variation among countries. Sri Lanka and the Maldives had the lowest MMRs in the region at respectively 29 and 31 per 100,000 live births in 2013. While Afghanistan had the highest MMR in the region at 400 per 100,000 live births in 2013 (see figure 2.3).

The regional MMR reduction rate varies widely by country. Most SAR countries had an MMR reduction rate above 65 percent between 1990 and 2013. Three countries—Bhutan, Maldives, and Nepal—are among the 19 countries worldwide that have reduced maternal deaths by 75 percent or more by 2013, thereby achieving MDG 5A much earlier than the target year of 2015. In 2010, Nepal received the Millennium Development Goal Award for its commitment and progress toward achieving MDG 5 (maternal health). Another group of countries consisting of Afghanistan, Bangladesh, and India have reduced maternal mortality by 65 percent or more. Sri Lanka has achieved considerable success in reducing MMR consistently since the 1940s and has maintained a low MMR since that time (figure 2.4).

The countries with the greatest share of the decline in the number of maternal deaths in the region are India (74.1 percent), Bangladesh (12.0 percent), and

Figure 2.2 Regional Maternal Mortality Ratios, 1990–2013

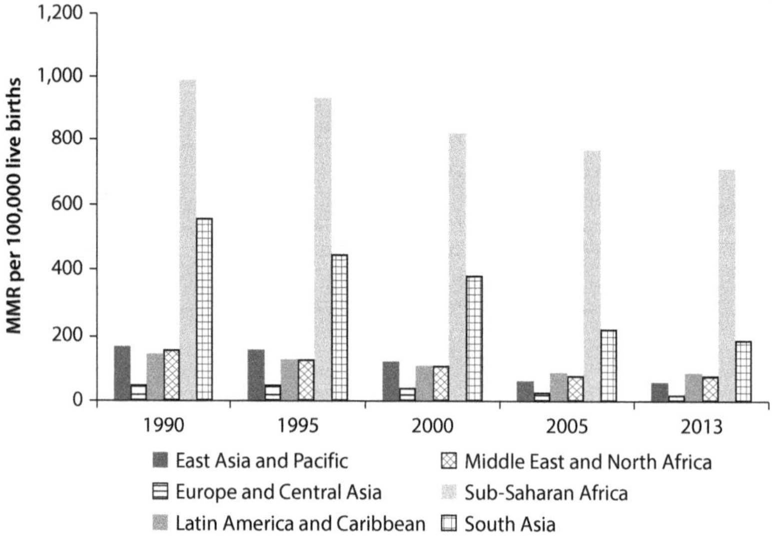

MMR per 100,000 live births
1,200
1,000
800
600
400
200
0
1990
1995
2000
2005
2013

East Asia and Pacific
Europe and Central Asia
Latin America and Caribbean
Middle East and North Africa
Sub-Saharan Africa
South Asia

Source: WHO et al. 2014.

Figure 2.3 MMR Trends among SAR Countries

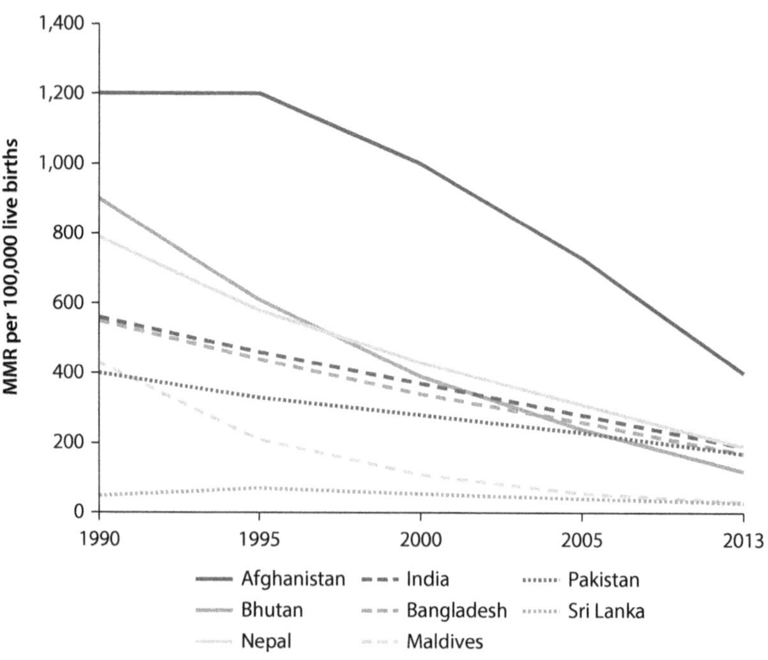

Source: WHO et al. 2014.

Figure 2.4 Proportion Reduction in MMR among SAR Countries, 1990–2013
Percent

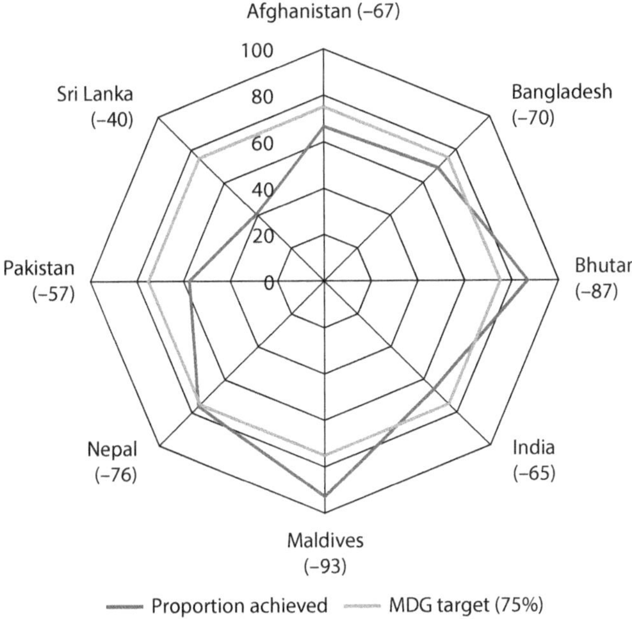

Sources: WHO et al. 2014.

Table 2.1 Trends in the Number of Maternal Deaths among SAR Countries, 1990–2013

Country	*1990*	*1995*	*2000*	*2005*	*2013*	*Decline in MMR from 1990–2013*	*Decline in MMR from 1990–2013*	*Rank by Greatest Decline*
Afghanistan	7,900	10,000	11,000	8,100	4,200	(3,700)	2.8%	5
Bangladesh	21,000	16,000	12,000	8,800	5,200	(15,800)	**12.0%**	2
Bhutan	180	110	61	35	17	(163)	0.1%	6
India	14,8000	123,000	97,000	73,000	50,000	(98,000)	**74.1%**	1
Maldives	38	16	7	4	2	(36)	0.0%	8
Nepal	5,400	4,200	3,300	2,200	1,100	(4,300)	3.3%	4
Pakistan	18,000	15,000	13,000	10,000	7,900	(10,100)	**7.6%**	3
Sri Lanka	180	240	190	150	110	(70)	0.1%	7
Total	200,698	168,566	136,558	102,289	68,529	(132,169)	100%	

Sources: WHO et al. 2014; World Development Indicators, the World Bank.

Pakistan (7.6 percent) (table 2.1). Because of their population size and achievements in MMR reduction, these countries contributed the most to the decline of maternal mortality in South Asia. Within India, the states of Uttar Pradesh/Uttarakhand, Bihar/Jharkhand, and Rajasthan had more than 50 percent of the total decline in India's maternal deaths. Despite country-level successes, India still accounts for 17 percent of all global maternal deaths and successes have been

http://dx.doi.org/10.1596/978-1-4648-0963-7

Figure 2.5 Causes of Maternal Deaths in SAR, 2013
Percent

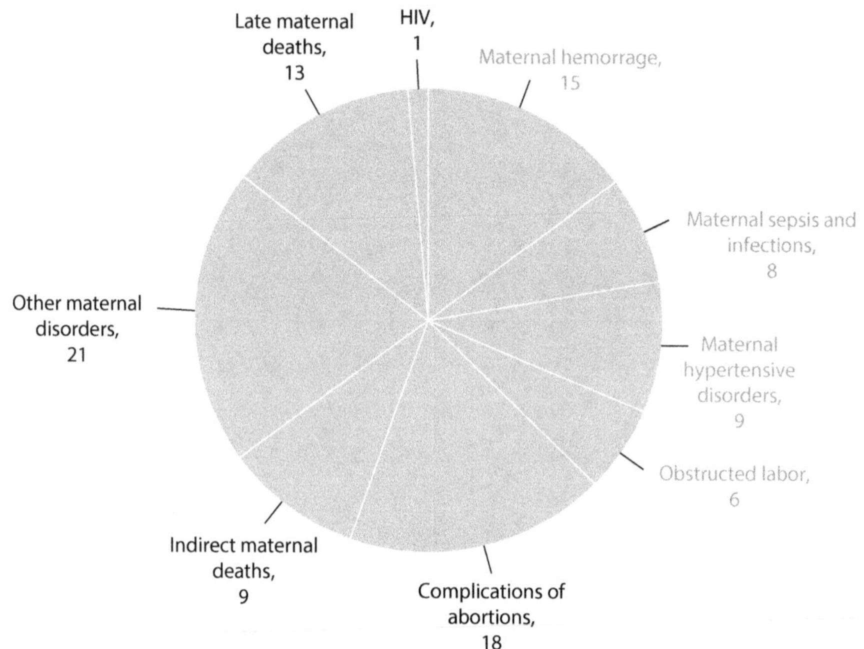

Source: Compiled from http://vizhub.healthdata.org/gbd-compare/.

Figure 2.6 Performance of SAR Countries in Achieving MMR with Level of Health Expenditure

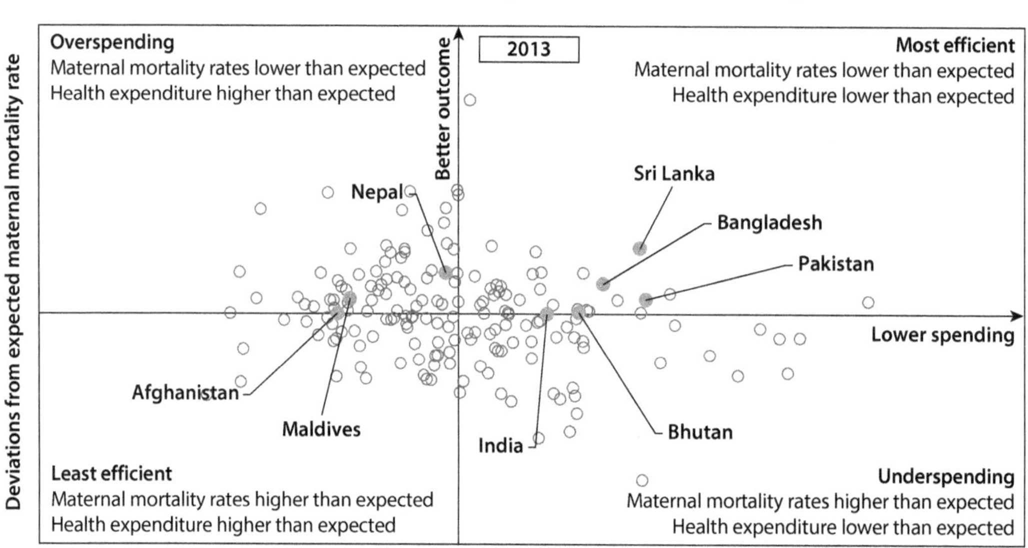

Source: Calculations based on World Bank 2015a.

http://dx.doi.org/10.1596/978-1-4648-0963-7

uneven across the states and income groups. Pakistan's decline in its MMR has been relatively slower than other countries in South Asia.

Causes and their share of maternal deaths in SAR follow the global trend. In SAR, 38 percent of maternal mortality occurs during the intra-partum stage, which is due to hemorrhage, sepsis, hypertensive disorders, and obstructed labor (figure 2.5).

SAR countries achieved lower MMR levels with different degrees of efficiency. Sri Lanka, Bangladesh, and Pakistan were the most efficient among all SAR countries, while Nepal achieved a lower MMR level but with higher spending compared to other countries (figure 2.6).

Maternal Health

The use of maternal health services, namely ANC and skilled birth attendance, has increased in SAR. However, inequity in access to maternal health services remains a major barrier to achieving MDG 5. Wide disparities in service use remain in SAR, especially across wealth quintiles and by residence.

ANC is an opportunity to reach pregnant women with vital interventions and information. In South Asia, 71 percent of women receive ANC, which includes at least one visit to a doctor, nurse, or midwife during pregnancy. However, only 35 percent of women make a minimum of four ANC visits, as recommended by the World Health Organization (UNICEF 2009). ANC coverage is highest in Sri Lanka (99.4 percent), Maldives (99.1 percent), and Bhutan (97.3 percent). Afghanistan has the lowest ANC rate at 63.4 percent. South Asian women in the wealthiest quintile are almost twice as likely as women in the poorest quintile to have at least one ANC visit with a skilled provider: 95 percent versus 50 percent (UNICEF 2009).

Along with frequency of ANC visits, the quality of ANC is important to assess the effectiveness of ANC. A recent study from Punjab, Pakistan, shows that 51.6 percent of expected pregnancies were reporting for their first ANC visit. Of those, 33 percent did not return for follow-up. More than 50 percent of the clients were not satisfied with the ANC services they received (Majrooh et al. 2014).

South Asia is lagging behind all other regions in skilled birth attendance, except for Sub-Saharan Africa (figure 2.7). Skilled birth attendance increased from 36.2 percent in 2000 to 49.8 percent in 2010. Skilled birth attendance is highest in Sri Lanka (98.6 percent) and the Maldives (94.8 percent) and lowest in Bangladesh (31.7 percent) (figure 2.8).

Although access to skilled birth attendance has increased in SAR, disparities remain throughout the region, especially across wealth quintiles. The largest gaps in service access between the richest and the poorest are in Nepal, India, and Afghanistan. Sri Lanka's distribution of access to skilled birth attendance is very equitable with only 2 percentage points separating the poorest from the richest quintiles. For example, the disparity between the richest and poorest quintiles in Bangladesh is more than 5.5 times (table 2.2). While significant inequity in

Figure 2.7 Skilled Birth Attendance by Region

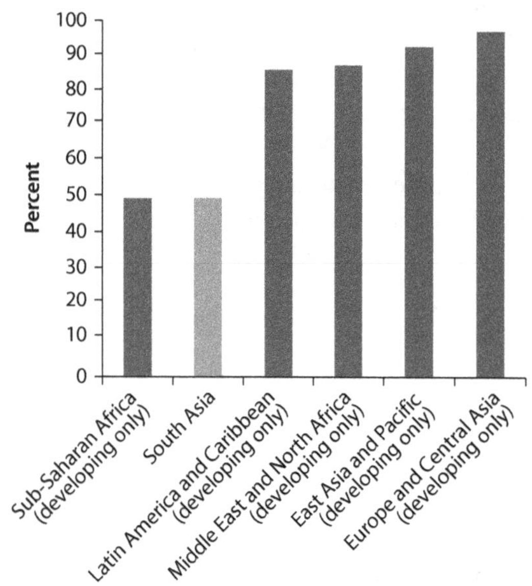

Source: World Bank 2014a.

Figure 2.8 Skilled Birth Attendance in SAR

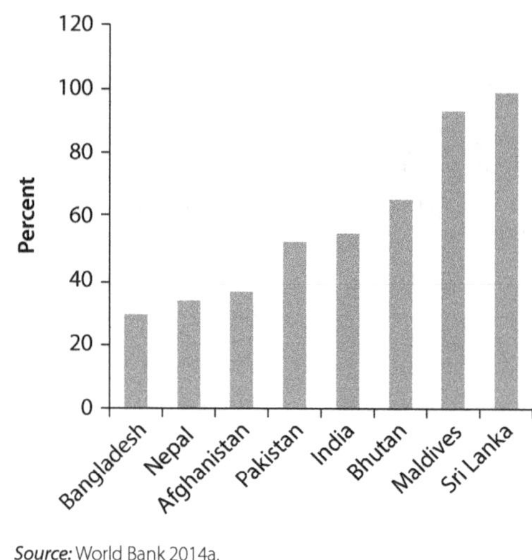

Source: World Bank 2014a.

Table 2.2 Skilled Birth Attendance across Wealth Quintiles in South Asian Countries

	Poorest	*Second*	*Middle*	*Fourth*	*Richest*
Afghanistan	11.7	21.2	32.7	40.7	80
Bangladesh	11.5	18.6	28.2	43.2	63.7
Bhutan	34.3	43.3	67.3	80.9	95.1
India	19.4	31.8	49	67.2	88.8
Maldives	88.6	92.6	95.4	98.4	99.3
Nepal	10.7	23.7	35.9	53	81.5
Pakistan	29.8	38.1	51.2	68.9	85.2
Sri Lanka	97.4	98.4	98.9	99.2	99.4

Sources: Afghan Public Health Institute, Ministry of Public Health [Afghanistan], Central Statistics Organization [Afghanistan], ICF Macro, Indian Institute of Health Management Research [India], and World Health Organization Regional Office for the Eastern Mediterranean 2011; National Statistics Bureau 2011; Department of Census and Statistics and Ministry of Healthcare and Nutrition 2009; International Institute for Population Sciences and Macro International 2007; Ministry of Health and Family [Maldives] and ICF Macro 2010; Ministry of Health and Population [Nepal], New ERA, and ICF International Inc. 2012; National Institute of Population Research and Training, Mitra and Associates, and ICF International 2013; National Institute of Population Studies [Pakistan] and ICF International 2013.

access to skilled birth attendance is found in the majority of SAR countries, except for Sri Lanka and Maldives, its disparities have narrowed over time. The poorest in Pakistan, for instance, had less than 10 percent of the access to skilled birth attendance that the richest enjoyed in 1990/91. With a greater increase among poorer populations, inequity between the poor and rich has diminished over time, though the level of access among the poor is still low (figure 2.9).

http://dx.doi.org/10.1596/978-1-4648-0963-7

Disparities in access to skilled birth attendance also exist by residence. The largest rural-urban service gaps exist in Afghanistan and Nepal. Access to skilled birth attendance in urban Afghanistan is almost three times the availability in rural areas. However, gaps in skilled birth attendance access in Sri Lanka and the Maldives are negligible (figure 2.10).

Figure 2.9 Skilled Birth Attendance across Wealth Quintiles in Pakistan, 1990–2013

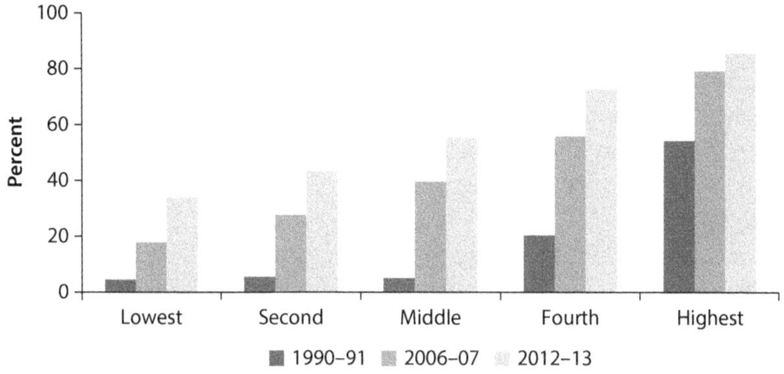

Percent
100
80
60
40
20
0
Lowest
Second
Middle
Fourth
Highest
1990–91 2006–07 2012–13

Source: Using Stat Compiler, Demographic and Health Survey, Macro International.

Figure 2.10 Skilled Birth Attendance by Residence in South Asian Countries

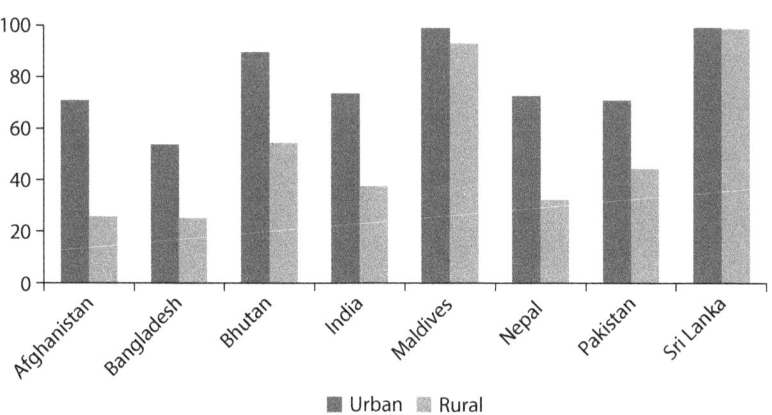

Sources: Afghan Public Health Institute, Ministry of Public Health [Afghanistan], Central Statistics Organization [Afghanistan], ICF Macro, Indian Institute of Health Management Research [India], and World Health Organization Regional Office for the Eastern Mediterranean 2011; National Statistics Bureau 2011; Department of Census and Statistics and Ministry of Healthcare and Nutrition 2009; International Institute for Population Sciences and Macro International 2007; Ministry of Health and Family [Maldives] and ICF Macro 2010; Ministry of Health and Population [Nepal], New ERA, and ICF International Inc. 2012; National Institute of Population Research and Training, Mitra and Associates, and ICF International 2013; National Institute of Population Studies [Pakistan] and ICF International 2013.

Reproductive Health

South Asia is close to reaching replacement fertility. The TFR declined from 4.2 in 1990 to 2.6 in 2012. Five SAR countries have achieved a replacement level fertility of 2.3: Bangladesh (2.2), Bhutan (2.3), Maldives (2.3), Nepal (2.3), and Sri Lanka (2.3), while India (2.6) is close (figure 2.11). The pace of TFR reduction has been steady but slow in Pakistan. Afghanistan has a TFR of 5.1, the highest in the region.

Contraceptive prevalence is increasing in the region. The average contraceptive prevalence rate (CPR) increased from 41.3 percent to 52.3 percent between 1990 and 2010. The countries with the highest CPRs are Bangladesh (61.2 percent), Bhutan (65.6 percent), and Sri Lanka (68.4 percent). Afghanistan has the lowest CPR at 21.2 percent.

While contraceptive prevalence has increased throughout South Asia, the unmet need for contraception is relatively high. It is highest in Maldives (28.1 percent), followed by Nepal (27 percent), and Pakistan (20.1 percent), while the lowest rates are in Sri Lanka (7.3 percent), Bhutan (11.7 percent), and India (12.8 percent).

Patterns of disparities in access to modern contraceptive methods within a country vary across countries. Bangladesh, for instance, has done an excellent job in achieving equitable access in modern contraceptive methods across rural-urban and poor-rich spectrums (~52 percent); however, negligible increase in urban areas as well as among the richest population needs to be addressed. In India and Pakistan, disparities by residence are about 10 percentage points

Figure 2.11 TFR and CPR among SAR Countries

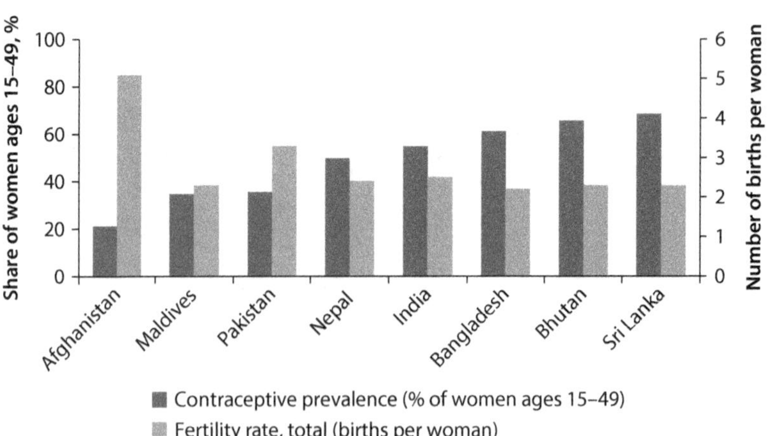

Sources: Afghan Public Health Institute, Ministry of Public Health [Afghanistan], Central Statistics Organization [Afghanistan], ICF Macro, Indian Institute of Health Management Research [India], and World Health Organization Regional Office for the Eastern Mediterranean 2011; National Statistics Bureau 2011; Department of Census and Statistics and Ministry of Healthcare and Nutrition 2009; International Institute for Population Sciences and Macro International 2007; Ministry of Health and Family [Maldives] and ICF Macro 2010; Ministry of Health and Population [Nepal], New ERA, and ICF International Inc. 2012; National Institute of Population Research and Training, Mitra and Associates, and ICF International 2013; National Institute of Population Studies [Pakistan] and ICF International 2013.

(urban 55.8 percent and rural 45.3 percent in 2005–06 for India; urban 32 percent and rural 23.1 percent in 2012–13 for Pakistan). However, available data from Pakistan shows that access by the poorest is only a half that of the richest, and there is no increase in access among the richest since 2006–07.[1]

The reproductive health needs of South Asian youth require particular attention and resources. Forty percent of youth report having unprotected sex and half of all abortions are performed in unsafe conditions. An estimated 50 percent of Human Immunodeficiency Virus (HIV) infections are believed to be in the 15–24-year age group. Tobacco use is increasing among the youth population, which increases the risk factors for pregnant teens (World Bank. Key Statistics).

Early marriage and pregnancy negatively affect maternal health outcomes. Pregnancy at an early age is risky for the mother and child. Bangladesh has the lowest median age at first marriage (15.5 years) and at first birth (18.1 years). The adolescent fertility rate (AFR) for South Asia is 38.8 births per 1,000 women aged 15–19 years. AFR is highest in Afghanistan and Bangladesh at respectively 86.8 and 80.6 births per 1,000 women aged 15–19 years. AFR is lowest in Maldives (4.2).

Young South Asian women face additional health-related problems. Many young women are malnourished and more than 80 percent of adolescent girls suffer from anemia. Social and cultural pressures force adolescents and teenagers into early marriage and child bearing, for which they are physically and mentally unprepared. Teen mothers are twice as likely to die of pregnancy-related causes as mature women are. Their babies are also at higher risk of illness and death. Young women and girls are increasingly becoming victims of sexual exploitation and human trafficking, especially girls in poor rural areas (World Bank 2015).

Note

1. Data were calculated by authors using StatCompiler website at: http://dhsprogram.com/data/STATcompiler.cfm.

http://dx.doi.org/10.1596/978-1-4648-0963-7

CHAPTER 3

Household Drivers

Key Messages

- Demand-side barriers within households—including unequal gender relations, poor access to information, low levels of female education, and poor household income—affect women's access to health care and impede further reduction of maternal mortality.
- Evidence suggests that household income and the education level of female household members are critical drivers of MMR reduction in SAR and globally.
- Interventions targeting increased male participation in maternal and reproductive health services and improved spousal communication may lead to improved service usage.
- Information campaigns are important channels to communicate gender transformative messages, inform male and female family members about critical maternal and reproductive health services, and stimulate demand for services.
- Key household drivers of improved maternal and reproductive health outcomes in SAR countries result from and are dependent on the broader social, economic, and political contexts where households are situated.

Introduction

Demand for life-saving MRH services is fundamentally tied to household dynamics and the degree to which women are empowered socially, economically, and educationally to make decisions (Ensor and Cooper 2004). Access to and use of MRH services are affected by a number of factors, including the role of men in decision-making, the manner in which health information reaches households, the educational and social status of female family members, and the level of household income (Ensor and Cooper 2004). In SAR countries, household factors—especially those related to household gender relations and women's level of education—play a key role in limiting or facilitating national progress on maternal survival and improved reproductive health outcomes.

This chapter describes how household factors contribute to maternal mortality reduction in SAR countries and elsewhere. It also describes projects, programs, and policies in the health sector and other sectors that target households and may support efforts to reduce maternal mortality ratio (MMR) and improve reproductive health outcomes.

Household Gender Dynamics

Gender relations and cultural norms in SAR have a significant impact on women's access to and use of MRH care. The role of husbands in household decision-making is often an important factor in their wives' access to maternal health services. The role of a husband's female family members, especially the mother-in-law, is also an important factor. For example, in Bangladesh a survey to determine the reasons why women do not seek care during obstetric emergencies found that 35.6 percent of women listed the objections of in-laws and 17 percent listed the objections of husbands (Ensor and Cooper 2004). In Pakistan, husbands and older female in-laws often play a decisive role in determining women's treatment seeking, for example, which services are necessary, what health conditions require medical attention, and whether household resources should be spent on health care (Sheikh and Hatcher 2004; Mumtaz and Salway 2009).

However, the role of men and female in-laws is not always negative. In urban Uttar Pradesh, India, households in which wives lived in their husbands' natal home or with their mothers-in-laws were more likely to use modern family planning and institutional delivery than women who did not live in the husbands' natal home or with their mothers-in-law (Speizer et al. 2015). A recent study found that Punjabi men seem more concerned about their fertility intentions and behavior than they were in the early 1990s (box 3.1). Nevertheless, the importance of the impact of husbands and mothers-in-law on household and health care decision-making complicates analyses of women's autonomy in SAR and contributes to a range of barriers to health care access, such as restrictions on women's unaccompanied movement and perceptions about isolation during the postpartum period (United Nations Secretariat Division for the Advancement of Women 2008). In acknowledgement of the prevailing notions of gender segregation, reproductive and maternal health programs in SAR countries have often historically targeted women exclusively (Greene et al. 2006). As a result, many men in SAR are often unaware of family planning and maternal health services or they think the information is irrelevant to them (Singh, Bloom, and Tsui 1998; Mullany 2005; Nasreen et al. 2012).

Reproductive and maternal health programs in SAR countries have increasingly emphasized the importance of including men. The SAR countries were among the 180 countries at the 1994 International Conference on Population and Development in Cairo affirming that male involvement is essential to improve MRH and reduce maternal mortality (UN Secretariat Division for the Advancement of Women 2008). Since then, MRH programs have increasingly incorporated men as reproductive health agents,

Box 3.1 Role of Men in Punjab, Pakistan

A 2013 study in four districts of Punjab province set out to explore the dynamics of couples' decision-making processes concerning their fertility intentions and practices, understand community perceptions of male-focused family planning interventions, and elicit men's suggestions for future intervention strategies. It also examined the readiness of men to be involved in family planning programs through different male-centered interventions.

The study found that Punjabi men seem more concerned about their fertility intentions and behavior than they were in the early 1990s. Since men are considered the primary earners and decision makers in Pakistani households, their primary motivating force is the growing economic challenge leading to an inability to meet household costs. This concern has increased spousal communication about family size and contraceptive use and has encouraged Punjabi men to practice family planning. The findings suggest that wives are no longer exclusively responsible for initiating discussions on their fertility intentions.

Punjabi men showed great interest in participating in male-focused interventions in family planning programs. Men and women suggested male group meetings as the most appropriate intervention for providing men with method-specific knowledge; emphasizing the importance of family planning use; and changing couples' fertility intentions and practices. Appreciating the role and effectiveness of the LHW program, men suggested recruiting male health workers in communities, with roles similar to LHWs and with a focus on providing services to men at the community level (Kamran, Mumraiz, and Tasneem 2014).

recognizing both partners as equal decision makers (Hou and Ma 2013). For example, the Ministry of Health in the Maldives began collecting information in 2004 on ever-married men aged 15–49 years in its national reproductive health survey (Cockcroft et al. 2011). In India, before 2000, there was no mention of male involvement in many of the country's key national policy and program documents (Khan and Panda 2004). However, after 2000, the National Population Policy (2000) and subsequent waves of national Five Year Plans have mentioned the importance of men as have many key state health and population policy documents, specifically with regard to planned parenthood, contraception, and sexually transmitted infection/Reproductive tract infections control (Khan and Panda 2004). Nepal's Health Sector Programme-2 Implementation Plan 2010–2015 includes targeting adolescent boys and men to provide comprehensive and correct information and knowledge about sexual, maternal, newborn, and child health; family planning; and gender equality and social inclusion through media, interpersonal communication, and Information, Education, and Communication/Behavior Change Communication (IEC/BCC) activities (Government of Nepal 2010). In many SAR countries, positive steps at the policy level have led to greater engagement of men in MRH, although many countries are still struggling to put policies into practice and to scale up successful projects nationwide.

Strategies used in SAR countries to improve male participation have included holding male-specific meetings, targeting male community leadership, distributing contraceptives, and disseminating information as part of male engagement activities. For example, in Sindh Province, Pakistan, the "Male Involvement to Promote Safe Motherhood" project held seminars facilitated by male leaders for men living in remote areas in 2001. The seminars educated men on risk factors for maternal mortality—such as postpartum hemorrhage (PPH), eclampsia, and high levels of fertility—using videos, informational pamphlets, and group discussion (WHO 2001). Punjab Province, Pakistan, served as one of the sites of the global "Men as Partners" project which sought to increase men's knowledge and responsibility for participating in family planning and sexual and reproductive health and to improve men's access to sexual and reproductive health services (WHO 2001). Participating organizations and facilities created targeted IEC materials for men, mobilized men's groups, used religious leadership for health messaging, and conducted health education events in workplace settings (WHO 2001). Afghanistan's Accelerating Contraceptive Use (ACU) project attempted to address high rates of maternal mortality, high rates of total fertility, and low contraceptive uptake by including men and male religious leaders in outreach activities across three project sites. Information on the benefits, use, and risk factors associated with contraception was updated and made relevant to religious teachings. Written materials were prepared about oral injectable contraceptives targeting couples and included quotes from the Quran approved by religious leaders to advocate for birth spacing and to provide simple instructions for use (Huber, Saeedi, and Samadi 2010).

In SAR countries where interventions have prioritized male participation, the involvement of men has improved antenatal care (ANC) and postnatal clinic attendance, births attended by skilled birth attendants (SBAs), and interest in family planning and pregnancy outcomes. During the eight months of Afghanistan's ACU project, contraceptive use increased by more than 24 percent at three project sites, and the Ministry of Public Health adopted the project for scale-up (Huber, Saeedi, and Samadi 2010). In Kathmandu, Nepal, a high proportion of men (40–50 percent) already accompanied their wives to ANC visits and other maternal health services. A project targeting married couples at ANC visits with maternal health education and information found that women receiving education alongside their husbands were more likely to make birth preparedness plans (60.7 percent versus 48.6 percent) and to attend more than three postpartum visits (21.8 percent versus 16.8 percent) (Mullany, Becker, and Hindin 2007). The "Men in Maternity" project in Delhi found that male attendance increased significantly at ANC and postpartum clinics and family planning consultations following interventions that explicitly encouraged the husband's participation. The interventions also resulted in increased male presence during labor and delivery and inter-spousal communication and joint decision-making related to MRH (Varkey, Mishra, and Khan 2008). In Bangladesh, a two-year project sought to integrate reproductive health services for men into public sector Health and Family Welfare Centers across the country (Al Sabir et al. 2004). Activities included promoting awareness of reproductive health issues among men, public announcements, male-focused group discussions, IEC/BCC materials, and the provision of reproductive health services. The project resulted in increased uptake of reproductive health services by men and their increased knowledge of reproductive health issues (Al Sabir et al. 2004).

The failure to involve men in MRH programming was related to negative maternal health outcomes in other regions. For example, from 2006 to 2012, Ethiopia's unmet need for family planning was 26 percent, and its contraceptive prevalence rate was only 29 percent (WHO 2014). One key impediment to women seeking reproductive health services in Ethiopia was found to be the failure of family planning programs to address the interests, needs, and concerns of men who disagreed with their wives about fertility decisions (Bongaarts et al. 2012). Spousal communication about family planning choices was also found to be poor (Bongaarts et al. 2012). While Ethiopia has managed to more than halve its MMR since 2000, it was still 420 per 100,000 live births in 2013. While low contraceptive prevalence is not the only factor affecting the high MMR, when combined with low levels of maternal health service coverage, it is a contributing factor. Similarly, the Republic of Yemen has the highest MMR in the Middle East and North Africa region and an unmet need for contraception (Marie Stopes International 2008). Knowledge, Attitude, and Practices studies have found that 67 percent of women and 59 percent of men said the mother-in-law exerted pressure on the couple to bear a child quickly after marriage. Only 20 percent of women felt that they were able to access MRH services freely. The majority of women felt that they did not have the prerogative to make decisions about their own health, and the majority of men felt that they were the key decision makers about the number of children born within a family (Marie Stopes International 2008). In Kenya, male approval of contraceptive use and male family size desires were found to be key factors in influencing family planning options, while men's attendance at ANC clinics was found to be a positive predictor of women's use of SBAs (Kimuna and Adamchak 2001; Mangeni et al. 2013). In some parts of Uganda, there are strong beliefs that men should not involve themselves in maternal or reproductive health, except for providing funds. Nonetheless, Ugandan men's discussions about family planning with community health workers, for example, are associated with significant increases in the use of modern contraceptive methods (Kabagenyi et al. 2014; Singh, Lample, and Earnest 2014).

The effect of improved male participation in MRH services on national MMR reduction is unclear. There is some evidence that suggests that male involvement was significantly associated with reduced odds of postpartum depression and with improved use of SBAs and postnatal care. Male involvement during pregnancy and at postpartum appeared to have greater benefits than male involvement during delivery. However, more rigorous studies are needed to improve this area's evidence base (Yargawa and Leonardi-Bee 2015). Also, in almost all instances cited in this section, the evaluation of program success involving male engagement is based on pilot projects.

> *Some studies indicate that men's involvement may lead, for example, to increased uptake of contraception, but it remains unclear whether this leads to more equitable gender norms or the empowerment of women. Other studies have shown positive change in attitudes towards gender norms as reported by men, but precisely how these attitudes affect key health behaviors and outcomes and to influence them, remains unclear. Does male involvement help men become capable of resisting social norms of male dominance, or isolate them from their peers? What are the effects of male involvement on the lives of men beyond straightforward health outcomes? Finally is long-term attitudinal change sustainable? We are unable to answer these questions given the lack of long-term, large-scale evaluation efforts* (Greene et al. 2006).

Further research is needed to explore the links between gender-based barriers to MRH use, men's role in overcoming such barriers, and how both contribute to MMR reduction at the national level. A better understanding of how men's negative and positive involvement in women's health influences maternal mortality also will be achieved when programs engaging men are implemented at a larger scale.

Access to Information and Increased Use of Services

One means to increase knowledge, change attitudes, and stimulate demand for MRH services in SAR countries and globally is by improving household access to information through community-level and mass media information, and IEC/BCC campaigns. In particular, IEC/BCC strategies through entertainment education, social marketing, and advocacy have played an important role in uptake of family planning and other MRH services and may indirectly contribute to declining MMR within populations targeted by such campaigns (Vijaykumar 2008). The effectiveness of a single communication medium, for example, a radio campaign, is sometimes difficult to isolate, because campaigns often involve a package of strategies rolled out simultaneously (Hornik and McAnany 2001). Additionally, campaigns and other IEC/BCC interventions are often rolled out alongside additional health sector programs and in the context of broader social, political, and economic change. In spite of the difficulty of measuring the impact of improved access to information on MMR reduction, there are nevertheless clear indications that household access to information is a key contributor to changing treatment-seeking behavior and attitudes toward family planning and pregnancy care (Hornik and McAnany 2001). For example, there are strong correlations between television or radio ownership and reductions in fertility rates, including in low-income countries (Retherford and Mishra 1997; Johnson 2001; Jensen and Oster 2009; Westoff and Koffman 2011).

The correlation between integrated IEC/BCC packages—often with mass media components—and increased uptake of family planning services in SAR is well documented. In Nepal, the multi-media Radio Communication Project ran from 1995 to 1997 and involved entertainment-education radio serials, that is, one soap opera and one learning program for health workers, as well as radio

http://dx.doi.org/10.1596/978-1-4648-0963-7

advertisement and promotion, and print materials to support the media campaign (Storey et al. 1999). Over the next several years, there were measurable improvements in quality of client-provider interactions, increased client self-efficacy in dealing with health workers, increased uptake of family planning, and increased use of family planning services (Storey et al. 1999). In India, data from the National Family Health Survey suggest that access to radio, television, and newspapers is correlated positively with current and intended use of contraception (Retherford and Mishra 1997). In 2002, All India Radio launched a 52-episode serial radio drama *Taru* in Bihar, Jharkhand, Madhya Pradesh, and Chattisgarh states. The radio drama's broadcast was rolled out alongside increased reproductive service provision and other BCC activities, such as listening groups and participatory theater performances. In Bihar state where the program was evaluated, not only did *Taru* lead to measurable changes in perceptions of gender equality and self-efficacy to use contraception, but awareness and use of various family planning methods also increased. Sales of condoms, contraceptives, and pregnancy dipsticks more than doubled in a number of the evaluated villages (Singhal et al. 2003). In Pakistan and Bangladesh, data suggest similar correlations. Increased exposure to television, radio, and print media is correlated with positive attitudes toward family planning, increased use of modern contraception, and spousal discussion of fertility desires (Olenik 2000). However, multivariate studies fail to describe the policy and programmatic context in which mass media messages on family planning are rolled out. In the SAR countries where strong associations exist between access to information through mass media and improved reproductive health indicators, the countries likely have simultaneously taken other measures to educate couples, increase service coverage and quality, and improve supply of essential family planning commodities. Nevertheless, exposure to positive family planning messages through television, radio, and print media is a key component of demand generation for reproductive health services.

The integrated IEC/BCC packages, which often have mass media components, were associated with improved uptake of MRH services in SAR. In urban India, 55 percent of women in the lower economic groups have no mass media exposure compared to only 1.5 percent in the richest economic group. They were also less likely to attend at least three antenatal checkups and less likely to have an institutional delivery (Goli, Doshi, and Perianayagam 2013). Employing media was more effective in improving maternal health service uptake in India when combined with a package that includes advocacy, social marketing, and service provision. The White Ribbon Alliance launched Safe Motherhood India to reduce the high levels of maternal mortality. The package combined public rallies and nationwide "Know your birth rights" and "No mother should die giving life" media campaigns, which included print advertisements, newspaper stories, television spots, radio drama, and a postcard campaign (Vijaykumar 2008). While the direct impact of this campaign on health service use is unclear, the campaign did lead to the development of evidence-based guidelines and protocols for an essential package of MCH services. It also led to the creation of a technical working group for maternal health, the establishment of guideline documents on prenatal

http://dx.doi.org/10.1596/978-1-4648-0963-7

care, skilled birth attendance, and the management of obstetric complications targeting auxiliary nurse midwives (ANMs) and lady health workers (LHWs). These in turn led to task shifting of maternity care to community-level health worker cadres in specified circumstances (Vijaykumar 2008).

In Bangladesh, an analysis of Demographic and Health Survey (DHS) data found that exposure to radio, television, or print media was associated with uptake of MRH services. Nearly 60 percent of women and over 80 percent of men had weekly access to the media, which along with education level and household income was correlated with increased probability of women using an SBA, seeking care for pregnancy related complications, and obtaining post-natal checkups for home deliveries (Das 2008). In rural Rajshahi district, greater exposure to mass media was seen among Bangladeshi men aged 15–54 years who accompanied their wives to ANC (Rahman et al. 2015). In rural Jhang district, Pakistan, exposure to mass media once a week, such as television or radio at least, was likewise strongly correlated with use of ANC and institutional delivery. Of women exposed to mass media at least once a week, 49 percent made at least three ANC visits compared with 30 percent of women with less frequent media exposure. Nearly 58 percent of women with media exposure delivered in a facility compared to 36 percent with less frequent exposure (Agha and Carton 2011). Nepal's Safe Motherhood Program included IEC/BCC interventions such as outreach worker visits, radio programs, mass media dissemination of information, and promotion of female education. All were correlated with increased use, although female education and outreach worker visits correlated more strongly than exposure to media, and household income correlated more strongly than any of the program variables (Sharma, Sawangdee, and Sirirassamee 2007).

Access to information has been also correlated with increased MRH service usage elsewhere. In Kenya, Nigeria, and Tanzania, for example, institutional delivery was closely tied to women's media exposure, along with the mothers' education level and household wealth (Tey and Lai 2013; Exavery et al. 2014). Indonesia implemented a six-month *Suami SIAGA* entertainment-education campaign to help address the "three delays" in access to emergency obstetric care (Shefner-Rogers and Sood 2004). *Suami SIAGA* (or "Alert Husband") broadcast and printed media as well as provided IEC materials for interpersonal communication between service providers and husbands (Shefner-Rogers and Sood 2004). Messages focused on increasing household knowledge of the three delays and birth preparedness. Husbands who had access to print media resources were five times more likely to report taking action than those who did not have access, while husbands who had the benefit of interpersonal communication with providers were 10 times more likely to report taking action (Shefner-Rogers and Sood 2004). The MaiMwana project (2009–2011) in Mchinji District, Malawi sought to increase the uptake of MCH care services (Zamawe, Banda, and Dube 2015). The project identified lack of health information at the household and community levels as a key barrier to access (Zamawe, Banda, and Dube 2015). MaiMwana launched a local radio program called *Phukusi la Moyo* that was broadcast via community radio (Zamawe, Banda, and Dube 2015). The target audience was women of child-bearing age, but special programs were also prepared to reduce barriers to men's engagement in MCH (Zamawe, Banda, and Dube 2015). At the end of the project, 81 percent of the men whose wives listened to *Phukusi la Moyo* participated in ANC compared to 73 percent of those whose wives did not listen; 76 percent of husbands whose wives listened were involved in child-birth compared to 64 percent of those whose wives did not; and 60 percent of husbands whose wives listened were engaged in postnatal care, compared to 44 percent of those whose wives did not (Zamawe, Banda, and Dube 2015). Brazil's Programa H, initially implemented by the NGO *Instituto Promundo*, has used mass media as well as developed postcards, banners, and comics that drew on mass media and youth culture to help raise the status of women, promote gender equity, and convey the various social and health costs of traditional perceptions of masculinity (Ricardo et al. 2010). The program has led to higher rates of condom use, self-efficacy among young women, more gender-equitable behavior, and improved couple communication (Ricardo et al. 2010). The Program H manual has since been adopted by Ministries of Health in Brazil, Costa Rica, Mexico, and Nicaragua. Versions of the program have been rolled out in Mexico, Jamaica, Columbia, Costa Rica, and Nicaragua, and are now being replicated in India, Tanzania, and Vietnam (Ricardo et al. 2010).

Access to information alone is insufficient to guarantee improved access to and use of MRH services. Mass media and other IEC/BCC campaigns can greatly contribute to stimulating demand for RMNCH services. However, in the absence of other drivers, for example, household income, female education, and the availability of quality RMNCH services, such campaigns will not realize their full impact, and in fact, they may have adverse effects (Wakefield, Loken, and Hornik 2010). Health communications experts caution that:

> *[C]ampaign messages can fall short and even backfire; exposure of audiences to the message might not meet expectations, hindered by inadequate funding, the increasingly fractured and cluttered media environment, use of inappropriate or poorly researched format (e.g., boring factual messages or age-inappropriate content), or a combination of these features; homogeneous messages might not be persuasive to heterogeneous audiences; and campaigns might address behaviours that audiences lack the resources to change* (Wakefield, Loken, and Hornik 2010).

The full impact of IEC/BCC campaigns—whether they involve one-on-one or group discussions, or deploy more widely disseminated television, radio, or print media—is often difficult to measure. The link of such interventions to national MMR reduction is also difficult to ascertain since so many of them have been carried out as short-term pilot projects and have not been scaled up and sustained. Nevertheless, access to information is persistently cited as a primary contributor to MRH service use and thus can be seen as having an indirect influence on maternal health outcomes.

http://dx.doi.org/10.1596/978-1-4648-0963-7

Women's Education and Household Income

Adult female literacy rates in SAR range widely. Adult female literacy is nearly universal in Sri Lanka and Maldives, while Afghanistan is below 20 percent. The rate for other SAR countries ranges between 40 and 55 percent. As depicted in figure 3.1, the relationship between adult female literacy rate and gross domestic product (GDP) per capita has a positive correlation ($R^2 = 0.5931$). For the level of GDP per capital, adult female literacy rates in SAR are mixed. Only the Maldives and Sri Lanka achieved adult female literacy rates that are higher than countries with comparable income while Bangladesh, India, and Nepal were close to other countries at similar income but Pakistan and Afghanistan were markedly lower.

A mother's education level is a significant predictor of health service use and maternal mortality in SAR countries. Among Indian women, the level of maternal education was a predictor of their choice of location for childbirth. Compared with other interventions, such as cash incentives, maternal education has been suggested as a priority intervention for increasing facility-based deliveries in India (Aggarwal and Thind 2011). The level of maternal education in India is also associated with increased use of reproductive health services, such as family planning and ANC. Twenty-nine percent of women with no education received at least one ANC visit as opposed to 88 percent among women with 12 years or more of education. The fertility rate among women with no education was 3.6 compared to 1.8 among women with 12 years or more education (IIPS and Macro International 2007). Likewise in Bhutan, women with secondary or higher education are more likely than women with no education or only primary education to deliver with the assistance of a skilled attendant or at a health facility. Whereas 93 percent of women with secondary education or more delivered in a health facility, only 51.5 percent of women with no formal education

Figure 3.1 Adult Literacy Rate, Population 15+ Years, Female, 2013

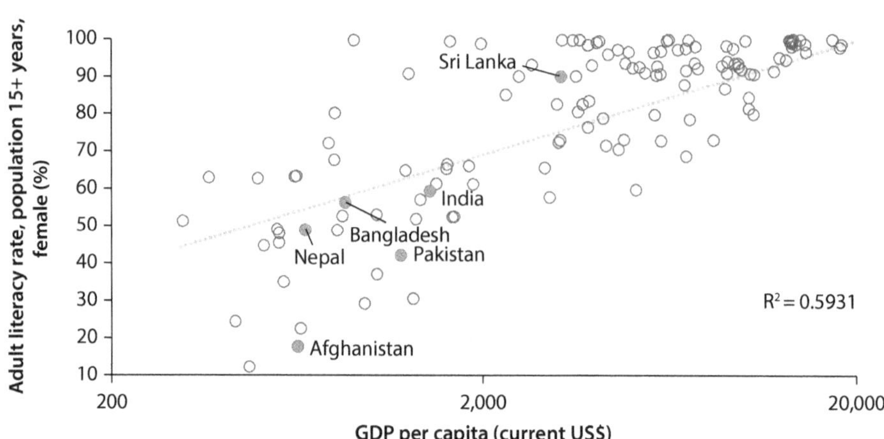

Source: World Bank 2014a.

http://dx.doi.org/10.1596/978-1-4648-0963-7

delivered in a health facility (National Statistics Bureau 2011). In addition, maternal education in Bangladesh has been linked with the probability of using maternal health services, with the strength of the relationship rising steadily with the level of education (Das 2008). Bangladeshi women with education are substantially more likely to use ANC and skilled birth attendance than women without education (Munsur, Atia, and Kawahara 2010). Similarly, for maternal mortality, improving education level of women of reproductive age in Bangladesh was one of the key contributors to MMR reduction in the country (Das 2008). When measured over a period of 30 years, women in the Matlab study area with eight or more years of formal education had an MMR of less than 150 per 100,000 live births. This was almost three times lower than women with no formal education (Chowdhury et al. 2009b). Throughout the whole of Bangladesh, women with some education were also substantially more likely to use ANC and SBAs than women without education (Munsur, Atia, and Kawahara 2010). In Nepal, the improved educational status of women giving birth is cited as one of the most plausible explanations for changes to the country's national MMR, as measured in the 1996 and 2006 Nepal DHS surveys (Hussein et al. 2011). The slow and regionally inequitable improvements to female education in Pakistan and India has been cited as one of the most important barriers preventing those countries from attaining their MMR targets (Bhutta et al. 2013). In Pakistan and India, the level of maternal education was also a significant predictor of the choice of location for childbirth, even in the context of other interventions to increase facility-based delivery, such as cash incentives through voucher schemes (Agha 2011).

Globally, women's educational status is a well-known driver to improve MRH indicators and to reduce maternal mortality. In the Yunnan and Henan Provinces in China, the Arab Republic of Egypt, Mongolia, and Namibia, women's educational status has been positively correlated with use of maternal health services (Li et al. 2007). In Namibia, the rate of use of SBAs among those women with post-secondary education is almost 100 percent. For those women who have completed primary school, the rate is around 60 percent and for those with no education around 50 percent (Zere et al. 2010). The rate of caesarian section is 35.5 percent in women with post-secondary education, compared to 5 percent in women with no education. Caesarean rates in Namibia among highly educated women are twice the recommended threshold. Nevertheless, women's education has a major impact on access to and uptake of emergency obstetric services and has contributed to reducing the disparity in maternal mortality across regions and wealth strata (Zere et al. 2010). Brazil has positively correlated reduction in maternal education disparity with the country's progress on its MDG 4 and 5 targets. The percentage of women in the lowest wealth quintile with eight or more years of schooling increased from 5.6 percent to 29.4 percent between 1996 and 2007 while the percentage of women without any school decreased from 11.8 percent to 5.9 percent (Barros et al. 2010). Over the same period, the MMR dropped from 100 to 73 deaths per 100,000 live births. Currently, the MMR is 68, a 2.4 percent reduction per year (Barros et al. 2010).

http://dx.doi.org/10.1596/978-1-4648-0963-7

Over a 50-year period in Chile, the MMR decreased by 93.8 percent in parallel with a significant increase in the number of years of women's education. For every additional year of maternal education, Chile's MMR decreased correspondingly (Koch et al. 2012).

Another key household driver that has been correlated with MMR reduction is household income. For example, since 1993, national income per household head in Bangladesh has almost doubled, reducing the percentage of the population living below the poverty line by 36 percent (El Arifeen et al. 2014). Poverty rates in Bangladesh declined rapidly between 2000 and 2005. The proportion of the population living in extreme poverty dropped from 34 percent in 2000 to 25 percent in 2005 (Faguet 2007). Growth in per capita consumption has also increased relatively equitably across all wealth groups (Faguet 2007). There is clear evidence that improved household economic status has contributed to Bangladesh's success in reducing the MMR, which in part is because wealthier households are willing and able to pay for private sector maternity services (El Arifeen et al. 2014). Nepal also has reported improved household incomes. It has been observed that "adjusting for education and wealth [shows] that changes in these factors explain" part of the reduction in the country's MMR and, together with changes to women's education and empowerment levels, account for more than 10 percent of district variation in the MMR (Hussein et al. 2011).

Household income is also positively correlated with improved MMR globally. Household income growth and reduced household income disparity have been attributed to improved MMR in China's Yunnan, Guizhou, and Henan Provinces and in Egypt, the Philippines, Mongolia, and Namibia (Barros et al. 2010; Du et al. 2015). One of the best examples of a household income's contribution to MMR reduction is Brazil. During the 1990s, Brazil achieved a 3.4 percent annual reduction in its MMR. Nonetheless, this progress masks deep inequities. The MMR is still high among the lowest wealth quintiles and poorer regions of the country (Victora et al. 2011). Since 2000, Brazil's growing economy and its commitment to implementing progressive social policies—including increasing the minimum wage and expanding conditional cash transfer programs—have all helped contribute to an overall reduction in income inequality (Victora et al. 2011). Reduced income inequality helped Brazil avoid stagnation in its progress on maternal mortality, a challenge that other rapidly growing economies have experienced (Victora et al. 2011).

http://dx.doi.org/10.1596/978-1-4648-0963-7

CHAPTER 4

Program Drivers

Key Messages

- Programmatic interventions focused on improving skilled birth attendance coverage, increasing institutional delivery rates, and scaling up access to emergency obstetric care (EmOC) have all had a direct impact on-reducing maternal mortality in the SAR countries and elsewhere.
- The SAR countries that have invested in family planning programs, policies, and legislation have often greatly reduced their maternal mortality rates.
- SAR countries that have successfully reduced their MMR frequently cite increased access to antenatal care (ANC) as an important correlate, but there is little evidence to support its impact.
- Access to safe abortion and post-abortion services has been correlated with maternal mortality reduction in some countries.
- Maternal health programs often greatly benefit from supportive interventions to improve access, such as those involving emergency transportation or maternity waiting homes.
- The success of programmatic interventions is associated with and dependent on investing and improving national health systems, such as those related to human resources for health, health facility infrastructure, and health commodity supply chains.

Introduction

In 1994, delegates to the International Conference on Population and Development in Cairo adopted a 20-Year Program of Action. The program was designed around four mutually reinforcing goals: reducing maternal mortality, increasing access to reproductive and sexual health services, achieving universal education, and reducing child mortality. Since then, countries across SAR have expanded and initiated policies and programs to reduce maternal mortality, improve the health of women and children, and establish comprehensive and integrated health programs. A number of programmatic interventions have effectively reduced maternal mortality as pilot programs or at the regional or national levels.

This chapter focuses on maternal and reproductive health (MRH) program drivers across the continuum of care that are linked to reduced maternal mortality ratio (MMR) in SAR countries. The program drivers reviewed include skilled birth attendance programs, the promotion and facilitation of institutional delivery and EmOC, family planning and reproductive health initiatives, access to safe abortion, and ANC services.

Cross-country analysis reveals that there is low to moderate correlation between a country's gross domestic product (GDP) per capita level and MRH indicators. There is moderate correlation between GDP per capita and SBA. With the exception of the Maldives and Sri Lanka, all other SAR countries had lower levels of SBA compared to countries with similar income (figure 4.1). There is relatively low correlation between GDP per capita and contraceptive prevalence rate (CPR). In SAR, CPR among reproductive age female population varies between 22 percent in Afghanistan to 68 percent in Sri Lanka. However, Bangladesh, Bhutan, India, Nepal, and Sri Lanka had higher CPR compared to other countries with similar income while Afghanistan, the Maldives, and Pakistan had lower levels (figure 4.2). The correlation between ANC coverage and GDP per capita is weak. In SAR, ANC varied between 47.9 percent in Afghanistan and 99.4 percent in Sri Lanka, which together with Bhutan and the Maldives outperformed other countries with similar income while the other SAR countries had lower levers (figure 4.3). Sri Lanka is the only country that has consistently had higher levels of all three indicators, which may partly explain its achievement of very low MMR. Out of the three countries that drove the regional reduction in MMR, India and Bangladesh had much higher contraceptive prevalence rates than comparable countries, which is a strong predictor of lower MMR.

Figure 4.1 Births Attended by Skilled Health Staff, 2011

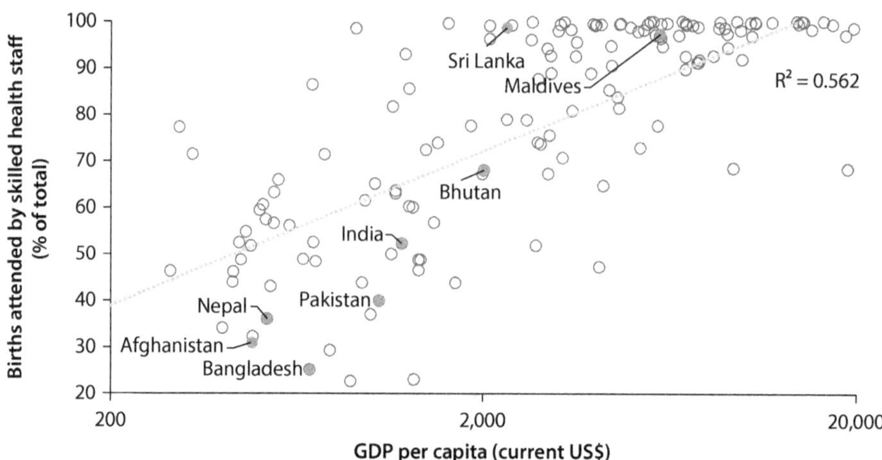

Source: Calculations based on World Bank 2015a.

http://dx.doi.org/10.1596/978-1-4648-0963-7

Figure 4.2 Contraceptive Prevalence Rate, 2011

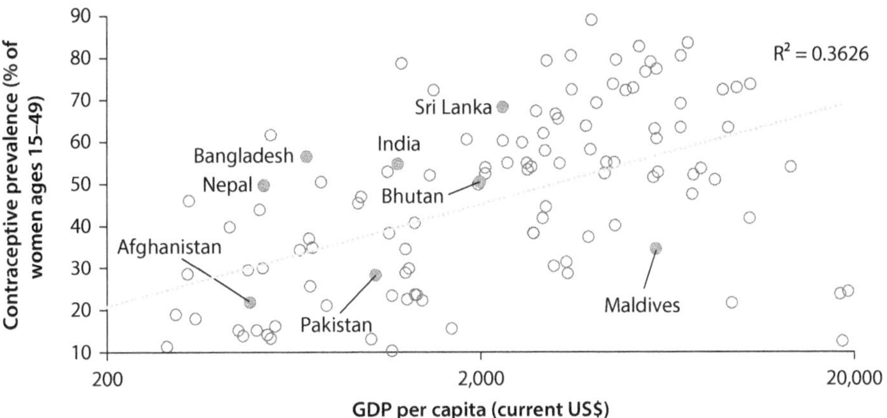

Source: Calculations based on World Bank 2015a.

Figure 4.3 Pregnant Women Receiving ANC, 2011

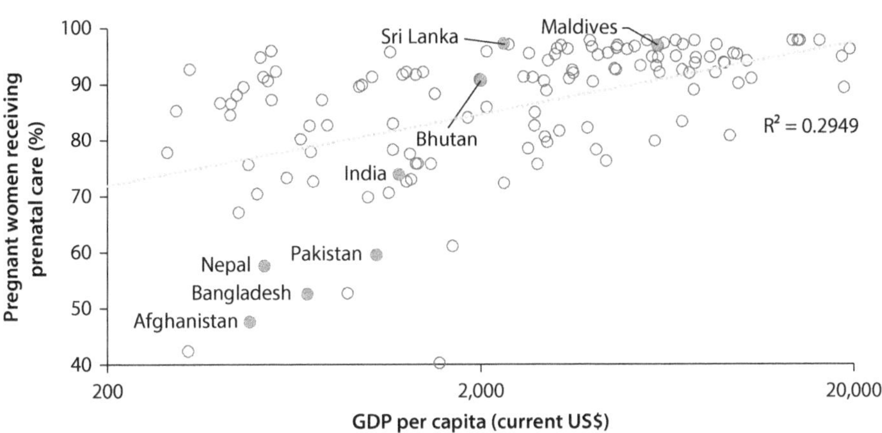

Source: Calculations based on World Bank 2015a.

Skilled Birth Attendance

Skilled attendance at birth is essential for safe delivery and is linked to reduced maternal mortality rates—particularly when it is combined with improved rates of institutional delivery. As depicted in figure 4.4, there is a strong correlation between maternal mortality decline and increased births attended by skilled health staff. SBAs are health workers trained to conduct normal delivery, identify any signs of complications, provide initial management of complications, and refer pregnant women to appropriate facilities to obtain medical care for complications. Programs may involve training existing workers in maternal health and midwifery skills or alternatively developing entirely new cadres of health workers, such as midwives and community-based birth attendants. Most of the

http://dx.doi.org/10.1596/978-1-4648-0963-7

Figure 4.4 Correlation between Maternal Mortality Ratio and Skilled Birth Attendance, 2013

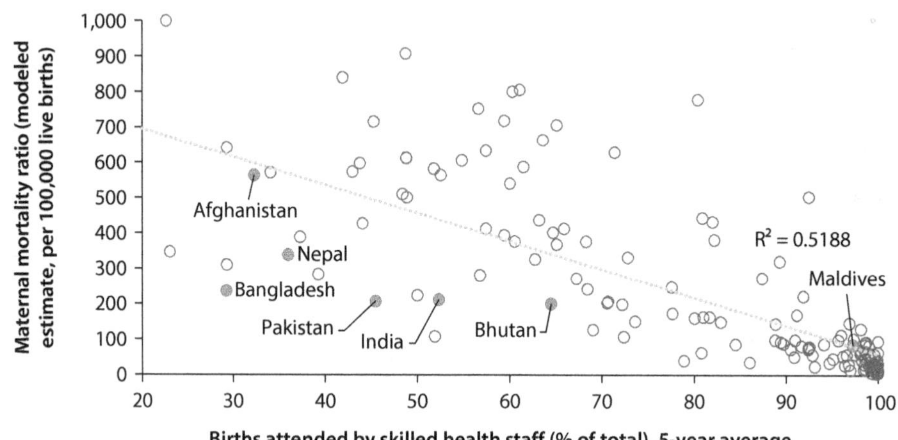

Source: Calculations based on World Bank 2015a.

SBA programs are focused on "centrifugal" strategies, which sought to bring services to the women as opposed to "centripetal" strategies, which sought to bring women to the services and entail increasing institutional delivery. The contribution of traditional birth attendants (TBAs) to maternal mortality reduction is well documented. Sri Lanka is one of the earliest examples of national prioritization of TBAs among the SAR countries.

In Sri Lanka, every household is covered by a public health midwife (PHM). The country began professionalizing midwifery services in the 1940s, leading to an increase in skilled attendance from 27 percent to more than 50 percent between 1940 and 1950 (Pathmanathan et al. 2003). From 1950 onwards, maternal deaths were reduced by 50 percent every 8–13 years. The country virtually eliminated maternal deaths from sepsis and hypertension (Pathmanathan et al. 2003). Midwives provide family planning, prenatal, maternity, and ANC services, as well as refer cases onwards for more specialized obstetric services (Pathmanathan et al. 2003). In 2010, more than 98 percent of deliveries in Sri Lanka occurred in hospitals with midwives in attendance, while 85 percent of women delivered in facilities with access to specialist obstetricians and gynecologists (Senanayake et al. 2011). Midwives are members of their respective communities and are trained over an 18-month period to care for a population of 3,000–5,000 (Senanayake et al. 2011). The Sri Lanka College of Obstetricians and Gynecologists and the Family Health Bureau collaborate to design policies and guidelines and train midwifery and nursing staff (Senanayake et al. 2011).

More recently, Afghanistan has developed the community midwife education (CME) program that contributed to a reduction of its high maternal mortality (Currie, Azfar and Fowler 2007). Midwives are trained to partner with women to promote their health, overcome harmful cultural practices, and focus on health promotion and disease prevention. The CME program led to a rapid increase in the use of SBAs—particularly among women in urban areas, educated women, and those from wealthier households. The use of SBAs increased from 26 percent from 2005–07 to 42 percent in 2009–10. The CME program is likely to be an important factor in the sharp reduction in the country's MMR from 1,600 in 2002 to 327 in 2010—a decrease of 80 percent (Rasooly et al. 2014).

Bangladesh developed a skilled birth attendance strategy in 2001 that contributed to reduction in maternal mortality. To address the issues of inequalities in accessing skilled birth attendance between the rich/poor and rural/urban, Bangladesh set a coverage target of one six-month trained community SBA for 6,000–8,000 people (Mridha, Anwar, and Koblinksy 2009). The implementation of this strategy was supported by the SBA training program, which began as a pilot in 2003 and employed a task shifting approach. The program aimed its efforts at existing family welfare assistants and female health assistants at the community level. They were trained in midwifery skills, to identify danger signs in pregnant women and to refer potential complicated cases (Koblinsky et al. 2008). Seventy-four essential skills were included in the curriculum, including those recommended by the Safe Motherhood Inter-Agency Group (Ahmed and Jakaria 2009). While the program did not reach its training and coverage targets, it nevertheless managed to train 3,000 SBAs. Little improvement in skilled birth attendance has been seen among poor, uneducated rural women. Skilled birth attendance overall among women aged 15–49 years, however, has increased from 9 percent in 1996 to 32 percent in 2011 (National Institute for Population Research and Trainng (NIPORT), Measure Evaluation and icddr,b, 2012). Maternal mortality decreased by more than 50 percent over this same period, although it is likely that a variety of factors contributed to this reduction.

In Bhutan, SBA-assisted deliveries have increased from 33.7 percent to 85.6 percent between 1990 and 2013. Over the same period, MMR has fallen from 390 to 120 per 100,000 live births (Maternal Mortality Estimation Inter-Agency Group 2014). While the number of health workers in Bhutan remains extremely low, the country has managed to increase nurses in the country from 335 in 2002 to 827 in 2014, of which about half were midwifery professionals (Kingdom of Bhutan 2014). The Government of Tamil Nadu State in India hired, trained, and deployed both auxiliary nurse midwife (ANMs) and Village Health Nurses to improve coverage in rural and tribal areas (one per 5,000 rural people and one per 3,000 people in tribal areas) to carry out ANC, home delivery, postnatal, and reproductive health visits at the community level (Padmanaban, Raman, and Mavalankar 2009). These cadres were incentivized with small payments based on the number of services delivered (Padmanaban, Raman, and Mavalankar 2009).

SBAs also have played a role in reducing maternal mortality in other countries. For example, Nigeria's Midwifery and Midwives Service Scheme has contributed to reducing the country's extremely high maternal and neonatal mortality rates, although the reduction was inconsistent across regions and facilities (Adogu 2014). The scheme provides for the temporary (12 month) placement of graduated, unemployed, and/or retired midwives to provide basic obstetric care in rural primary facilities and create improved chains of referral to EmOC-enabled secondary facilities (Adogu 2014). The program has been hampered by inadequate incentivization, disrupted supply chains for essential obstetric commodities, and poor infrastructure. Nevertheless, it succeeded in producing a sharp downward trend in maternal mortality among patients attending the facilities where the scheme was implemented (Adogu 2014).

Evidence of the impact of SBA on maternal mortality is moderate. A systematic review of SBA programs in 41 countries found that SBA was associated with significant reduction of maternal mortality (Berhan and Berhan 2014a). Another systematic review of impact evaluation of SBA programs in a few countries found that there was no evidence that solely improving the proportion of SBA improved mortality outcomes; however, it found that combining SBA with quality and access elements can improve mortality outcomes (IEG 2014).

Institutional Delivery

Much of the progress achieved by countries that reduced national MMR to less than 50 per 100,000 live births is due to the development of referral networks and the increased uptake of institutional delivery. Although some SBA programs support home-based delivery, the large reductions in MMR are often the result of situating SBAs in health facilities, increasing the number of women who deliver in those facilities, and creating a means of referring pregnant women from the community to primary and secondary facilities for either basic or comprehensive obstetric care (Koblinsky 2003). However, institutional delivery is a complex issue that is influenced by characteristics of the pregnant woman herself, her immediate social circle, the community in which she lives, the facility that is closest to her, and context of the country in which she lives (Moyer and Mustafa 2013).

Sri Lanka is perhaps the best example of the promotion of institutional delivery. Sri Lanka has promoted institutional delivery since the 1950s (Senanayake et al. 2011). By 2010, less than 1 percent of deliveries took place at home, and 85 percent of women delivered in a facility with specialist obstetric services (Senanayake et al. 2011). Comprehensive obstetric services coverage is approximately 1 per 460,000 people, which far surpasses the recommended coverage rate (Senanayake et al. 2011). A partogram tool for tracking each woman's labor and delivery was adopted and used since 1998 (Senanayake et al. 2011). The MMR in Sri Lanka is now 29 per 100,000 live births, the lowest among SAR countries, and far better than the MMR in many countries in the Caribbean, Central and South America, and Central Asia (WHO 2014).

Bangladesh's increased SBA coverage has occurred concurrently with improvements in access to and use of institutional delivery. Rates of home delivery in Bangladesh remain very high (more than 70 percent) (Hotchkiss, Godha, and Do 2014). Nevertheless, from 1996 to 2011, the percentage of women using institutional delivery increased from 5 percent to 29 percent (Hotchkiss, Godha, and Do 2014). Although this is partly due to increased uptake of women using private sector maternal health facilities—which grew from 2 percent to 17.1 percent in 2011—the percent of women using public facilities to deliver during this period

http://dx.doi.org/10.1596/978-1-4648-0963-7

increased from 2.9 percent to 12 percent as well (Hotchkiss, Godha, and Do 2014). During this period, Bangladesh decreased its MMR by an annual rate of 5–6 percent (El Arifeen et al. 2014). While the decrease in MMR cannot be entirely credited to institutional delivery, Bangladeshi women are nonetheless six times more likely to deliver in facilities now than they were in 1990 (Anwar et al. 2014). The country has improved institutional delivery rates across all wealth quintiles, reduced the rich to poor ratio from 15.8 to 6.8, and markedly decreased home delivery among the highest three quintiles (Hotchkiss, Godha, and Do 2014).

The Government of Tamil Nadu in India has also prioritized the increase of quality institutional deliveries. It increased institutional deliveries to 97.7 percent in 2008 from 64.7 percent in 1996 (Padmanaban, Raman, and Mavalankar 2009). Deliveries at home by trained personnel dropped over the same period from 20.9 percent to 2.1 percent, while deliveries at home by untrained personnel dropped from 14.4 percent to 0.2 percent (Padmanaban, Raman, and Mavalankar 2009). To promote 24-hour institutional delivery in rural areas, the government piloted a program where 90 primary health center (PHCs) were equipped with three staff nurses who were incentivized for each delivery conducted. Tamil Nadu has one of the lowest rates of maternal mortality in India, having reduced the MMR from 380 per 100,000 live births in 1993 to 90 per 100,000 live births by 2007. The emphasis on institutional delivery has been promoted throughout India, even though the country has struggled to reach its overall MMR targets (Chatterjee and Paily 2011). National initiatives such as the National Rural Health Mission (NRHM) and schemes like the JSY have sought to scale up institutional deliveries countrywide by increasing and improving first referral units (FRUs), training staff, and incentivizing patients (Chatterjee and Paily 2011). A coverage evaluation survey by UNICEF indicates that such schemes have had a major impact on increasing institutional deliveries in India from 40.7 percent in 2005 to 76 percent in 2009 (Chatterjee and Paily 2011).

Other countries have also reduced maternal mortality by increasing institutional delivery and improved referral networks along with SBAs. In Yunnan Province in China, for example, demographic, economic, and geographic characteristics contributed to an MMR that was almost twice the national average (Li et al. 2007). The rate of institutional delivery in Yunnan was about 57 percent compared to 79 percent nationally (Li et al. 2007). National and provincial authorities undertook a number of measures to improve institutional delivery rates among poor pregnant women. The MMR in Yunnan was reduced from 149 deaths per 100,000 live births to 63.3 deaths per 100,000 live births between 1995 and 2005, a 3.0 percent annual decline, although rates are higher in the Yunnan's more inaccessible mountainous regions (Li et al. 2007). Although the MMR in Yunnan is still almost twice that of the national average, multivariate analysis strongly correlates the percentage of pregnant women who delivered in hospitals—along with access to ANC and systematic management of pregnancy—with the reduction of the MMR in the province (Li et al. 2007). Likewise, in Cambodia, institutional births assisted by SBAs increased from 11 percent in 2000 to 55 percent in 2010 across the four lowest wealth quintiles (Liljestrand and Pathmanathan 2004).

Health system factors that contributed to this rapid change include the availability of health centers staffed with midwives (Liljestrand and Pathmanathan 2004).

There is strong evidence of the effectiveness of institutional delivery on reducing maternal mortality. In addition to the above examples, a systematic review of 70 papers that covered SBA and institutional delivery in Sub-Saharan African countries found a strong inverse correlation between institutional delivery and maternal mortality rates Sub-Saharan Africa of −0.69 ($p = .008$) (Moyer, Dako-Gyeke, and Adanu 2013). However, as with SBA, the rates of institutional delivery often depend on simultaneous investment in the broader health system, including increasing coverage, stocking, staffing, and quality control of facilities offering maternity care. For example, Sri Lanka, Bangladesh, and Tamil Nadu greatly increased the number of health facilities, which decreased the distance between households and clinics (see chapter 5 for details). They also established quality control measures to improve service performance. All of these efforts contributed to SBA and institutional delivery outcomes. Although one goal of such measures is to improve maternal health services, they also contributed to strengthening health systems overall, above and apart from targeted programmatic interventions.

Emergency Obstetric Care

EmOC initiatives are key to reducing MMR. EmOC is a central component of most Safe Motherhood Programs. Rollout of EmOC has proven to be an important targeted means to address the quality of maternal health services and improve maternal mortality indicators. EmOC teaches health workers a number of skills, including management of pregnancy-related complications by administering antibiotics, uterotonic drugs (oxytocin) and anticonvulsants (magnesium sulfate), manual removal of the placenta, removal of retained products following miscarriage or abortion, assisted vaginal delivery (preferably with vacuum extractor), and basic neonatal resuscitation care. PPH is a leading cause of maternal death and it can be effectively managed with EmOC. Countries in SAR are improving their efforts to deliver EmOC as part of the continuum of care. A World Bank study estimated that access to essential obstetric care accounts for more than half the maternal deaths averted (Wagstaff and Claeson 2004).

Nepal has made great strides in ensuring training for and coverage of EmOC through its Safe Motherhood and Newborn Health Long Term Plan, 2002–17. The Support for Safer Motherhood Programme funded by the U.K. Department for International Development (DfID), initiated in 2005, has supported Nepal's efforts in providing services to the poor and marginalized. A central component of this program has been basic, comprehensive, and emergency obstetric care training of health workers, along with information and education campaigns for the recognition of danger signs and the creation of emergency referral networks (Bhandari, Gordon, and Shakya 2011). By 2010, the number of health and sub-health posts offering 24-hour delivery increased from close to 0–537 (Bhandari, Gordon, and Shakya 2011). The met need for EmOC grew by 2–3 percent per year and the met need for caesarean section grew by 2–9 percent per year (Bhandari, Gordon,

http://dx.doi.org/10.1596/978-1-4648-0963-7

and Shakya 2011). One important element of Nepal's EmOC efforts includes working with the Red Cross to increase availability and distribution networks of safe blood for PPH. PPH is the leading cause of maternal deaths in the country, accounting for an estimated 19 percent of maternal deaths (Bhandari, Gordon, and Shakya 2011). Nepal has also worked to scale up access at health facilities of two important uterotonics for PPH, oxytocin and misoprostol. Distribution of the drugs by trained female community health volunteers (FCHVs) has been particularly effective in reaching women who are poor, illiterate, or living in remote areas. (Rajbhandari et al. 2010). Community-based distribution of misoprostol tablets has been scaled up since 2010. As of 2013, it had reached 31 of 75 districts in the country (Government of Nepal 2014). However, surveys have found that health worker and patient awareness remains low and stockout is high, so it is difficult to judge misoprostol's contribution toward MMR reduction in the country (Government of Nepal 2014). Oxytocin is perceived by health workers to be in adequate supply and was deployed in 63 percent of facilities surveyed for PPH, but it is frequently poorly stored (Government of Nepal 2014).

Bangladesh has implemented a comprehensive EmOC program at the community and facility levels since the 1990s (El Arifeen et al. 2014). These efforts gained momentum during the 2001 Women's Right to Life and Health Initiative. During the program, trainings, facility renovations, supply chain and information systems, quality assurance mechanisms, community and social mobilization activities, and staff retention initiatives related to EmOC were rapidly rolled out in all the country's 59 district hospitals and 120 of the 400 sub-district hospitals (El Arifeen et al. 2014). The program was integrated into the country's SBA strategy, enabling referral for emergency care starting at the community level (Koblinsky et al. 2008). The program now includes management of PPH through community-level distribution of oxytocin and misoprostol by community-based SBAs, although drug stockout remains a problem (Bergeson-Lockwood, Leahy Madsen, and Bernstein 2010). Distributing misoprostol tablets is well-suited for Bangladesh since it can be self-administered as the majority of births take place at home (Bergeson-Lockwood, Leahy Madsen, and Bernstein 2010). By 2004, 70 sub-district hospitals and 53 district hospitals were able to provide comprehensive EmOC, and another 35 sub-district hospitals were able to provide basic EmOC (Islam et al. 2005). In a very short time, EmOC coverage increased from 0.23 in 1998 to 1.04 per 500,000 people in 2002, achieving the minimum United Nations (UN) standards on coverage of comprehensive EmOC services (Islam et al. 2005). The proportion of births at EmOC facilities also increased during this time from 5.3 percent to 11.7 percent, while the met need for EmOC increased from 11.1 percent to 26.6 percent (Islam et al. 2005). By 2008, the number of facilities able to provide EmOC had expanded to 1,463 (El Arifeen et al. 2014). In 2013, the MMR in Bangladesh was estimated at 120 per 100,000 live births, a more than 50 percent reduction since 2000 (El Arifeen et al. 2014; WHO 2014).

India has prioritized EmOC since 2005 in the NRHM. Since then, the government has collaborated with numerous domestic and international nongovernmental organizations (NGOs) to develop guidelines and train health workers

http://dx.doi.org/10.1596/978-1-4648-0963-7

in EmOC. The EmOC initiatives include a four-month competency-based curriculum and training system for doctors to provide services in rural areas, the creation of guidelines for SBAs, staff nurses, and ANMs, and the development of instructions to operationalize field referral units (Vora et al. 2009). Task shifting enabled SBAs, ANMs, and nurses to administer oxytocin, misoprostol, magnesium sulfate, and antibiotics for the treatment of complications (Vora et al. 2009). In the case of oxytocin and misoprostol, this move has been critical as a proportion of maternal deaths due to PPH has increased from 16 percent in 1985 to 38 percent in 2009 (Chatterjee and Paily 2011). MMR in India has subsequently dropped from 280 in 2005 to 190 per 100,000 births in 2013 (Maternal Mortality Estimation Inter-Agency Group 2014). This reduction, however, has not been enough to ensure that India meets its MDG targets for 2015, and variations in the MMR between states are great. For example, Tamil Nadu, Kerala, Andhra Pradesh, and other southern states have achieved far greater progress in reducing maternal mortality than predominantly northern states such as Uttar Pradesh, Rajasthan, Assam, and others designated as "Empowered Action Group" states due to their weaker performance on health and development indicators. Providing comprehensive EmOC to rural areas remains a challenge due to a severe shortage of specialists. Of the 20,000 obstetricians in India, only 780 work in rural areas at the sub-district level (Ministry of Health and Family Welfare 2004). Furthermore, 30 percent of facilities lack labor rooms and only around half are open 24 hours a day (Kumar and Dansereau 2014).

Rollout of EmOC, SBAs, institutional delivery, and other maternal health services with the aim of reducing the MMR are frequently accompanied by supportive interventions that facilitate access. For example, Sri Lanka was one of the pioneers of the maternity waiting home. Women were admitted to health facilities before their due date so they could be close to clinics or hospitals before delivery. This service was first initiated in the 1950s (Pathmanathan et al. 2003). Community-based emergency transport has often been part of a targeted maternal health response. In India, the JSY scheme has focused on free transport for obstetric emergencies, the development of an ambulance network, and the incentivization of mothers to deliver institutionally by helping to finance transportation costs (Chatterjee and Paily 2011). In 11 states, maternal transport schemes have been linked to a centralized call center (Chatterjee and Paily 2011). In 2006, Gujarat State supported financial protection to families below the poverty line and out-of-pocket cost recovery on transport for maternity cases through its Chiranjeevi Project. The project contributed to a drop in the MMR from 218 per 100,000 live births in 2005 to around 122 in 2010 (Chatterjee and Paily 2011). Since 2008, this project has been replicated by Uttar Pradesh, a state with the highest maternal mortality burden in India (Chatterjee and Paily 2011). In a number of countries, health commodity distribution of iron/folic acid supplementation, tetanus toxoid immunization, and other critical drugs and supplies have been carried out at community level in Nepal (Padmanaban, Raman, and Mavalankar 2009; Bhandari, Gordon, and Shakya 2011); Bangladesh (El Arifeen et al. 2014); India (Chatterjee and Paily 2011); and Pakistan (Bhutta et al. 2013).

http://dx.doi.org/10.1596/978-1-4648-0963-7

Assurance of EmOC and supportive interventions are a priority among other countries. Improving access to basic care and EmOC, scaling up maternity waiting homes (Koblinsky 2003), and rolling out essential maternal health commodities have been cited as key contributing factors to reducing the MMR in countries around the world (Koblinsky 2003; Campbell et al. 2005). However, all those interventions require strong health systems to ensure their effectiveness, sustainability, and access.

There is strong evidence that EmOC has significantly contributed to maternal mortality reduction. A systematic review and meta-analysis of 62 studies representing 51 countries assessed the global met need for EmOC, which was 45 percent (inter quartile range: 28–57 percent), with significant disparity between low-income (21 percent [12–31 percent]), middle-income (32 percent [15–56 percent]), and high-income countries (99 percent [99–99 percent]), ($P = 0.041$). This review found a strong inverse correlation between met need of EmOC and MMR ($r = -0.42$, $P < 0.001$) as depicted in figure 4.5, which provides robust evidence of the effectiveness of EmOC but also points out to the challenge of its scaling up in LMICs (Holmer et al. 2015).

Safe Abortion Services and Post-Abortion Care

Countries have leveraged safe abortion services and post-abortion care to support national maternal mortality reduction. Such services can prevent deaths from unsafe abortion and its subsequent complications (Padmanaban, Raman, and Mavalankar 2009; Bhandari, Gordon, and Shakya 2011). For example, in Nepal, unsafe abortions accounted for a high proportion of maternal deaths throughout the 1990s (Henderson et al. 2013). Advocates estimated the abortion rate at 117 per 100,000 women, while some facility-based studies found upwards of 20 percent of maternal deaths and over 50 percent of obstetric complications

Figure 4.5 Correlation between Met Need of EmOC and MMR

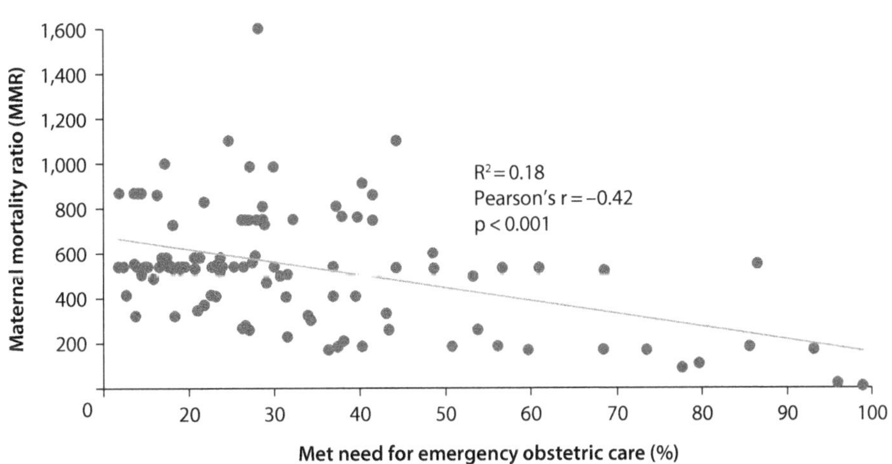

Source: Holmer et al. 2015.

due to unsafe abortion (Samandari et al. 2012). In 2002, following a period of advocacy, Nepal amended its constitution to legalize abortion during the first 12 weeks of pregnancy and up to 18 weeks in cases of incest, rape, fetal malformation, or risk of death to the mother (Samandari et al. 2012). Over the next two years, a National Safe Abortion Policy was created which stipulated free services for poor and marginalized women. The eligibility criteria, however, was not well defined, posing a challenge to service use. A Safe Abortion Advisory Committee was also established and health workers (including mid-level ANMs) were trained when the first clinic opened in 2004 (Samandari et al. 2012). This was followed by rapid expansion of facilities and training of health workers. Safe abortion services are now available nationwide in the public sector and through public-private partnerships. Since 2010, all 75 districts had at least one safe abortion site with one qualified provider, and more than 400,000 women made use of the service (Samandari et al. 2012). During this period, Nepal also achieved large reductions in maternal mortality (Padmanaban, Raman, and Mavalankar 2009; Bhandari, Gordon, and Shakya 2011).

Safe abortion services are one of the maternal mortality reduction strategies in India's Reproductive and Child Health Program (RCH-II). Successive legislative controls in 1971, 1994, and 2002 have led to a demonstrable decline in abortion-related deaths. A 2001–2003 survey found that the number of maternal deaths due to unsafe abortions declined from 11.5 percent in 1985 to 8 percent in 2001 (Registrar General of India and Centre for Global Health Research 2006). Despite the fall in abortion-related deaths, challenges persist, including informal fees, service availability, quality of care, low levels of awareness of services, and social stigma (Hirve 2004). As a result of shortfalls in public investment, only 25 percent of abortion facilities are public and 87 percent of the abortion market is controlled by the private sector. The cost of seeking an abortion in the private sector is typically 7.5 times higher than in public facilities, and post-abortion medication imposes additional costs (Hirve 2004).

Even in Bangladesh, where abortion remains illegal except to save the life of a mother, the country has managed to reduce the risks associated with unsafe abortions. Menstrual regulation (MR) refers to the induction of menstruation to ensure non-pregnancy after a missed period (Vlassoff et al. 2012). Bangladesh's MR program was first introduced in 1974, following parliament's lifting of a ban on abortion to reduce the number of clandestine abortions sought by victims of rape during the war. MR has been available free of charge in the public sector since 1979. There is some indication that MR has reduced maternal mortality from unsafe abortion. In the mid-1980s, one study estimated that in rural areas, unsafe abortions accounted for 15 percent of maternal deaths. By 2001, the estimated rate declined to 5 percent and then to 1 percent in 2010 (Vlassoff et al. 2012). In 2006, the government reported 124,045 MR procedures, evenly distributed across government and NGO facilities (Johnston et al. 2010). While the MR program reduced the number of clandestine abortions, many barriers remain, including user fees, availability, quality of care, and lack of knowledge about the service. For example, women who are financially better off and live in urban areas

http://dx.doi.org/10.1596/978-1-4648-0963-7

are more likely to access abortions from trained providers than their counterparts (Vlassoff et al. 2012). In 2010, 43 percent of facilities that could potentially offer MR were not providing the service due to the lack of funding for the program (Johnston et al. 2010).

Family Planning

Access to family planning services and modern contraception contribute to a decrease in the overall birth rate, a reduction in the total number of pregnancies per woman (birth parity), an improvement in birth spacing, and a decline in rates of pregnancy among women over the age of 35. These indicators are linked to a higher risk of pregnancy and delivery-related complications and, thus, maternal mortality. For this reason, reproductive and sexual health interventions represent a critical rung on the continuum of care. A number of SAR countries have been able to attribute large reductions in maternal mortality rates in part to the introduction and expansion of family planning and reproductive health policies and programs. As depicted in figure 4.6, global trends also indicate a strong correlation between increased contraceptive prevalence and maternal mortality reduction.

In SAR countries, there are strong correlations between increasing family planning coverage and declining maternal mortality. Since its independence in 1971, Bangladesh maintained and expanded the Family Planning program (Nag 1992). Increased access to and uptake of family planning services is now part of the country's Essential Service Delivery Package and is one of several factors attributed to Bangladesh's success in reducing its MMR from 322 to 194 deaths per 100,000 live births between 1998 and 2010 (Koblinsky et al. 2008; El Arifeen et al. 2014). During this same period, the percent of currently married women using modern contraception increased from 43 percent to 54 percent, and the fertility rate dropped from 3.2 to 2.5, especially among

Figure 4.6 Correlation between MMR and Contraceptive Prevalence Rate, 2013

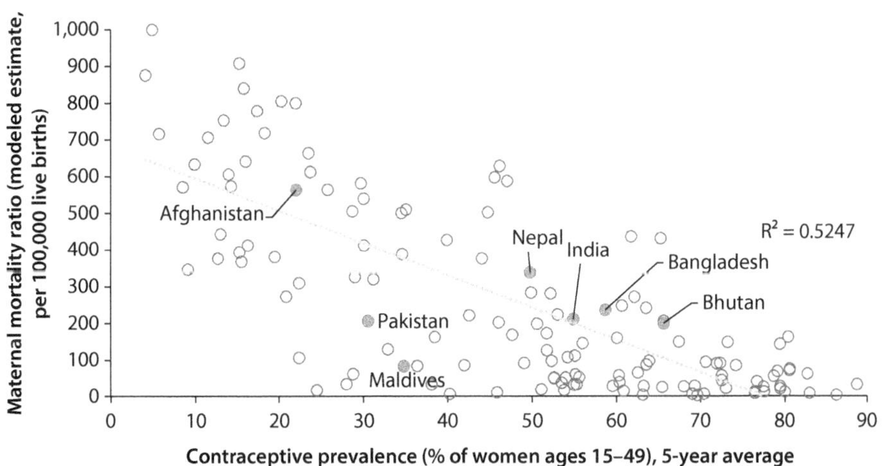

Source: Calculations based on World Bank 2015a.

older, higher parity women (El Arifeen et al. 2014). It is calculated that this decrease in fertility rate contributed to 21 percent of deaths averted, with an additional 7 percent of deaths averted due to shifts in parity and age of mothers (El Arifeen et al. 2014). In Tamil Nadu State in India, for example, the percentage of couples using various family planning methods increased from 44.7 percent in 1993 to 60.0 percent in 2006, while the MMR declined by over 70 percent during the same period. Interestingly, it was the presence of female doctors that helped rural women accept family planning services (Padmanaban, Raman, and Mavalankar 2009). Between 1990 and 2008, 35.4 percent of maternal deaths averted and 32.3 percent of the MMR reduction across India has been attributed to fertility decline resulting from increased contraceptive uptake (Jain 2011). From 1996 to 2006, a similar trend was seen in Nepal, where modern contraceptive use increased from 26 percent to 44 percent, with a corresponding decline in the TFR from 4.6 to 2.1 (Bhandari, Gordon, and Shakya 2011). In Afghanistan and Pakistan, where MMR is still high, contraceptive prevalence rates also increased but at lower levels. In Afghanistan, modern contraceptive use increased from 10 percent in 2003 to 20 percent in 2010, particularly among the more educated women and those in wealthier households. The TFR dropped from 6.3 to 5.1 (Rasooly et al. 2014). Pakistan's contraceptive prevalence rate rose from 5.2 percent in 1974 to 30 percent in 2007, with social marketing playing an important role in the provision of contraceptive methods, while the TFR declined from 6.2 to 4.1 in the same period (Mahmud et al. 2011).

In other regions, a focus on targeted MRH interventions, like in the SAR, are often delivered as integrated packages along the continuum of care. For example, Mongolia's maternal mortality fell from 210 deaths per 100,000 live births in 1994 to 98.8 in 2004 and to 68 in 2013 (Hill, Dodd, and Dashdorj 2006). The use of modern family planning increased from 46 percent in 1998 to 58 percent in 2003, with a 14 percent increase in hormonal methods (Hill, Dodd, and Dashdorj 2006). Mongolia is seen as a "fast track" country for declining MMR (Cohen et al. 2014) and it came very close to reaching its MDG 5 goal of 50 deaths per 100,000 live births. Even though the Lao People's Democratic Republic was struggling to meet its MMR goal, it nevertheless managed to halve its MMR from 1,200 deaths per 100,000 live births in 1990 to 580 deaths in 2008 (Scopaz, Eckermann, and Clarke 2011). In part, these gains are attributable to great improvements in access to contraception. In 13 of the country's 17 provinces, more than 50 percent of women have their contraceptive needs met (Scopaz, Eckermann, and Clarke 2011).

Family planning programs, while not directly affecting maternal mortality outcomes at the intra-partum stage, play an important role in the inter-partum stage that contributes to maternal mortality reduction. Family planning provides a prevention strategy for reducing the exposure, incidence, and risks associated with pregnancy, especially when parity is high. They also help reduce the risks associated with unsafe abortion due to unwanted pregnancy, which is another main cause of death (Ahmed et al. 2012). While the evidence base from

http://dx.doi.org/10.1596/978-1-4648-0963-7

systematic reviews on the subject is limited, there are a few important studies that observe the relationship between family planning and maternal mortality. For example, one study in SAR countries found that fertility decline caused a 39 percent of the decline in MMR in Bangladesh, 32 percent in India, and 22 percent in Pakistan (Jain 2011). Interestingly, these are the three countries that are responsible for most of the maternal death decline in SAR between 1990 and 2013. Another study found that increased contraceptive use and declining fertility reduced over 1 million maternal deaths between 1990 and 2005, suggesting that a change in at risk births could mean a decline in MMR by 450 points (Stover and Ross 2010). In an analysis of 172 countries, contraceptive use was found to have averted 44 percent of maternal deaths worldwide in 2008, and for individual countries, the reduction ranged between 7 and 60 percent. The same study also found that if unmet need was satisfied, another 29 percent of deaths per year could be avoided (Ahmed et al. 2012).

Antenatal Care and Female Community Health Workers

SAR countries that have successfully reduced their MMR frequently cite increased access to ANC as an important correlate, but there is little evidence to support its impact. ANC provides an opportunity to establish contact between the services provider and the patient. For example, in Nepal, ANC coverage reached 73.7 percent in 2011 (Hussein et al. 2011). In Tamil Nadu State in India, the percentage of women attending at least three ANC visits rose from 18 percent in 1992 to 95.9 percent in 2006 (Padmanaban, Raman, and Mavalankar 2009). In comparison, nationwide estimates in India show that only 19 percent of women received at least three ANC visits, according to the District Level Household and Facility Survey, 2007–2008 (Rai and Tulchinsky 2015). Afghanistan increased the percentage of births with ANC from a skilled provider from 57 percent during 2005–2007 to 68 percent in 2009–2010. As with family planning, ANC use was highest among urban, educated, and wealthier women (Rasooly et al. 2014). Sri Lanka began providing ANC services in the 1920s, extending antenatal clinics to the community level by the early 1930s (Pathmanathan et al. 2003; WHO 2014). Supported by PHMs, ANC coverage is 93 percent for four visits and 99 percent for at least one visit (Senanayake et al. 2011.) Bangladesh has also improved ANC coverage. The proportion of women attending at least one ANC consultation increased from 27 percent in 1991 to 60 percent in 2007 to 71 percent in 2010. Socioeconomic status, education, and residence are significant predictors of ANC use in Bangladesh. (Koblinsky et al. 2008).

Increased use of ANC interventions are often the result of the establishment of volunteer or nominally incentivized female community-based MRH workers (Koblinsky et al. 2008). In this case, ANC care is part of a broader focus on a continuum of care providing an integrated package of services spanning reproductive health to pregnancy, labor and delivery, postnatal, neonatal, and child health. For example, even though Pakistan is struggling with armed conflict, political insecurity, and natural disaster, the country has nevertheless had some

http://dx.doi.org/10.1596/978-1-4648-0963-7

success with its LHW Program. Rolled out in 1994, the LHW program involves the training of a cadre of female community health workers to carry out a wide range of activities. LHWs link women to reproductive, maternal, and child health care by providing contraceptives, micronutrient supplementation, immunization, and health education messaging. They also act as liaisons between TBAs and skilled providers in local facilities (Bhutta et al. 2013; Malik and Kayan 2014). In spite of concerns about quality of care and financial sustainability, Pakistan has deployed over 100,000 LHWs to cover 60 percent of the country's rural population (Bhutta et al. 2013). In 1988, Nepal began deploying community-based volunteers, known as FCHVs, to link the community with the health system and to provide advice to community members on family planning and MCH (Karkee 2011). Now, over 48,000 FCHVs work across Nepal (Karkee 2011).

Globally, increasing access to ANC is also cited as a component of integrated maternal health programs. The Arab Republic of Egypt, for example, is on track to meet its MMR targets with a 62.5 percent decline in MMR between 1990 and 2013—from 120 per 100,000 live births to 45 per 100,000 live births. Improving, expanding, and increasing ANC has been a priority for the Egyptian Ministry of Health (Campbell et al. 2005). ANC in Egypt consists of information, education, and communication (IEC) and behavior change communication (BCC) campaigns, treatment of existing conditions, and screening for risk factors (Campbell et al. 2005). The IEC/BCC component is understood as a major factor in improving women's use of maternity services. Media campaigns and community outreach contribute to increased women and families' awareness of maternal danger signs and reduced delays in seeking treatment for complications, especially those related to antepartum hemorrhage (Campbell et al. 2005).

The evidence of the impact of ANC on reducing maternal mortality is limited. Although the availability, content, and quality of ANC vary enormously among developing countries, they are generally much lower in countries with high maternal mortality. Hospital case series, confidential enquiries into causes of maternal death, and case-control studies of maternal deaths in developing countries show an association with "lack of" ANC. Despite the consensus from different studies in favor of ANC, reservations about the extent of its true effectiveness remain unknown. However, there may be real benefit from at least some of the elements of ANC, and the absolute scope for benefit may be greater in developing countries where morbidity and mortality are higher (Carroli, Rooney, and Villar 2001).

http://dx.doi.org/10.1596/978-1-4648-0963-7

CHAPTER 5

Health Sector Drivers

Key Messages

- Women's access to and use of maternal and reproductive health (MRH) services depend on broader health system inputs.
- In most South Asia Region (SAR) countries, the percentage of general government spending on health—as a proportion of total government spending—is below the global average. However, the association between maternal survival and low levels of government spending on health, combined with high levels of out-of-pocket payments, and reliance on private providers is weak.
- There is strong evidence of the impact of supply- and demand-side health financing schemes on the use of MRH services but little evidence of their effect on maternal mortality.
- The removal of user fees for maternal health services had mixed results and the robust evidence quantifying impact remains scant. Health insurance was found to have a positive relationship with the use of MRH services.
- Coverage of MRH services has improved in the public sector in SAR but gaps still remain. On the other hand, the private sector is increasingly providing a larger share of MRH services.
- Countries in SAR have made efforts in hiring and training midwives, other skilled birth attendant (SBAs), and obstetrics/gynecology specialists as well as cadres of semiskilled volunteers and community workers to support maternal health services, which may have contributed to increased service usage. The evidence of the impact of training of health workers on maternal health is mixed.
- The SAR countries have also attempted to prioritize the delivery of drugs and commodities; invested in their health information systems by rolling out maternal death registration and implementing facility-based and community-based verbal autopsy and audits; and laid the policy and governance structures, although the impact of these on maternal health outcomes is not evident.

Introduction

Maternal mortality is an important marker of how well a country's health system is functioning (Béhague and Storeng 2008; Muldoon et al. 2011). Women's access to and use of MRH services are dependent on a number of broader health system inputs that buttress the provision of MRH services. The World Health Organization's (WHO's) "health systems building blocks" define the key pillars required for building better health systems. They include increased health care financing, greater service delivery, better availability of human resources for health (HRH), investment in health information systems, enhanced leadership and governance, and improved access to essential drugs and health commodities (WHO 2007). These building blocks support the activities, services, and programs proven effective in improving MRH indicators and, thus, improved maternal survival.

Cross-country analysis reveals that level of inputs to the health systems in SAR vary widely. Health expenditure per capita increases as gross domestic product (GDP) per capita increases, depicting a strong correlation, as shown in figure 5.1. In SAR, the level of health expenditure per capita is generally low and varies widely from less than US$40 per capita in Bangladesh, Pakistan, and Nepal to US$720 in Maldives. Compared to other countries with similar income level, Afghanistan, Nepal, and Maldives had a higher level of health expenditure per capita while all other SAR countries had lower level of spending (figure 5.1). On the other hand, the correlation between the level of government health expenditure (as a percentage of total health expenditure) and GDP per capita is low. In SAR, it ranges from 21.2 percent in Afghanistan to 57.6 percent in Bhutan. Compared to countries with similar income, only Bhutan had a higher level of government health expenditure as a percentage of total health expenditure and Maldives and Nepal had the same levels while all other SAR countries had lower levels (figure 5.2). Hospital beds per 1,000 people ranges from 0.6 beds in Pakistan and Bangladesh to 4.3 beds in Maldives.

Figure 5.1 Health Expenditure per Capita, 2013

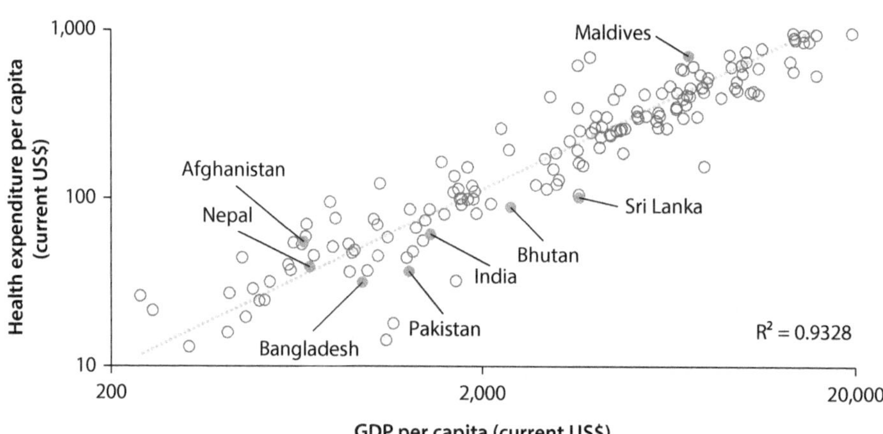

Source: World Bank 2015a.

Figure 5.2 Public Health Expenditure as a Share of Total Health Expenditure, 2013

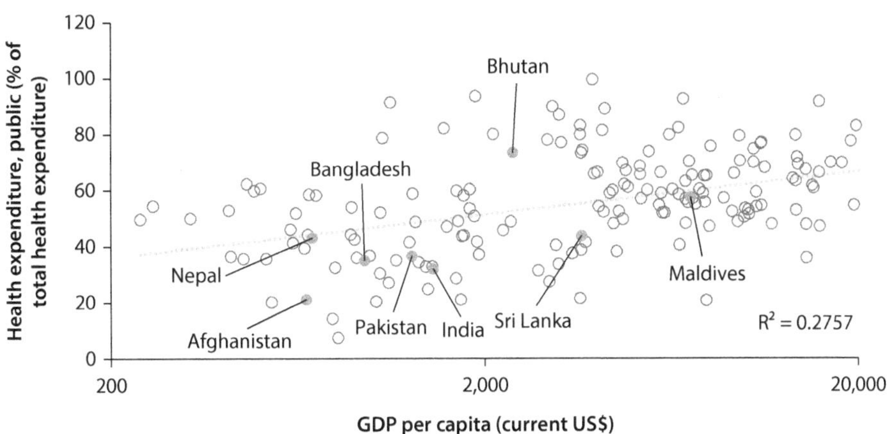

Source: World Bank 2015a.

Figure 5.3 Hospital Beds per 1,000 People, 2012

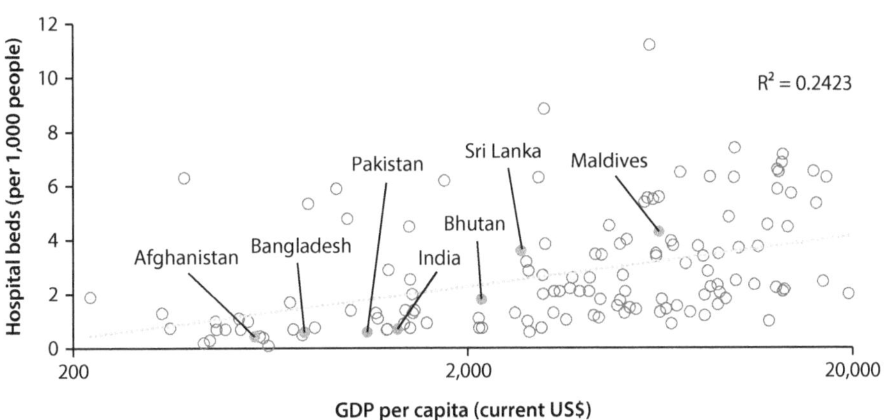

Source: World Bank 2015a.

Compared to other countries with similar income, Maldives and Sri Lanka had higher levels of hospital beds while the other SAR countries had much lower levels (figure 5.3). With regard to the health workforce, the correlation between availability of physicians and nurses/midwives per 1,000 people and GDP per capita is moderate. In SAR, the number of physicians per 1,000 people ranges from 0.023 in Bhutan to 1.4 in Maldives. Compared to countries with similar income, only Pakistan had a higher level of physicians and Afghanistan, Bangladesh, and India had the same levels of physicians while Bhutan, Sri Lanka, and Maldives had much lower levels of physicians per 1,000 people (figure 5.4). Nurses and midwives per 1,000 people ranges from 0.1 in Bhutan to 5.0 in Maldives. Compared to countries with similar income, only Maldives had a higher level of nurses and midwives while all the other SAR countries had lower levels (figure 5.5).

http://dx.doi.org/10.1596/978-1-4648-0963-7

Figure 5.4 Physicians per 1,000 People, 2010

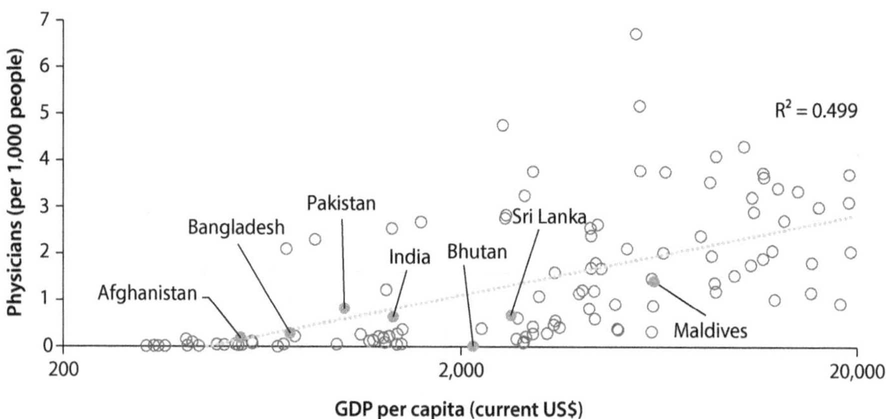

Source: World Bank 2015a.

Figure 5.5 Nurses and Midwives per 1,000 People, 2010

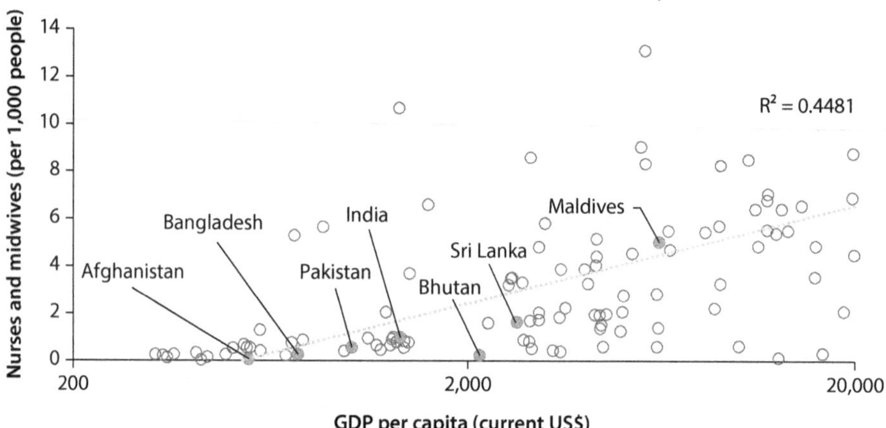

Source: World Bank 2015a.

Health Care Financing

Although SAR countries and their development partners have been investing in MRH programs, in most instances, the percentage of general government spending on health—as a proportion of total government spending—is below the global average. The proportion of private expenditure and out-of-pocket expenditure remains high. For example, 2013 estimates in India indicate that general government expenditure on health as a percentage of total government expenditure increased slightly from 7.4 percent in 2000 to 9.6 percent in 2013, while private expenditure as a percentage of total expenditure fell from 73 percent to only 67.8 percent (WHO Global Health Observatory 2015). Of this, 86.3 percent was out-of-pocket expenditure (WHO 2014). Globally, the increase

http://dx.doi.org/10.1596/978-1-4648-0963-7

Figure 5.6 Correlation between MMR and Out-of-Pocket Expenditure, 2013

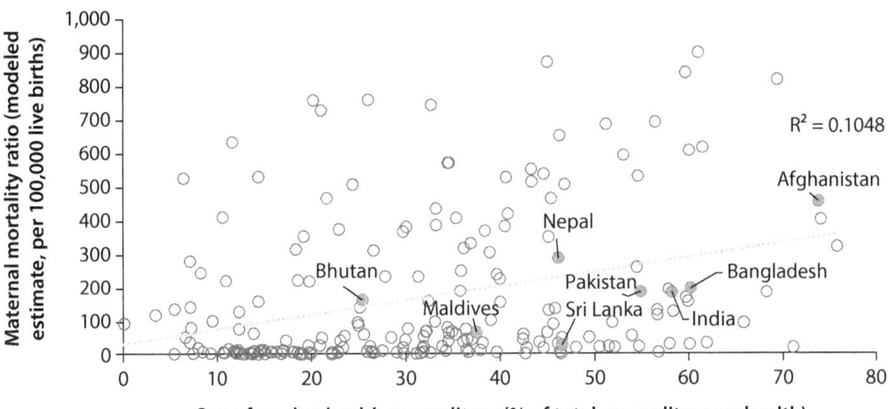

Source: World Bank 2015a.

in out-of-pocket spending as a percentage of total health spending was not strongly associated with the increase in maternal mortality ratio (MMR), and most SAR countries achieved better MMR compared to other countries at the same level of out-of-pocket spending (figure 5.6).

In 2004, over 80 percent of Indian households reported paying out of pocket for maternal health services. Of those, four times the number were using private maternity services rather than public services (Leone, James, and Padmadas 2013). This high level of private and out-of-pocket expenditure is surprising given the fact that the Indian government more than doubled its per capita expenditure on health from US$17 in 2000 to US$44 in 2011. A significant portion of government expenditure has been directed to public sector MRH services (WHO 2014). For instance, the proportion of spending on the *Janani Suraksha Yojana* (JSY) program—as a total of the National Rural Health Mission (NRHM)—increased from about 9 percent in 2005–06 to 36 percent in 2012–13. RCH flexipool expenditures have grown exponentially, from less than US$50 million in 2005–06 to over US$1 billion in 2012–13.[1] However, progress in reducing the MMR and improving other MRH health indicators in India remain off target, and households in India frequently choose to opt out of many of these public sector services.

Since 2000, the Bangladesh government's general expenditure on health as a percentage of total government spending has only increased from 7.4 percent to 7.8 percent. Yet private expenditure on health as a percentage of total expenditure on health increased from 59.3 percent to 64.7 percent over the same period. Out-of-pocket expenditure as a percentage of private expenditure on health is 93 percent (WHO Global Health Observatory 2015). In 2012, total expenditure on maternal, newborn, and child health (MNCH) patient services in Bangladesh represented an estimated 12 percent of total recurrent expenditures on health. The government only financed 28 percent of MNCH expenditure (Rannan-Eliya, Kasthuri, and De Alwis 2012). Of the total expenditure on MNCH patient services, only 28 percent went to childbirth care. This is partly because a large proportion of women in Bangladesh continue to deliver at home with traditional birth attendants (TBAs), whose fees are much lower than those for institutional delivery (Rannan-Eliya, Kasthuri, and De Alwis 2012). The estimated breakdown of sources for childbirth financing indicate that more than 70 percent came from out-of-pocket payments for either delivery at a private provider, out-of-pocket purchase of medicines at the Ministry of Health and Family Welfare (MOHFW) facilities, out-of-pocket purchases of medicines, or informal out-of-pocket payments at MOHFW facilities (Rannan-Eliya, Kasthuri, and De Alwis 2012). Pakistan (86.8 percent), Afghanistan (93.6 percent), and Nepal (81.4 percent) also have disproportionately high out-of-pocket expenditures as a percentage of private expenditure, a significant share of which is estimated for private maternity services (WHO Global Health Observatory 2015).

The association between maternal survival and low levels of government spending on health, combined with high levels of out-of-pocket payments, and reliance on private providers is weak. In Bangladesh and Nepal, this combination of factors has not prevented a sharp reduction in the MMR over the last 15 years. In Afghanistan, Pakistan, and India, however, political and socioeconomic factors distort any analysis of the impact of financing on MMR reduction. Nevertheless, it is clear that additional investment in public sector MRH service delivery has not consistently resulted in progress on reducing MMR, improved maternal health outcomes, or improved public services usage.

A commitment to free maternal and child health (MCH) services is one of the most important steps a country can take to reduce its MMR (Amibor 2013). Countries that have been most successful in reducing high MMR, such as Brazil, China, Cuba, and Malaysia, have all attributed their progress in part to the availability of free MRH services (Barros et al. 2010; Koblinsky 2003; Li et al. 2007; Victora et al. 2011; You et al. 2012). Evidence suggests that even in countries that have struggled with high MMR, providing free services can have a tremendous impact on MRH service usage. In Haiti, the expansion of the free *Soins Obstétricaux Gratuits* and *Soins Infantiles Gratuits* schemes helped to double the number of institutional deliveries from 2007, before the devastating earthquake of 2010 (Amibor 2013).

The removal of user fees for maternal health services had mixed results and the robust evidence quantifying impact remains scant. Countries in SAR that have attempted to remove user fees for reproductive, maternal, newborn, and child health (RMNCH) services to reduce financial barriers to use have had mixed success improving service uptake (Witter et al. 2000). In Sri Lanka, the most successful SAR country in improving maternal survival, the removal of financial barriers to health care is noted as a fundamental contributory factor to reducing national MMR (Pathmanathan et al. 2003). Since the 1930s, Sri Lanka has provided mostly free health services—including maternity and reproductive health services and drugs and supplies—to its population. It achieved high levels of equity with 70 percent of poor women using public sector hospitals (Koblinsky 2003; Pathmanathan et al. 2003). In 2009, Nepal eliminated fees for maternity services under the Aama Surakchhya Programme. Nevertheless, out-of-pocket expenditure for health as a percentage of private expenditure for health was 81.4 percent in 2013 (Bhandari, Gordon, and Shakya 2011). Technically, India has free maternity services available in public sector facilities, including free emergency transport in a number of states. Evidence exists that in public sector facilities, health workers demand excessive informal payments and quality issues exist. Both issues are key factors driving Indian families to pay private providers out of pocket for maternity services (Chatterjee and Paily 2011). In Bhutan, although basic primary health care is provided free of cost, households continue to pay out-of-pocket expenditures, especially for referrals. A systematic review of 20 studies in low- and middle-income countries (LMICs) found that the removal of user fees provided some evidence of an increase in facility delivery as well as possible increases in the number of managed delivery complications. There was little evidence of the effect on health outcomes or inequality in accessing care and, where available, the direction of effect varied (Dzakpasu, Powell-Jackson, and Campbell 2014).

SAR countries have used various health financing schemes to increase uptake of MRH services with considerable success. On the demand side, these programs have helped reduce the burden of out-of-pocket expenditures. Since 1989, Tamil Nadu has implemented the Dr. Muthulakshmi Reddy Memorial Maternity Assistance Scheme, which provides poor pregnant women with conditional cash transfers (CCTs) to compensate for loss of wages and to stimulate their use of services (Padmanaban, Raman, and Mavalankar 2009). Reimbursement is based on their (a) attending all required antenatal visits at the primary health facility; (b) delivering within government facilities; and (c) completing their child's third dose of relevant vaccinations (Padmanaban, Raman, and Mavalankar 2009). Additional information on health financing schemes in SAR can be found in box 5.1. There have also been financing programs to address the supply-side constraints. At the end of the Taliban regime in 2002, Afghanistan's network of public health services was extremely weak. Rather than trying to provide services itself, the Afghan government contracted with nongovernmental organization (NGOs) to deliver the basic package of services to specific geographic areas. NGOs working under 42 separate contracts were given responsibility for health care in areas that are home to 90 percent of the country's rural population (Benderly 2010). To ensure consistent performance across these contracts, with the Bank's support, a health facility level "performance-based partnership" was introduced to provide a further push for improving performance, particularly in MCH services. The partnership is being implemented for basic health services in 11 provinces and in 5 provincial hospitals (Benderly 2010). Incentives have also been offered to health workers in India to encourage providing skilled birth attendance. Since 1996, Village Health Nurses and auxiliary nurse midwifes (ANMs) in Tamil Nadu State received incentives for each patient that completed a five-visit antenatal care (ANC) checkup, for each institutional delivery, and for referrals (Padmanaban, Raman, and Mavalankar 2009).

http://dx.doi.org/10.1596/978-1-4648-0963-7

Box 5.1 Health Financing Schemes for Maternal Health

India's Janani Suraksha Yojana. The world's largest CCT program for poor pregnant women. Payments of INR 500 are made to women after their delivery at either a public or private facility for their first two births. It employs women from the community known as ASHAs who are also incentivized for correctly identifying and assisting eligible pregnant women, ensuring they access facilities for their delivery, and completing their postnatal treatments (Randive, Diwan, and De Costa 2013).

Nepal's Safe Delivery Incentives Program. Piloted in 2005, the government made financial incentives available to women to encourage them to have four antenatal care (ANC) visits followed by at least one postnatal visit. The cash transfers also covered the cost of transport to and from the facility. The incentives were also offered to SBAs, who were encouraged to perform home deliveries. Women were also entitled to US$5 if they sought health care before delivery at least four times, as recommended by international health standards. On the supply side, the scheme offers financial incentives to health facilities, encouraging the procurement of drugs and materials necessary to carry out deliveries. The program had a positive, albeit modest, effect. Women who had heard of the SDIP before childbirth were 4.2 percentage points (17 percent) more likely to deliver with an SBA. The treatment effect was positively associated with the size of the financial package offered by the program and the quality of care provided in hospitals and primary health care centers (Hanson and Powell-Jackson 2010; Saadat et al. 2014).

Bangladesh's Demand Side Financing Maternal Health Voucher Scheme provides cash incentives to pregnant mothers and providers of reproductive health services. Births attended by a qualified provider were significantly higher ($p < 0.001$) among women in the intervention group (63.7 percent) than the comparison group (27.1 percent). Institutional births were also significantly higher ($p < 0.001$) among the intervention group at 37.5 percent compared to the comparison group with 18.7 percent. ANC was especially high with 91.6 percent of women in the intervention group receiving at least one ANC visit compared to 75.6 percent in the comparison group. This program also helped reduce out-of-pocket costs in the intervention group where payments were 34 percent lower than the comparison areas (Nguyen et al. 2012)

Pakistan has used a P4P financing mechanism to increase health care uptake, which addresses supply and demand constraints in health services. On the demand side, women purchase subsidized vouchers to receive services from private providers in the Greenstar Social Marketing Network including family planning, antenatal and postnatal care, and delivery in health facilities. The program also funds the cost of transportation. On the supply side, providers receive a fee for services rendered under this program (Bashir et al. 2009).

A number of countries outside SAR have also implemented health financing schemes. Performance-based financing (PBF) or Results-based financing (RBF) approaches have been used to reduce the barriers that drive many MRH patients to private sector services. PBF and RBF approaches encompass several different systems to reward the delivery of outputs or outcomes by providing incentives upon verification. In Rwanda, PBF has been implemented nationwide since 2006. It has been a factor in driving increased maternity care coverage between 2000 and 2010 (Bucagu et al. 2012). PBF had the greatest effect on those health services that had the highest payment rates and the least effort from the provider (Basinga et al. 2011). Even though PBF had a positive effect on quality for all services, service use improved only for those activities that were not well organized, including institutional deliveries (Rusa et al. 2009). Demand-side interventions, in the form of vouchers or cash-based incentives, have been used to remove financial barriers to accessing MRH and to generate demand throughout South and Central America. Also, El Salvador's *Comunidades Solidarias Rurales* program provided cash transfers of US$15 conditional upon the prenatal monitoring of pregnant women. As a result, skilled birth attendance in the treatment group increased from 73.8 percent to 90.3 percent (de Brauw and Peterman 2011).

There is strong evidence of the impact of health financing schemes on the use of MRH services. Several systematic reviews provided ample evidence to this effect. One review found that CCTs in eight countries have helped increase antenatal visits, skilled birth attendance, institutional delivery, and tetanus toxoid vaccinations for mothers. The impact on maternal mortality was less clear as there was little evidence in this area (Glassman, Duran, and Koblinsky 2013). Another systematic review used the Joanna Briggs Institute approach to determine the effectiveness, feasibility, appropriateness, and meaningfulness of demand-side financing (DSF) programs. Based on the review of 83 studies from 17 countries, they identified that most DSF programs were effective in increasing use of MRH services. However, the evidence of the impact of unconditional cash transfers as well as the evidence on the effect on mortality and morbidity was also sparse (Murray et al. 2014). Similarly, another review of 19 DSF programs across 28 countries for impact on the supply and demand side found that most studies reviewed impact on use, which was substantial but very little explored the impact on maternal health status. It also noted that while the target of these programs is often the poorest of the population, the impact on this group is mixed (Gopalan et al. 2014). Costs and access to transportation are a common delay to in seeking care for maternal health emergencies, so another review assessed the impact of community- based loan funds to reduce this constraint, improve use of maternal health services, and reduce mortality. The review found evidence to suggest that community-based loan funds as part of a multifaceted intervention have positive effects. The results showed increases in use of health facilities for deliveries, with Odds Ratios (ORs) of 3.5 (0.97–15.48) and 3.55 (1.56–8.05) and an increase in use of emergency obstetric care with ORs of 2.22 (0.51–10.38) and 3.37 (1.78–6.37). Intervention groups also experienced a positive effect on met need for complications and a reduction in maternal mortality (Nwolise et al. 2015).

Community-based health insurance had a positive relationship with the use of maternal health services. Financial barriers can affect timely access to MRH services. Health insurance can influence the use and quality of these services and potentially improve maternal and neonatal health outcomes. In SAR,

http://dx.doi.org/10.1596/978-1-4648-0963-7

community-based health insurance schemes were implemented in India and were associated with increased use of health services, including those for pregnant women as well as ensuring better health outcomes (Aggarwal 2010; Devadasan et al. 2010). A systematic review of 29 studies in 16 LMICs, including India, found relatively consistent evidence that health insurance was positively correlated with the use of maternal health services. However, the available evidence on the quality and health outcomes was inconclusive (Alison, Peterson, Laurel 2013).

Health Service Delivery

Many South Asian countries have attempted to ensure that MRH is a priority by creating specialized administrative, service delivery, or programmatic streams within government ministries with an emphasis on maternal and/or reproductive health. Ideally, these structures would extend through the provincial, district, and community levels. Although the SAR countries differ in their degree of health sector decentralization and the degree to which public sector service delivery structures intersect with the private NGOs or for-profit sectors.

When MRH services are effectively institutionalized, a major impact on service coverage and use can occur. In Nepal, responsibility for MRH is under the Family Health Division of the Department of Health Services under the Ministry of Health and Population (MOHP). Under this system is a nested series of Regional Health Directorate facilities, as well as zonal, district, primary, and village facilities, with 3,134 subhealth posts overseeing community activities, such as female community health volunteers (FCHVs) and 13,811 Primary Health Care Outreach Clinics (Government of Nepal 2015). The Family Health Division oversees the key programs targeting MRH in the country: Safe Motherhood and Newborn Health, Safe Abortion Services, Family Planning, Adolescent and Sexual Reproductive Health, FCHVs, and Primary Health Care Outreach, including family planning and safe motherhood outreach (Government of Nepal 2015). One of the strengths of this structure is that safe motherhood and family planning is now institutionalized at the lowest levels of the health system and working with local NGOs and district Reproductive Health Coordinating Committees. It is also becoming a part of villages' development plans (Bhandari, Gordon, and Shakya 2011).

Sri Lanka's MRH services are overseen by the Family Health Bureau within the Ministry of Health and Indigenous Medicine. In the 1920s, MRH was initially institutionalized at the lowest levels of the health system by establishing a network of institutions—ranging from teaching hospitals to rural hospitals and maternity homes—to create comprehensive and universal access to maternal health services (Pathmanathan et al. 2003). At the heart of this system of delivery is the subprovincial Health Unit, an administrative unit that oversees facilities down to the primary health level (Family Health Bureau 2015). A health medical officer is responsible for each health unit, with the assistance of public health nursing sisters, public health inspectors, and public health midwifes (PHMs)

(Pathmanathan et al. 2003). Before 1968, and through this system of subprovincial Health Units, the country managed to reduce the MMR from 2,136 deaths per 100,000 live births in 1930 to 245 in 1963—even in the absence of an established MRH program (Pathmanathan et al. 2003). In 1968, to further capitalize on its progress, the Ministry of Health launched the Maternal and Child Health Bureau, which later evolved into the Family Health Bureau (Family Health Bureau 2015). The Family Health Bureau oversees a number of specialized Technical Units, including the Antenatal and Postnatal Care Unit, the Intranatal and Newborn Care Unit, the Family Planning Unit, and the Reproductive Health Unit, all of which provide technical and programmatic support to services provided through the Ministry of Health's Provincial Health Services and the Health Units. Sri Lanka rapidly expanded these administrative Health Units and the primary health center (PHCs) and "field" antenatal clinics that are within its responsibility, from the 1920s through the 1960s. The number increased from 30 health centers per 100,000 live births in 1931 to 271 health centers per 100,000 live births by 1965 (Pathmanathan et al. 2003). With such high rates of coverage and access, the country turned its attention to improved quality assurance in the 1980s (Pathmanathan et al. 2003).

Bhutan dramatically reduced its MMR between 1990 and 2012, from 900 deaths per 100,000 live births in 1990 to 120 in 2013 due, in part, to more than doubling the number of basic health units (BHUs) since 1995 (WHO 2014). MRH programming in Bhutan is overseen by the Reproductive Health Program under the Ministry of Health's Department of Public Health. Nonetheless, programs are implemented at the primary level by BHUs, which are overseen by the District Health Services Program under the Department of Medical Services (Royal Government of Bhutan 2015). BHUs are staffed with three health assistants who have completed two years of training, including training in MRH (Torgay et al. 2011). The BHUs provide assistance for normal deliveries and deliver community prevention and sanitation activities. However, due to the mountainous geography of Bhutan, the government has extended the reach of BHUs by organizing monthly outreach clinics during which health assistants travel to remote communities to provide MCH services and primary health care coverage (Torgay et al. 2011). The health service delivery system now includes 28 hospitals, 156 BHUs, and 654 outreach clinics, all available free of charge under Bhutan's universal health coverage policy (Torgay et al. 2011).

The structure of service delivery can have a major impact on MRH service use. For example, in Bangladesh, MRH falls under the MOHFW, with responsibilities divided between two different directorates. The Directorate General of Health Services (DGHS) is responsible for implementing all health programs, provides support to the MOHFW, and advises hospitals and Upazila Health Complexes. The Directorate General of Family Planning (DGFP) is responsible for family planning programs and provides technical assistance on family planning to the ministry, as well as oversees district-level maternal and child welfare centers and Union Health and Family Welfare Centers (Nasreen et al. 2007). MRH services are included within Bangladesh's free Essential Health Package. MRH services are budgeted for through the Sector-Wide Approach (SWAp)–financed Health and Population Sector Program (HPSP), which is in its third iteration. Since the HPSP's inception, the DGFP has overseen services comprising far more than family planning. The DGFP responsibilities include all safe motherhood services, that is, ANC, SBA, emergency obstetric care, post-abortion care, postnatal care, and vitamin supplementation, as well as family planning and contraception and adolescent reproductive health. However, some of these activities will be implemented by facilities under the DGHS. Even though the DGFP and DGHS are independent, they are often tasked with joint implementation of MRH programs. This public sector service delivery structure has fallen short of its target indicators. The percentage of professionally assisted deliveries increased from 8 percent in 1997 to only 13.2 percent in 2004, with many of the gains made through NGO-provided services, while the use of government services declined (Nasreen et al. 2007). The HPSP is scheduled to run through 2016. However, the separation of MRH services across the two directorates of the DGHS and DGFP staff and the reported lack of cooperation between them results in inefficient MRH service delivery (Nasreen et al. 2007).

The private sector is increasingly providing a larger share of MRH services. India's private health care system has grown significantly. In 2004, the share of the private sector in total hospitalized treatment was about 58.3 percent in rural areas and 61.8 percent in urban areas. Government sources account for only 22 percent of nonhospitalized treatment in rural areas and 19 percent in urban areas (Planning Commission 2008). The nonpublic sector, which is composed of 16.6 percent private providers and 0.6 percent NGOs, provides 17 percent of contraceptives to users, making it the second-largest source of contraceptives behind the state. The private sector and NGOs also account for 21 percent of facility-based births (IIPS and Macro International 2007). India's private medical sector remains the primary source of health care for the majority of households in urban (70 percent) and rural areas (63 percent) (IIPS and Macro International 2007). Only 25 percent of abortion facilities are public, while 87 percent of abortions are carried out by the private sector (Hirve 2004). A 2013 study of 14,000 urban and rural households in 12 states indicated a steady increase in the usage of private health care facilities for outpatient and inpatient services over the last 25 years (Kannan 2013). In Bangladesh, the quality of private health services is perceived to be higher than public sector services. The private sector—38.4 percent private medical providers and 4.3 percent NGOs—provides 43 percent of contraceptives to users. It is the second major source of contraceptives behind the public sector. The majority of ANC services (52 percent) are provided by groups other than the state: 43 percent are provided by the private sector while 9 percent are provided by NGOs. The increase in facility-based births is largely due to an increase of deliveries in private sector facilities. Currently, the majority of facility-based births occur in private sector facilities (NIPORT, Mitra and Associates, and ICF International 2013).

Though large numbers of nonpublic organizations are involved in health care delivery, they do not fill the gap left by inadequate public health.

http://dx.doi.org/10.1596/978-1-4648-0963-7

In Bangladesh, more than 400 NGOs are engaged in maternal health and family planning (Robinson and Ross 2007). NGOs are often contracted through public-private partnerships to deliver services. NGOs have also been actively involved in the design of the National Maternal Health Strategy (Bergeson-Lockwood, Leahy Madsen, and Bernstein 2010). *Gonoshasthaya Kendra* (GK) is one such large NGO provider of health care in Bangladesh. The broad range of health services provided by GK reach over 1 million people. Areas served by GK attained an MMR of 186 deaths per 100,000 live births by 2002. This was 42 percent lower than the national average. Part of the reason for GK's success in reducing MMR is that it takes a multisectoral approach to the issue by implementing interventions that affect health, primary education, and women's development. Local health workers receive extensive specialized training before returning to their villages to train additional cohorts of health workers. By establishing these long-term local relationships, GK gains a deep understanding of local health issues (Faguet 2007). More than 7,000 voluntary agencies are involved in health-related activities in India though relatively few provide a full range of services. They are unevenly distributed within and between states and have limited areas of operation. Some NGOs implement government programs and others run basic or integrated health services programs. Health care activities are also carried out by agencies such as the Red Cross, Industrial Establishments, the Lions Club, and HelpAge India. Currently, the Department of Family Welfare funds 97 "mother" NGOs, which are larger NGOs with filial branches. The mother NGOs are responsible for 412 districts and over 800 smaller NGOs. However, states with high maternal mortality rates, and also high fertility rates, still have a large number of districts without any NGO presence (Planning Commission 2008).

Large disparities in quality of care persist in SAR countries and have a major impact on MRH indicators and national MMR reduction. In India, there remains a dearth of available skilled manpower and significant mismanagement of available human resources, especially in the rural public health system (Bhat et al. 2009). Though there are an adequate number of PHCs and doctors at the national level, the distribution across states is uneven, with an absolute shortage in many rural areas. Despite prioritizing rural health care since independence, coverage remains significantly higher in urban areas. In addition, a facility survey conducted by the Department of Family Welfare in 1999 showed that a majority of PHCs lack essential infrastructure and inputs, affecting the quality of care (Ministry of Health and Family Welfare 2010). Tamil Nadu is one state that has taken initiatives to improve maternal health services, leading to a faster-than-average reduction in maternal mortality, from 380 deaths per 100,000 live births in 1993 to 90 in 2007. Initiatives include establishment of maternal death registration and audit, establishment and certification of emergency obstetric and newborn-care centers, 24/7 delivery services, and policy innovation, such as attracting medical officers to rural areas by offering incentives of places for postgraduate study. Dedicated public health officers also

http://dx.doi.org/10.1596/978-1-4648-0963-7

helped improve the authorities' management capacity (Padmanaban, Raman, and Mavalankar 2009). Tamil Nadu also expanded coverage with concomitant quality improvements by strengthening the infrastructure of sub-centers and primary health and community health centers (Padmanaban, Raman, and Mavalankar 2009). Tamil Nadu's quality improvements are notable. One of the main findings of research into the expansion of RMNCH health services elsewhere in India is that increased coverage and access is not equated with higher quality service delivery. Thus, the expansion of RMNCH health services has not resulted in a rapid nationwide reduction in the MMR (Chatterjee and Paily 2011). Likewise, in Pakistan, the expansion of RMNCH services has not been accompanied by quality improvements. In fact, poor quality of care is listed as one of the most significant factors contributing to maternal deaths (Bhutta et al. 2013).

Other regions have also consistently sought to increase the coverage and quality of primary and community health services in part to support improved MCH service delivery. For example, maternal mortality in Malaysia declined from over 1,100 deaths per 100,000 live births in the 1920s, to 282 in 1957, to 20 in 1995 (Pathmanathan et al. 2003). This sharp decline in part was achieved by the rapid scale-up of service coverage. In the mid-1950s, it is estimated that there was roughly one MCH clinic for every 1,000 live births in Malaysia (Pathmanathan et al. 2003). The government embarked on a rural health services program that focused first on the construction of additional clinics, hospitals, training facilities, and staff accommodation, thereby increasing hospital bed capacity by 38 percent (Pathmanathan et al. 2003). This was followed in the 1970s and 1980s by a period of upgrading during which facilities were improved, management strengthened, and quality assurance emphasized (Pathmanathan et al. 2003). By the mid-1990s, 86 percent of Malaysia's population lived within 3 kilometers of a facility and 71 percent of poor people lived within 5 kilometers (Pathmanathan et al. 2003). Improved coverage helped ensure that by 1997, 87 percent of births were hospital based (Pathmanathan et al. 2003). The Arab Republic of Egypt in the 1990s embarked on a program of upgrading facilities, improving standards and guidelines, and retraining medical personnel in an attempt to reduce maternal deaths attributable to substandard infrastructure and care (Campbell et al. 2005; Gipson et al. 2005). In each of four countries that have reduced their maternal mortality since 1990—Burkina Faso, Cambodia, Indonesia, and Morocco—a similar pattern of health systems strengthening of four components occurred: expansion of the network of health facilities with increased uptake of facility birthing, scaling-up of the production of midwives, reduction of financial barriers, and attempts to improve quality of care (Van Lerberghe et al. 2014). The focus on quality of care came about well after the other three components were introduced. It remains a challenge in the four countries, particularly the quality dimension of respectful woman-centered care (Van Lerberghe et al. 2014).

Human Resources for Health

Health workforce bottlenecks are fundamental barriers to national efforts to improve MRH service delivery and reduce MMR. Common bottlenecks in HRH include staff shortages in rural areas; weak management systems; an unregulated private sector; and the brain drain of health workers from public sector facilities to the private sector, NGO sector, or migration out of the country altogether (Afzal, Cometto, and Rosskam 2011; WHO 2006).

To address HRH issues, national and regional Ministries of Health in some SAR countries have succeeded in professionalizing the maternal health workforce and in hiring and training increasing numbers of health providers. In Sri Lanka, the role of the PHMs was expanded and professionalized. The country's coverage has improved from 1 midwife per 157 live births in 1955, to 1 per 51 live births in 1995. Specialist obstetricians in government hospitals per 1,000 live births meanwhile increased from 6.6 in 1950 to 23.0 in 1995 (Pathmanathan et al. 2003). A special cadre of PHMs is recruited specifically for rural areas and areas with poor health indicators. Each region in Sri Lanka has a PHM training center, and PHMs are incentivized with professional development opportunities, as well as special financial incentives to work in remote areas (Pubudu de Silva 2011). There is also a specialized cadre of Public Health Nursing Sisters, serving as nurse-midwives in hospitals (Pathmanathan et al. 2003). Even though Sri Lanka has long met its MMR targets and skilled birth attendance exceeds 97 percent, the country continues to improve health worker coverage. The rate of PHMs per 100,000 population has grown from 24.9 in 2005 to 30.8 in 2007 (Medical Statistics Unit 2008). As part of upgrading PHCs in Tamil Nadu State in India, efforts were made to improve the availability of HRH. Each upgraded center was to be staffed with at least five medical officers, three staff nurses, and two ANMs. The state sought to address shortfalls of specialist health workers in rural areas by having First Referral Unit hospitals contract local private sector or retired anesthetists who were incentivized at a rate of INR 1,000 per caesarean section/emergency obstetric care (EmOC) operation. Eventually, this program was extended, allowing PHCs with operating theaters to contract anesthetists for tubectomies (Padmanaban, Raman, and Mavalankar 2009). In Afghanistan, the number of nurses and midwives increased in 2002 from 566 and 467 to 3,651 and 3,100, respectively, in 2011. By 2011, an estimated 77 percent of health facilities had at least one female health provider—which is essential for women's access to health services given their mobility constraints (Rasooly et al. 2014).

Still, a number of SAR countries struggle to ensure that investment in human resources translates into usage. In Nepal, for instance, the National Policy for Specialist Birth Attendants was established to boost the number of SBAs and to improve their skills through in-service training by increasing the duration of midwifery training to three years. Though the number of health care assistants and medical facilities has increased, Nepal continues to face recruitment challenges, particularly in relation to midwives. A government-produced health human resources plan for 2011–2015 found that although the total population of Nepal had grown by 45 percent over the past decade, the number of public health staff had only increased by 3 percent. By 2013, only 35 percent of births in Nepal were attended by SBAs (WHO 2014). Likewise, in Bangladesh, a community-based skilled birth attendant (CSBA) strategy was launched in 2003 with the aim of training 13,500 family welfare assistants and female health assistants in midwifery skills (Ahmed and Jakaria 2009; Islam, Islam, and Yoshimura 2014).Though the program has been expanded to 56 of the 64 districts (Ahmed and Jakaria 2009), most women still deliver without the presence of an SBA. Therefore, Bangladesh's remarkable progress in reducing its MMR cannot be attributed to the CSBA program (El Arifeen et al. 2014). This issue is detailed further in chapter 6.

In some cases, semiskilled volunteers and community workers can partially make up for the shortage of skilled health professionals. Pakistan's lady health worker (LHW) program was established in 1994 and involves training, incentives, and support for almost 100,000 new health workers. The LHW program covers 60 percent of the rural population and costs over US$150 million, which is primarily funded by government sources (Bhutta et al. 2013; GHWA 2008). More recently, Pakistan has also established a cadre of community midwifes (CMWs) for home deliveries. By 2012, 45 percent of the targeted 12,000 CMWs had been trained and another 30 percent enrolled in training (USAID 2012). In Nepal, the FCHV program accounts for a large part of community-level service provision (USAID 2007). More than 48,000 FCHVs are serving the country and more than 50 percent have held their positions for over 10 years (Schwarz et al. 2014). The annual turnover rate is only 4 percent (Schwarz et al. 2014). Because of the low rate of turnover, the investment in human resources is considered extremely cost-effective (USAID 2007). Both these programs are discussed in greater detail in chapter 6.

Countries in other regions also have focused on improving their health human resources capacity. In Brazil, the government introduced a number of human resource-based initiatives to improve access to health services. The Family Health Program (1994) aimed to increase equity by expanding and restructuring coverage of doctors, nurses, and community health workers to primary health levels in poor regions of the country (Barros et al. 2010). Between 1996 and 2007, skilled birth attendance increased in the poorest wealth quintile, from 72.6 percent to 96.8 percent. ANC in the same quintile also increased from 52.5 percent to 92.7 percent (Barros et al. 2010). Brazil was undertaking a number of other health sector reforms at the same time that contributed to the countries' success in reducing national and regional maternal mortality. Likewise, between 1990 and 1997, safe motherhood efforts in Honduras were accompanied by the government increasing the number of doctors by 19.5 percent, nurses by 66.4 percent, and auxiliary nurses by 41.9 percent (Shiffman, Stanton, and Salazar 2004). China, Thailand, and Malaysia made similar investments in human resources to increase the numbers and aptitude of health workers providing maternal services at the community and primary levels (Li et al. 2007).

http://dx.doi.org/10.1596/978-1-4648-0963-7

The evidence of the impact of training of health workers on maternal health is mixed. Training TBAs was an early strategy to improving HRH for MRH. A systematic review of six studies involving over 1,345 TBAs, more than 32,000 women and approximately 57,000 births found the evidence of the impact of such programs to be limited; however, there was some impact on maternal mortality as the maternal death rates were lower, although not significantly (adjusted OR 0.74, 95 percent CI 0.45–1.22) among trained TBAs than non-trained TBAs (Sibley, Sipe, and Barry 2012). Another review of 53 studies to determine the effectiveness of mid-level health workers did not find a difference in care provided by mid-level providers and higher-level providers for MCH though the quality of evidence was found to be low. However, satisfaction of care was significantly higher for midwives than their counterparts (Lassi et al. 2013). As most births occur at home, a systematic review found that community-level and clinical interventions are needed to reduce maternal mortality in Sub-Saharan Africa. The review of 15 studies found that effective interventions are the administration of specific drug regimens (for example, magnesium sulfate for pre-eclampsia or eclampsia). TBA training was also reviewed; however, the intervention did not significantly reduce maternal deaths (Piane 2009). On the other hand, moderate evidence has been found in support of training providers in Essential Obstetric and Newborn Care to reduce institutional mortality (Ni Bhuinneain and McCarthy 2015).

Essential Drugs and Health Commodities

One important pillar of national health systems is the supply chain for drugs and other medical commodities—of which MRH commodities is a vital component (Wilson et al. 2012). In 2013, the leading causes of maternal mortality in SAR countries included maternal hemorrhage (1st), hypertension (3rd), and sepsis (4th), all conditions treatable with essential obstetric medicines (Kassebaum et al. 2014). Thus, progress on national or regional MMR is indirectly related to strengthening the availability of and access to key MRH commodities. Reducing the MMR requires creating supply chains for critical medicines such as magnesium sulfate for eclampsia, oxytocin or misoprostol for postpartum hemorrhage (PPH), tetanus toxoid immunization, iron and folic acid supplements, antibiotics for sepsis/postpartum infection, antiretrovirals to prevent mother-to-child transmission of HIV, and antimalarials for intermittent preventive treatment for malaria (Wilson et al. 2012). A range of other health products contribute to MMR reductions from bed nets for malaria prevention, to anesthesia for caesarian section, to contraceptives and barrier protection for reproductive health.

In the SAR countries, health commodity supply chains are frequently described as barriers to successful outcomes of key programmatic interventions such as ANC, SBA/CSBA, or EmOC. Persistent stockouts of MRH commodities have been identified as a contributing factor in Pakistan's struggle to reduce its MMR (Bhutta et al. 2013). In one district in Pakistan, a maternal

http://dx.doi.org/10.1596/978-1-4648-0963-7

essential drug survey and supply survey found that no partographs were available in any facility; magnesium sulfate was only available at the tertiary hospital; and iron and folate tablets, broad spectrum antibiotics, oxytocin, gloves, and sutures were not available at either primary or secondary facilities (Fikree, Mir, and Haq 2006). Moreover, many health care workers did not understand how to manage obstetric complications with such commodities (Fikree, Mir, and Haq 2006). In Bangladesh, facility-based studies have shown that one of the main patient complaints about quality of care regarding the provision of MCH services was the inadequate supply of medicines (Chowdhury, Hossain, and Halim 2009a). A survey of pharmacies, private clinics, and public facilities in two districts in the northwest of Pakistan found that while pharmacies had 100 percent coverage of all essential EmOC medicines, public clinics experienced serious shortages of EmOC stock. Among public clinics, only 57 percent had magnesium sulfate, 71 percent had IV solution with infusion set, 56 percent with uterotonics, and 7 percent with partographs (Sikder et al. 2015). Private clinics outperformed public clinics in all categories except partographs, with 100 percent of private clinics having magnesium sulfate, 100 percent having IV solution with infusion set, and 58 percent having uterotonics (Sikder et al. 2015). No centralized blood bank was available in any of the districts surveyed (Sikder et al. 2015). Issues with essential MRH commodities in Bangladesh exist upstream as well. In 2010, the Health, Population and Nutrition Sector Program's special budget line for MRH commodities was reported to be underspent by about 55 percent in spite of reports of stockouts of key commodities around the country (Bergeson-Lockwood, Leahy Madsen, and Bernstein 2010).This suggests critical problems with procurement systems, supply and demand forecasting, and stock inventory systems at the national, district, and facility levels (Bergeson-Lockwood, Leahy Madsen, and Bernstein 2010).

SAR countries have attempted to prioritize the delivery of key MRH commodities. For example, in Nepal and Bangladesh, iron/folic acid supplements and tetanus toxoid immunization (Bhandari, Gordon, and Shakya 2011; El Arifeen et al. 2014; Padmanaban, Raman, and Mavalankar 2009) are critical maternal health commodities. Community health volunteers have been engaged by national maternal health programs to deliver the supplements. Also, creating access to safe blood supply has been a key element of Nepal's facility-based EmOC programs (Bhandari, Gordon, and Shakya 2011) and India's NRHM (Chatterjee and Paily 2011), as well as subnationally in various Indian states, such as Tamil Nadu (Padmanaban, Raman, and Mavalankar 2009). In Tamil Nadu, the state government established the parastatal Tamil Nadu Medical Services Corporation in 1995 to coordinate the purchase, storage, and distribution of public sector health commodities and to ensure accountability and transparency in the medical supply chain with one key focus being essential RMNCH commodities (Padmanaban, Raman, and Mavalankar 2009). In Afghanistan, an EmOC needs assessment in 2009–2010 found that, in spite of insecurity, facilities around the country had the drugs and supplies needed to treat severe pre-eclampsia and eclampsia, including magnesium sulfate (Kim et al. 2013). Between 2001 and 2009, the government of Pakistan spent an average of US$5 million to US$6 million per year on contraceptive procurement. This has since increased to US$52 million for 2010–2012 with in-kind donations from USAID (2013). To strengthen the supply chain, warehouse capacity was increased and an online logistics information system was launched to monitor monthly data (USAID 2013). Contraceptive use increased as a result of the increase in supplies and met the needs of 17 million couples throughout the country. Further analysis showed that this intervention averted 5 million unintended pregnancies, 2 million births, and 5,000 maternal deaths (USAID 2013). To address PPH, Bangladesh has trained health workers in dispensing the oral drug misoprostol as a cost-effective way to prevent PPH. Misoprostol is an inexpensive oral drug that can be administered by health workers without requiring much skill. It is an alternative to injectable uterotonics, which require cold chain storage. Access to Misoprostol is especially important since the majority of births in Bangladesh take place at home. It was added to the Essential Drug List in 2008 and efforts are being made to scale up distribution (Bergeson-Lockwood, Leahy Madsen, and Bernstein 2010).

Other countries with notable reduction in MMR have also prioritized supply chains for essential maternal health commodities. For example, the promotion and improved use of magnesium sulfate for eclampsia is documented in Egypt (Campbell et al. 2005) and Jamaica (Koblinsky 2003). Iron/folic acid supplements and/or tetanus toxoid immunization have been cited in a review of successful Countdown to 2015 countries (Bryce et al. 2008), including Egypt (Gipson et al. 2005) and Nigeria (Adogu 2014). In many African countries, improved access to antiretroviral therapy for prevention of mother-to-child transmission of HIV, as well as roll out of bed nets, and intermittent preventive treatment in pregnancy for malaria have been cited as key contributing factors to MMR reductions (Bryce et al. 2008).

Health Information Systems

A critical pillar in national health systems is the national information system. Many countries do not have a centralized means to register births or deaths. Therefore, the MMR is frequently calculated using modeling. A lack of statistics measuring coverage of targeted interventions means that coverage rates for SBA, institutional delivery, and EmOC often also have to be estimated. Countdown to 2015 has noted that of the 68 priority countries for maternal and newborn mortality that feature in their research, "none…had health-information systems that were able to produce coverage estimates for all the standard indicators" (Bryce et al. 2008). Linking such interventions to MMR is therefore difficult. Nonetheless, accurate statistical information is vital for national strategic planning and for improving the quality of service delivery.

A number of countries in SAR have attempted to improve their information systems through RMNCH programs. They have done so by rolling out maternal death registration and implementing facility-based and community-based verbal autopsy and maternal death and adverse event reviews and audits. Sri Lanka was a pioneer in this process. It introduced maternal death audits in 1985 (Pathmanathan et al. 2003). Based on the "three delay model," reviews are held at the district level quarterly and at the national level annually. The reviews involve government representatives, practitioners, academics, and other stakeholders (Pathmanathan et al. 2003). The intention is to identify clear systemwide failures and trigger change. Tamil Nadu State in India began compulsory audit of maternal deaths in 1996. Maternal deaths must be reported to the MNCH commissioner within 24 hours, and cases undergo community-based verbal autopsy and facility-based review (Padmanaban, Raman, and Mavalankar 2009). Findings are presented to the facility-based Medical Death Audit Committees as well as to the District Reproductive and Child Health Committees. Finally, the cases are logged at the district commissioner's office. A similar process is carried out for "near miss" maternity cases for which adverse maternity events occur but do not cause the mother's death.

Other regions have worked to improve national information systems, particularly maternal death registration and maternal death and adverse event reviews and audits. Assessing the burden of maternal death across various states of Brazil has been hampered by under-registration of cases and causes of maternal death, while simultaneously helped by the implementation and active participation of maternal death audit committees in a number of states (Barros et al. 2010). While less successful than Brazil at reducing maternal mortality, Jamaica has a Maternal Mortality Surveillance System requiring institutional delivery, death, and casualty registers, and maternal death notification (McCaw-Binns et al. 2007). This system has helped Jamaica ascertain the huge role that hypertensive disorders play in MMR and to implement targeted pilots to improve these issues (Koblinsky 2003). In 1988, the health bureau in Zhejiang Province, China, established an annual maternal death audit system that included the collation of all provincial information on live births and maternal deaths, as well as the establishment of a Provincial Prenatal Health Committee that investigated all maternal deaths. These changes have contributed to improving the reporting over the past two decades. The system now includes the reporting of migrant populations that have higher rates of maternal mortality than Zhejiang residents (Du et al. 2015). The 1990 RAMOS survey on maternal mortality in Honduras spurred rapid mobilization for safe motherhood, which had far-reaching impact in reducing maternal mortality in the country (Shiffman, Stanton, and Salazar 2004). In Egypt, the National Maternal Mortality Study of 1992–1993 helped the MOHP prioritize the reduction of maternal mortality, with an emphasis on regions with the highest rates (Gipson et al. 2005). Further research is needed to show how improved reporting has contributed to national successes in maternal mortality reduction, as the Countdown to 2015 group has emphasized the key role that vital statistics registries play in national policymaking and programming for maternal health (Bryce et al. 2008).

http://dx.doi.org/10.1596/978-1-4648-0963-7

Leadership and Governance

Leadership and governance in health is important to the development agenda in SAR countries and globally. Leadership and governance in the context of health systems involve ensuring that strategic policy frameworks exist along with effective oversight, coalition building, regulation, attention to system design, and accountability (WHO 2010b). Leadership and governance can be understood as rules based and therefore concerned that national health systems have appropriate policies, strategies, and guidelines. National health systems also need to be outcome based, with procedures and systems in place to ensure that such policies, strategies, and guidelines are implemented effectively, efficiently, and to the highest possible quality standards (WHO 2010b).

Even when struggling to meet their MMR targets, SAR countries have taken the important first step of laying the policy groundwork for RMNCH initiatives. These include Nepal's 1998 Reproductive Health Strategy and its National Safe Motherhood and Newborn Health Long Term Plan 2002–17 (Bhandari, Gordon, and Shakya 2011), as well as India's 2000 National Population Policy and its 2005 NRHM. In Pakistan, relevant policies are the 1994 National Programme for Family Planning and Primary Health Care, that is, Lady Health Workers, the 2003 MNCH Programme, and the 2005 MNCH Strategic Framework (Bhutta et al. 2013). In Afghanistan, the country has adopted a National Reproductive Health Policy (2012–2016) and its National Strategic Health Plan 2011–2015 has increased the proportion of women with access to emergency and routine Reproductive, Maternal, Neonatal, and Child health care as one of its strategic objectives (Government of the Islamic Republic of Afghanistan 2011).

Countries that have achieved large reductions in MMR share a common strong policy framework to guide service delivery—with extra attention to ensuring equity across regions, wealth quintiles, and other social categories (Koblinksy 2003). Honduras, for instance, managed to reduce MMR by 40 percent between 1990 and 1997, from 182 to 108 deaths per 100,000 live births, through a concentrated effort by the government to prioritize maternal health (Shiffman, Stanton, and Salazar 2004). Following a survey in 1990, which showed that maternal mortality was actually four times that of previous estimates, health officials mobilized to make safe motherhood a priority (Shiffman, Stanton, and Salazar 2004). A shared decision-making authority was set up, working groups were established, policies were created, and regional buy-in and mobilization was achieved (Shiffman, Stanton, and Salazar 2004). Financing was also solicited from donors to support maternal health programs (Shiffman, Stanton, and Salazar 2004). Likewise, Brazil's National Women's Health Program (1984), Unified Health System (1988), National Program for the Humanization of Pregnancy and Childbirth (2000), and its Pact for the Reduction of Maternal and Newborn Mortality (2004) provided clear policy guidelines and implementation strategies to achieve steady gains in maternal mortality reduction from the late 1980s and onward (Victora et al. 2011).

http://dx.doi.org/10.1596/978-1-4648-0963-7

Governance structures ensuring proper enforcement, accountability, and transparency have proven to be equally important in SAR and elsewhere, although the impact of such structures on maternal health outcomes is unclear. One way to improve accountability and transparency upstream is by adopting the Joint Annual Health Sector Reviews and International Health Partnership (IHP+) country compacts with development partners to improve mutual effectiveness in implementing commitments (Frost and Pratt 2012). Nepal was an early IHP+ partner, joining in 2007. In 2009, Nepal and seven development partners signed an IHP+ country compact which committed Nepal to having a national health plan in place, including a results framework, jointly assessed targets and budgets, joint coordination, monitoring and evaluation, financial management, and other assessment mechanisms, and mutual joint annual reviews of the health sector (IHP+Results 2015). The country compact also stipulates that civil society organizations should be involved in all aspects of planning (IHP+Results 2015). Nepal and its partners have been rated highly in terms of fulfilling commitments (IHP+Results 2015). In SAR, Pakistan (2010) and Afghanistan (2014) have since joined IHP+, although both countries and their partners face a number of challenges in fulfilling commitments.

The SAR countries have also initiated innovative downstream social accountability mechanisms to ensure that health officers and workers meet their professional commitments. For instance, absenteeism of health workers has undermined maternal health service quality in numerous countries in SAR. In India and Bangladesh, absenteeism rates are estimated at 40 percent and 35 percent, respectively (Deussom et al. 2012). In Punjab, Pakistan, the high rate of health officer and doctor absenteeism was attributed to political connections. Health officers and doctors were able to use their family and community connections to support politicians' political campaigns, and politicians were able to exert their influence to get health officers and doctors better postings and to protect them from being fired for absenteeism (Callen et al. 2013). A project called "Monitoring the Monitors" set about ensuring existing quality assurance systems functioned and that district health officers followed through on their monitoring functions of facility health staff (Callen et al. 2013). Android smartphones were distributed with a special application that required monitors to first have a picture taken with the staff they have marked present in front of the facility that they were instructed to visit (Callen et al. 2013). The application geo-tagged and time-stamped the picture. This information was sent by mobile Internet to a portal in which data was aggregated and made accessible to senior health officials through an online dashboard (Callen et al. 2013). Rates of inspection more than doubled over the first 10 months of the program and only 4 phones of 99 were lost. All facilities in the 18 district project areas were effectively monitored (Callen et al. 2013). In Thane District, Maharashtra State, India, the use of community monitoring tools such as village health report cards, village and primary health centers, taluka- and district-level meetings, and public hearings has led to a number of positive accountability outcomes, such as the end of illegal charges, increases in inpatient and outpatient service use, and increases in facility-based deliveries

http://dx.doi.org/10.1596/978-1-4648-0963-7

(Shukla 2012). These tools were initially part of a WHO-supported Empowerment of Rural Poor for Better Health project. Since 2007, they have been rolled out as part of India's larger NRHM strategy (Shukla 2012).

In other regions, strong accountability and transparency mechanisms have helped ensure that government and international policy, programmatic, and financial commitments to downstream patients and communities are met (Brinkerhoff 2004). In Zambia, for example, alongside its IHP+ compact, the country signed on to Countdown to 2015 to better track performance and commitment to its MDG 4 and 5 targets (Countdown to 2015: Maternal Newborn and Child Survival 2012). Zambia held its first event in 2008, bringing together government, civil society, development, and technical partners to raise awareness; identify gaps in programs, policies, and financing; improve monitoring and evaluation strategies; and ensure coordination and common purpose (Countdown to 2015: Maternal Newborn and Child Survival 2012). An MNCH road map was created, as was a specialized budget line for reproductive health and commodities; the national midwifery training was expanded; and RBF for MCH program was developed (Countdown to 2015: Maternal Newborn and Child Survival 2012). A project implemented in four regions in Uganda used community-based monitoring through a citizen report card pilot project (Bjorkman and Svensson 2009). Citizen report cards in local languages were created based on key findings from community surveys about quality of service, usage, and comparisons of different health facilities (Bjorkman and Svensson 2009). Community meetings were held to disseminate findings from the report cards, which included high rates of absenteeism, long wait times, poor quality of treatment, and concerns from staff (Bjorkman and Svensson 2009). Additional meetings were held to establish community monitoring systems going forward (Bjorkman and Svensson 2009). Over the duration of the pilot, usage of facilities increased, as did perceived quality of service provision and health outcomes related to child health (Bjorkman and Svensson 2009).

Note

1. District Level Health Survey (DLHS) 2 (2002–04) acts as the baseline for this analysis. DLHS 3 (2007–08) marks the beginning of the improvement in performance. The Coverage Evaluation Survey (CES 2009–10) was used for the most recent data, that is, 2009–10. Annual Health Surveys in the Empowered Action Group + A states provide updated information until 2012.

http://dx.doi.org/10.1596/978-1-4648-0963-7

CHAPTER 6

Community Enablers

Key Messages

- Community-based interventions aim to create an enabling environment to reduce maternal mortality and improve Maternal and Reproductive Health (MRH) outcomes by improving care-seeking practices, strengthening linkages to facility-based MRH services, and empowering communities to eliminate harmful cultural norms and community practices.
- Female community-based health workers recruited from and working in their communities help establish trust and provide frontline services to the remote and underprivileged. They help improve access to MRH services, which contribute to improved use of services.
- Community interventions such as participatory women's groups and community education group sessions led to improved use of MRH services. However, more evidence is needed of the impact of their scaling-up on reducing maternal mortality.
- Involving community leaders in the design and implementation of MRH services has led to the design of interventions that are more sensitive to local context, the development of awareness and trust among community members, and increased uptake of services in some South Asia Region (SAR) countries.
- Evidence suggests that community-based interventions in SAR and other countries work to "create an enabling environment" to improve maternal survival and reproductive health outcomes.

Introduction

Community enablers are interventions within communities that create an environment conducive to reducing maternal mortality and improved reproductive health outcomes. While increasing the provision and quality of facility-based maternal health interventions is essential for maternal survival, these services may not be acceptable or accessible to everyone (Kidney et al. 2009). This is particularly the case for the poorest and most marginalized women, as well as

http://dx.doi.org/10.1596/978-1-4648-0963-7

women living in the most remote communities. In these cases, interventions within communities that improve care-seeking practices, strengthen linkages to facility-based MRH services, and empower communities to address harmful cultural norms and community practices are needed to complement facility-based efforts. This chapter discusses community-based interventions that have been implemented in SAR and other countries. Interventions include female community health workers, demand-side interventions such as participatory women's groups, and efforts to engage community leaders to increase demand for and access to MRH services to enable maternal survival. To ensure equity in the reduction of maternal mortality, implementers of these interventions need to take particular care in ensuring that they are identifying and reaching the most economically and socially disadvantaged women.

Harmful cultural norms and community practices in SAR and other countries have acted as barriers to improving maternal health. For example, in Nepal, women of a lower caste have been denied access to obstetric care due to social norms that give higher caste groups preferential access to resources (Karkee 2011; Rath et al. 2007). Some Nepalese also believe that postpartum women should not leave the home or touch anyone for at least eleven days after delivery and that care seeking in pregnancy and childbirth is shameful (Karkee 2011). In some areas in Pakistan, women have restricted mobility and are not allowed to leave the house alone (Bhutta et al. 2013). In some settings in Pakistan, women's mobility is further influenced by class hierarchies. Unaccompanied mobility is higher among poorer women because of their necessity to travel for work, which has implications for their physical security (Mumtaz and Salway 2009).

The literature on countries in other regions also identifies cultural norms and community practices that inhibit maternal health gains. For example, in rural the Arab Republic of Egypt large discrepancies exist between uptake of antenatal services, which have increased, and postnatal checkups, which have remained low in Egypt. At the same time, while the number of deaths from antepartum hemorrhage decreased from 1992 to 2000, the number of deaths caused by postpartum hemorrhage (PPH) increased. This increase was related to poor emergency blood supply and to the persistence of traditional beliefs about women staying at home during the postpartum period (Campbell et al. 2005). Interventions at the community level can empower and support communities to address those cultural norms and community practices that perpetuate high levels of maternal mortality.

Deploying Community-Based Female Health Workers

Female health workers recruited from and working in their communities provide frontline services to the remote and underprivileged in SAR countries. They also help establish trust in and access to MRH services, thereby contributing to reducing maternal mortality. Pakistan's Lady Health Worker (LHW) Program was rolled out in 1994 and involves training a cadre of female community health workers to carry out a wide range of activities linking women to reproductive, maternal, and child health care. Their activities include acting as liaisons between traditional birth attendants (TBAs) and skilled providers in local facilities, and providing contraceptives, micronutrient supplementation, immunization, and health education messaging (Bhutta et al. 2013; Malik and Kayan 2014). The LHWs selected are young married women based in their communities with at least eight years of schooling. They receive a 15-month training course that prepares each of them to deliver services to approximately 1,000 people (GHWA 2008). As of 2013, the LHW program has deployed over 100,000 LHWs, covering 60 percent of the rural population (Bhutta et al. 2013). LHWs play a substantial role in providing preventive and promotive care and linking communities with emergency and referral care. Their impact on maternal mortality has not yet been assessed, however (Oxford Policy Management 2009). Areas served by LHWs have a higher prevalence of modern contraceptive use and tetanus toxoid vaccination. LHWs are appreciated by the communities they service (Oxford Policy Management 2009). The LHW program faces challenges related to general health system bottlenecks, including lack of support and poor performance from higher-level facilities and general health financing issues.

More recently, Pakistan has also established a cadre of community midwifes (CMWs) (USAID 2012). Beginning in 2006, the Ministry of Health sought to train 12,000 CMWs in home delivery (USAID 2012). CMWs are educated rural women between the ages of 18 and 36 and from the communities they aim to serve (USAID 2012). They cover a catchment area of 5,000 people (USAID 2012). By 2012, 45 percent of the targeted 12,000 CMWs had been trained and another 30 percent enrolled in training. In addition, 68 midwifery schools were upgraded (Middleton et al. 2012). The results of deploying the CMWs have yet to be assessed, including their acceptability to the community, their ability to provide services, and their effectiveness.

India began the ASHA program in 2006. The program provides a link between the local community and the public health system. ASHA volunteers are trained female community health activists selected from their villages and accountable to them. As of 2013, there were 820,000 ASHA volunteers (Gopalan, Mohanty, and Das 2012). They have a wide range of responsibilities including counseling women on birth preparedness and the importance of safe delivery. ASHAs also provide information on existing maternal and child health (MCH) and other services and act as the first port of call for the health needs of community members who have difficulty accessing services. Most states in India have introduced a performance-based payment system for ASHAs. It is linked with the government's *Janani Suraksha Yojana* (JSY) scheme to promote institutional deliveries. The JSY scheme provides cash payments to ASHAs for facilitating deliveries in a government facility. Despite the ASHA program's potential, it has encountered serious challenges, and its impact on maternal mortality rates is unclear (Bajpai and Dholakia 2011). Performance-based payments encourage ASHA volunteers to focus only on those activities that are tied to cash incentives, such as delivery and immunization, and to neglect tasks such as promotion of awareness of hygiene and sanitation and family planning counseling

http://dx.doi.org/10.1596/978-1-4648-0963-7

(Wang et al. 2012). ASHA volunteers report a high degree of work satisfaction, but they also report heavy workloads, poorly organized liaison with local officials, and insufficient involvement in future planning (Gopalan, Mohanty, and Das 2012). ASHA volunteers also find it difficult to persuade the most disadvantaged women to deliver in medical facilities because these women fear discrimination from health workers (Dongre and Kapur 2013).

In 1988, Nepal began deploying female community health volunteers (FCHVs) to link the community with the health system and to provide advice on family planning and MCH (Karkee 2011). FCHVs are recruited locally based on recommendations from Village Development Committees (Schwarz et al. 2014; USAID 2007). The FCHVs are provided financial and other incentives for their performance (Schwarz et al. 2014). A significant number of FCHVs over the age of 30 have not completed primary education and many are non-literate (USAID 2007). To overcome the lack of formal education, FCHVs are supported with frequent training, monitoring, and evaluation (USAID 2007). Over 48,000 FCHVs work across Nepal and 53 percent of FCHVs have held their posts for over 10 years (Schwarz et al. 2014). They have been deployed on initiatives ranging from community distribution of misoprostol for PPH to breast cancer screening to management of neonatal sepsis (Coffey et al. 2012; Hyoju et al. 2011; Rajbhandari et al. 2010; USAID 2007). FCHVs also provide counseling and advice to pregnant women. From 2001 to 2006, the FCHVs were linked to increases in iron supplementation from 23 percent to 59 percent, breastfeeding from 65 percent to 85 percent, and postpartum vitamin A from 10 percent to 29 percent. Additional evidence suggests that FCHVs have succeeded in providing services to underserved groups in Nepal and have contributed to maternal mortality reductions (Government of Nepal 2007). Despite these successes, challenges remain in ensuring that FCHVs deliver consistent quality of services between districts.

SAR countries have had successes and challenges with programs to train and deploy community-based skilled birth attendant (CSBAs) to increase accessibility to skilled delivery in communities where the majority of births still occur at home. Afghanistan launched a community midwife education (CME) pilot program in 2002 to increase its health resources in remote and underserved areas. It was scaled up nationwide in 2005. The program is structured as a public-private partnership with the government as steward. Implementation is largely conducted by nongovernmental organization (NGOs). After decades of war, the program sought to deploy urgently needed skilled female health workers, particularly midwives, to reduce the country's high maternal mortality rate (Speakman et al. 2014). Because of cultural norms, women in Afghanistan have traditionally sought health care from female medical professionals. As the majority of the population lives in remote, rural areas, midwives needed to be based at the community level. The CME curriculum trains midwives to partner with women to promote their health, overcome harmful cultural practices, and focus on health promotion and disease prevention. The CME program led to an enormous increase in trained midwives. In 2003, Afghanistan had 467 midwives

(Bartlett et al. 2011). By April 2013, the program had graduated 2,245 students. Midwives are selected by rural communities and agree to be deployed in their communities upon graduation. Communities report high ownership and acceptance of the CME program (Speakman et al. 2014). Maternal mortality fell by 80 percent between 2002 and 2010, from 1,600 per 100,000 live births to 327, in large part due to the CME program (Rasooly et al. 2014).

Bangladesh launched the CSBA program in 2003 to increase access to skilled delivery at home. By June 2014, nearly 9,000 CSBAs were trained. Nevertheless, despite their availability in rural areas, evidence suggests that CSBAs are not being used (DGHS 2011). CSBAs reported uncertainty about their role and lacked high acceptance from the community or a supportive work environment. Many community members continue to rely on TBAs because they are perceived as having more experience and living closer to the community (Turkmani and Gohar 2015). Pakistan set out to foster the formation of a cadre of CMWs under the National Maternal, Newborn, and Child Health (MNCH) Program in addition to its LHW program. Beginning in 2006, the program aimed to train 12,000 CMWs in home delivery. CMWs are educated rural married women aged 18–36 selected from the communities they serve. They receive 18 months of training in antenatal, intrapartum, postnatal, and newborn care. They cover a catchment area of 5,000 people (USAID 2007). As with Bangladesh, evidence shows that use of CMWs in Pakistan is low and there has been no major change in maternal health indicators (Sarfraz and Hamid 2014). CMWs have encountered challenges with inadequate training, lack of sufficient resources, and lack of facilitation into the community by LHWs and untrained TBAs. One study in a rural district of Pakistan found that CMWs struggled to gain the communities' trust in their abilities. In part, their relative youth led to a perception of inexperience. Community women had greater respect for the opinions of the local TBAs (Sarfraz and Hamid 2014).

In other countries, female community-based skilled and semiskilled health workers also are deployed to provide MRH services to their communities. For example, since 2003, Ethiopia has deployed a new cadre of paid female community-based health workers called Health Extension Workers (HEWs) to improve access to care in rural areas. HEWs are recruited from and serve in their communities and their activities include administration, promotion and prevention, basic treatment and referral, and dissemination of information, education, and communication (IEC). Reproductive and maternal health activities represent a major component of HEWs' work (Mangham-Jefferies et al. 2014). The program has generally been accepted by its stakeholders, including the communities in which HEWs serve, and has strong government and financial backing (GHWA 2010). In terms of providing an enabling environment for maternal mortality reductions, HEWs contribute to improving women's use of family planning, antenatal care (ANC), and HIV testing, but their contribution to increasing health facility delivery and skilled birth attendance has been limited (Medhanyie et al. 2012). In Rwanda, the Ministry of Health reformulated the community health system in 2007, with community health workers required to have a minimum of six years education and to be elected by their community.

http://dx.doi.org/10.1596/978-1-4648-0963-7

By 2014, there were 60,000 community health workers (CHWs)—three per village, with one of these designated as the female maternal health worker, the *Animatrice de Santé Maternelle*. Evidence suggests strong acceptance of the CHWs by communities, with the relationship between the CHWs and communities fostering support and respect, and community members regularly seeking CHWs for advice (Condo et al. 2014). The program is credited with extending the reach of the health system, improving coordination of care, and is one of a constellation of factors improving maternity care coverage in Rwanda. It has reduced its maternal mortality rate between 2000 and 2010 by 59.5 percent (Farmer et al. 2013). However, the CHW program faces challenges due to an irregular supervision and training and delays in providing incentives to CHWs through the country's Performance-based Financing (PBF) system (Condo et al. 2014).

Community-Based Interventions

In SAR countries, interventions have been implemented to mobilize and empower communities to utilize MRH services. The interventions have led to reduced neonatal mortality in most of the intervention sites, but their contributions to reducing maternal mortality is less clear. In Nepal's Makwanpur District, a women's group intervention—based on participatory learning supported by a local female facilitator—was implemented to reduce maternal and neonatal mortality (Condo et al. 2014). An action learning cycle was conducted in which women's groups identified local perinatal problems and designed strategies to address them. Likewise, in Hala and Matiari subdistricts of Pakistan, a community-based intervention was piloted to improve perinatal care using LHWs and TBAs and involved training in newborn care, community education group sessions, and support for the establishment of an emergency transport fund (Bhutta et al. 2008). In Bangladesh, women's groups, using a participatory action and learning methodology, were scaled up in three districts to increase the effectiveness in maternal and neonatal care services (Azad et al. 2010). Participatory women's groups were also used in Jharkhand and Orissa, India, to improve home-care practices and health-seeking behavior of pregnant and postnatal women (Tripathy et al. 2010). The interventions in Pakistan and India showed a significant effect on neonatal mortality but did not include enough women to sufficiently study the effect on the maternal mortality ratio (MMR) (Bhutta and Lassi 2010). For similar reasons, maternal mortality was not a predefined outcome of the Nepal study. However, the intervention suggested an effect because maternal mortality was found to be significantly lower in the intervention areas than in control areas. The MMR was 69 per 100,000 in intervention clusters compared to 341 per 100,000 in control clusters (Manandhar et al. 2004). The intervention in Bangladesh reported low coverage of newly pregnant women being enrolled in the women's groups. It did not show much effect on neonatal mortality and did not study impact on maternal mortality (Azad et al. 2010). Several systematic reviews focus in part or completely on community-based interventions because, they argue, these have the potential to improve outcomes by increasing the

http://dx.doi.org/10.1596/978-1-4648-0963-7

standard of care outside facilities or by improving care-seeking behavior access to facility-level care (Gilmore and McAuliffe 2013; Kidney et al. 2009; Lassi and Bhutta 2015; Piane 2009; Piane and Clinton 2014). These reviews find evidence that suggest community-level interventions can reduce maternal mortality and that benefits may extend across the continuum of care. However, studies for these reviews were limited and authors argue for more high quality, evaluated, community intervention trials examining maternal death in high-risk settings.

Similar interventions have been tried in other countries with varying results. For example, the main objective of the Mobilizing Access to Maternal Health Services in Zambia (MAMaZ)—funded by UKAid (formerly DFID—the UK Department for International Development) and operating in six districts between 2010 and 2013—was to design and test demand-side approaches to ensure access to and use of maternal health services, including emergency services, and home-based care of pregnant women and their babies. The community engagement approach of MAMaZ sought to reach the most vulnerable households by (a) using a "whole community" approach and generating social approval for behavior change; (b) training community volunteers to facilitate community discussion groups and integrate social inclusion into discussions; (c) developing or strengthening community systems, such as emergency transport; (d) conducting door-to-door visits to ensure everyone was included; and (e) soliciting the support of traditional leaders in the effort. MAMaZ increased skilled birth attendant rates from 43 percent to 70 percent in intervention districts compared to an increase from 39 percent to 46 percent in control districts. Antenatal and postnatal care, as well as modern contraceptive use, also increased more in the intervention districts (iERG 2013). Successes were due to the comprehensive approach used, a strong sense of ownership by communities, and a high level of commitment shown by volunteers (iERG 2013). In central Malawi, the MaiKhanda intervention was conducted in three districts to assess the effect of a combined intervention package involving community mobilization and facility-based quality improvement on maternal, perinatal, and neonatal mortality rates (Colbourn et al. 2013). As part of the intervention, 729 participatory women's groups were established to mobilize the community around maternal and newborn health using volunteer facilitators. Women's groups used many different strategies—such as health education, voluntary testing and counseling for HIV/AIDS, village savings and loans, bed nets, vegetable gardens, and bicycle ambulances—to take control of mother and child health issues (Colbourn et al. 2013). The combined intervention reduced neonatal mortality by 22 percent, but there was no effect on maternal mortality, which was potentially because the size of the intervention was too small to detect meaningful change (Colbourn et al. 2013). Also in central Malawi, the MaiMwana project assessed the effect of women's groups and health education delivered by peer counselors on maternal mortality (Lewycka et al. 2013). The women's groups were supported by cluster facilitators through an action cycle of 20 meetings in four phases and linked to government health surveillance assistants. Outcomes were monitored between 2005 and 2009. Women's groups led to a 74 percent reduction in the MMR in years two and three (Lewycka et al. 2013).

http://dx.doi.org/10.1596/978-1-4648-0963-7

Recent systematic reviews have found that small- and medium-scale community-based interventions have led to improved use of MRH services and reductions in maternal and neonatal mortality. A systematic review of the effects of women's groups that practiced a four-phase participatory learning and action cycle on maternal and newborn health found that interventions in Bangladesh, India, Malawi, and Nepal led to a 37 percent reduction in maternal mortality. With at least a third of pregnant women participating and adequate population coverage, women's groups practicing participatory learning and action may be a cost-effective strategy to improve maternal and neonatal survival; however, there is a need to assess which of the interventions conducted in small- or medium-scale projects could be taken to scale (Prost et al. 2013). A second systematic review looked at a broader set of community-based intervention packages to reduce maternal and neonatal morbidity and mortality, the majority of which were in SAR countries. These interventions were found to increase uptake of some MRH services and have a possible effect on reducing maternal and neonatal mortality (Lassi and Bhutta 2015). Another review assessed 10 interventions and found that community participation had largely positive impacts on maternal and newborn health as part of a package of interventions (Marston et al. 2013). Finally, another review showed that community-based intervention packages increased the uptake of several MRH services and had a significant effect on maternal morbidity reduction and a possible effect in terms of a reduction in maternal mortality (Lassi and Bhutta 2015). Nonetheless, these reviews had various definitions of "community-based interventions" and most of the studies were implemented on a small to medium scale. A clearer definition of "community-based interventions" and more evidence to assess the impact of scaling up these interventions in a range of settings are therefore needed.

Engaging Community Leaders

Involving community leaders in the design and implementation of MRH services has led to developing community trust, intervention designs that are more sensitive to local context, and increased uptake of services in some SAR countries. The Accelerating Contraceptive Use (ACU) project in Afghanistan, implemented by Management Sciences for Health, sought to strengthen contraceptive services in three project sites (Huber, Saeedi, and Samadi 2010). Project interventions were developed following dialogue with men and women community leaders, families, clinic staff, and religious leaders (*mullahs*), and included the introduction of modern contraceptives by community health workers with updated written information and guidance for each method. Project staff learned that *mullahs* were concerned about safety and infertility, rather than religion. Through continued dialogue, all the *mullahs* in the project sites accepted the concept of birth spacing using modern contraceptives and many began to emphasize the importance of birth spacing in Friday prayers. After eight months, contraceptive use increased by 24 to 27 percent in ACU project sites (Huber, Saeedi, and Samadi 2010). While the ACU project site was small and did not assess the impact of interventions on maternal mortality reductions, it did demonstrate the importance of involving religious and other community leaders for developing trust, designing project activities, and confirming acceptance by community members. The six-year Pakistan Initiative for Mothers and Newborns, funded by USAID, also worked with 800 religious leaders (*ulamas*) in its efforts to reduce maternal and neonatal mortality (Greene and Ostrowski undated). Consultations with *ulamas* were held—in the presence of senior religious scholars—during which they all learned about maternal health interventions and developed messages to share during sermons. The project estimates that more than 200,000 men and women were reached with these messages during sermons. The strategy was adopted as a best practice by the government and written into the Karachi Declaration signed by the Secretaries of Health and Population in 2009.

Programs in other countries around the world have also involved local leaders in their design and implementation. For example, a key component of the MAMaZ program in rural Zambia was to gain the support of traditional leaders. These leaders were informed and involved early on in community engagement leading to the introduction of "laws" to promote facility delivery, a supportive environment for implementation, and practical support for the program, such as communities being instructed to clear pathways for bicycle ambulances (Health Partners International 2013). Another example is the 2004–05 Skilled Care Initiative implemented in Ouargaye District, Burkina Faso, in which a community mobilization approach was used to guide the community to use quality delivery care (Hounton, Byass, and Brahima 2009). The approach centered on identifying and engaging influential traditional, administrative, and religious leaders, as well as local associations, through a structured participatory approach about the importance of skilled delivery care. The demand-driven intervention led to a 30 percent increase in institutional births in the intervention district compared to a 10 percent increase in the comparison district, with the community mobilization activities likely a key factor in this increase (Hounton, Byass, and Brahima 2009).

Reaching Economically and Socially Marginalized Women

Supply-side and demand-side community-based interventions to reduce maternal mortality often fail to reach the most economically and socially marginalized women because of difficulties identifying these women and fully addressing the obstacles they face. A study in a Punjab, Pakistan village illustrates this challenge (Mumtaz et al. 2014). The lowest caste in the village, the Kammis, has limited employment options and work for higher caste individuals or in a brick-making kiln for a meager wage. Kammi women are invisible in the community and stay silent to avoid bringing attention to their stigmatized identity. Even an NGO working in the community for women's economic empowerment and human rights overlooked these women in their projects because of the difficulties in identifying them (Mumtaz et al. 2014). Moreover, some government health care providers treat Kammi women poorly because they are perceived to be inferior. This problem, combined with limited financial means, leads pregnant Kammi women to deliver at home with the help of a relative or unskilled birth attendant. In the case of maternal health emergencies, Kammi families turn to higher caste individuals for loans which are sometimes (but not always) given. Kammi families are also systematically excluded from community-level cash transfer programs intended to address economic insecurity. Local political leaders who determine resource allocation do not include all Kammi families in the programs.

In Bolivia, the MMR is particularly high among poor indigenous women who face discrimination at health facilities. As a result, they are disincentivized from seeking care. Therefore, the majority of indigenous women deliver at home assisted by untrained family and friends. The United Nations Population Fund (UNFPA) midwifery training program in Bolivia intervened by recruiting and training prospective birth attendants from remote communities to work in those areas. The scheme offers women living in rural areas financial incentives to seek ANC and institutional deliveries, while those indigenous women being trained as midwives are offered courses in rural universities, with support from the Bolivian Society of Nurses and UNFPA (UN Population Fund 2009).

To reduce the risk of maternal death among the poorest and most marginalized women in communities, interventions must design equity-based strategies founded on an informed understanding of these women's lives. Careful, discreet, and sensitive strategies are needed to identify the most marginalized women in communities (Mumtaz et al. 2014). Providers and marginalized communities should be supported to ensure respectful maternity care. For example, a pilot project of the Academy for Nursing Study in Andhra Pradesh, India, sought to improve interactions between providers and lower caste women (George 2003). Women's groups were formed and trained to enable group togetherness, empowerment, self-esteem, and bargaining skills. Women in these groups were affirmed as community representatives with badges. When accompanying community women with obstructed labor to facilities, they used these badges to ensure access and respectful care at facilities. Additionally, cash transfer programs designed to facilitate MRH service uptake must use approaches that ensure the resources actually reach those most in need (Mumtaz et al. 2014). As the government is often unable to address the problems of excluded populations on its own, multisectoral action is required, particularly including the organizations of the excluded themselves (Kabeer 2006). More research is needed to better understand how "community empowerment" initiatives in SAR and globally can ensure that they are reaching the most economically and socially marginalized women (Mumtaz et al. 2014).

http://dx.doi.org/10.1596/978-1-4648-0963-7

CHAPTER 7

Multisectoral Enablers

Key Messages

- Multisectoral interventions such as in education, transport and communications, water and sanitation, nutrition, and energy contribute to maternal survival in South Asia Region (SAR) countries and worldwide. Nonetheless, many of the linkages between maternal mortality and interventions in these sectors are poorly documented and require more research.
- Educating girls and women a minimum of 12 years results in reproductive and maternal health benefits and has been a key factor in reducing maternal mortality.
- Strengthening transportation and communications infrastructure has increased uptake of and access to maternal health services and to the broader health system in the SAR, and, it has indirectly influenced maternal mortality rates.
- Better access to water and sanitation in health facilities and households has been correlated with improved maternal health in some SAR countries.
- Efforts to improve nutrition for women of childbearing age and pregnant women have seen successes, yet some challenges remain in SAR countries.
- Access to electricity has enabled the supply of maternal health services in some SAR countries. In households, electricity has led to greater awareness and use of maternal health services.

Introduction

Multisectoral interventions at the household, community, district, and national levels have enhanced health interventions and created an enabling environment to reduce maternal mortality in SAR countries over the past decades. This chapter focuses on interventions in the education, transport and communications, water and sanitation, nutrition, and energy sectors in SAR countries. Some of these interventions were designed and implemented by coordinated stakeholder actions in multiple sectors, while others were implemented wholly within non-health sectors and had a direct or indirect influence on maternal mortality.

While the link between maternal mortality and education has been shown, an understanding of the association between maternal mortality and interventions in other sectors is less clear, and more research is needed.

Education

Cross-country analysis reveals relatively strong correlation between female gross enrolment ratio in secondary education and gross domestic product (GDP) per capita. Compared to other countries with similar income, female gross enrolment ratio in secondary school in SAR is generally higher and it ranges from 31 percent in Pakistan to above 100 percent in Sri Lanka. Bangladesh, Bhutan, India, Nepal, and Sri Lanka had higher levels than income comparable countries while Afghanistan and Pakistan had lower levels (figure 7.1).

Educating girls improves their access to information, empowers them to make their own health and reproductive choices, and contributes to maternal mortality reduction. A higher level of education—secondary or more years of schooling—is linked with an increase in the age at which a woman marries and has children (Caldwell 2005). Marrying later tends to increase the age at which mothers deliver their first child, thereby decreasing the risk of maternal mortality from adolescent births and reducing the overall number of children born to a mother. Female education has been demonstrated to be associated with maternal mortality rates in global-level studies, which have also showed that lower levels of maternal education are associated with higher mortality rates, even among women who are able to access health care facilities (McAlister and Baskett 2006; Saffron et al. 2011). As shown in figure 7.2 and figure 7.3, the mean years of schooling and progression to secondary school for females were positively associated with maternal mortality ratio (MMR) reduction.

Figure 7.1 Gross Secondary Enrollment Ratio, Female, 2012

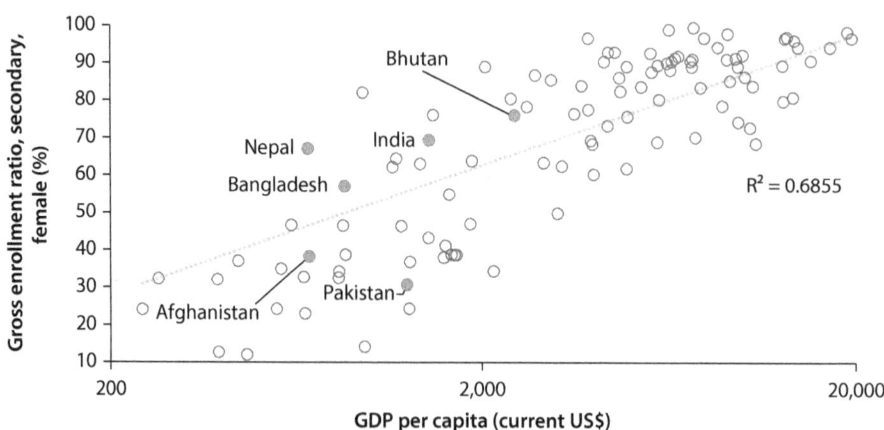

Source: Calculations based on World Bank 2015a.

Figure 7.2 Correlation between Mean of Years of Schooling for Females and MMR, 2010

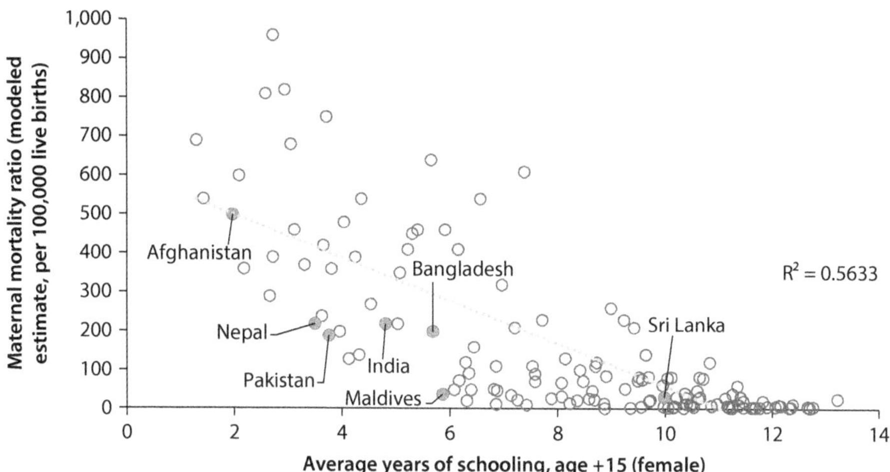

Source: World Bank 2015a.

Figure 7.3 Correlation between Progression to Secondary School for Females and MMR, 2013

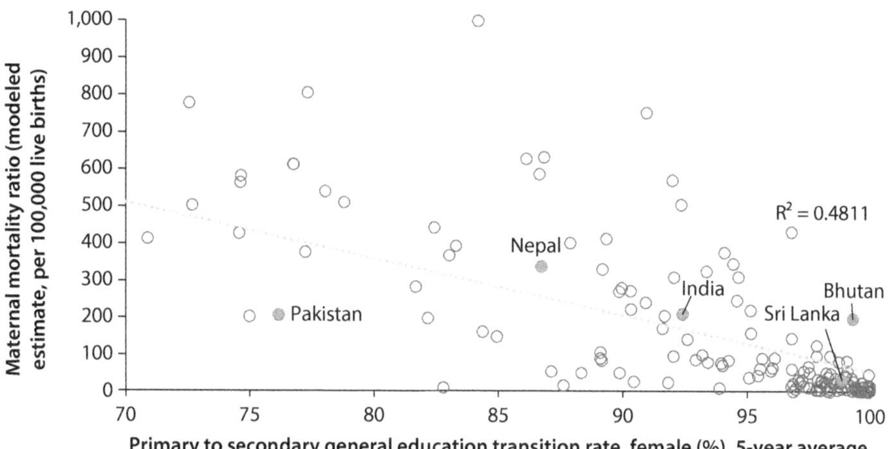

Source: World Bank 2015a.

In SAR countries, education has been a key non-health factor in the reduction of maternal mortality. In Nepal, women's education has been cited as a contributing factor to maternal mortality reductions, with women's literacy increasing from 35 percent in 2001, to 55 percent in 2006, and to 67 percent in 2011 (Barker et al. 2007a). Achievements in Sri Lanka in both child and maternal health are linked to the provision of free health care as well as free education, which started in 1931 and is provided up to the completion of university education (Pathmanathan et al. 2003; Senanayake et al. 2011).

Improving levels of education in Sri Lanka have contributed to women's empowerment in health and household decision-making and exposed them to media that has enabled them to have greater awareness about their own health (Seneviratne and Rajapaksa 2000). In India, the improvement in maternal mortality since 1990 is in part due to the country's progress in overall development, including education (Rai and Tulchinsky 2015). However, studies of MMR in India point out that further progress in maternal health requires an integrated approach, including the strengthening of education, particularly the education of adolescents, poor women, and women in rural areas (Rai and Tulchinsky 2015).

Completion of secondary education is a particularly strong predictor of women's use of antenatal care (ANC), skilled birth attendance, and facility delivery. In Bangladesh, the proportion of women of reproductive age with some secondary schooling increased from 26 percent to 44 percent between 2001 and 2010. Improved secondary education levels have likely improved women's negotiating power within the home and the health care system and increased women's awareness levels of pregnancy complications and maternal health services (El Arifeen et al. 2014). The secondary education of mothers has been credited as "the major driver of reductions in fertility and child malnutrition in Bangladesh." Some stakeholders have called for investing in female education as one of the most important means for Bangladesh to meet its maternal and child mortality targets (Faguet 2007). Of Bangladeshi women completing secondary school, 94 percent attended ANC, compared with 30 percent of women with no education, and 60 percent of women with primary education (Das 2008). In Nepal, women with no education dropped from 80 percent in 1996 to 62 percent in 2006, while the proportion of women completing secondary school doubled. Over the same period, MMR in Nepal dropped by over half (Bhandari, Gordon, and Shakya 2011). In Bhutan, women with secondary or higher education are more likely to have delivered with the assistance of a skilled attendant or at a health facility than women with primary or no education. Whereas 93 percent of women with secondary education or more delivered in a health facility, 51.5 percent of women with no formal education delivered in a health facility in Bhutan (National Statistics Bureau 2011).

Female education has been also a key non-health factor in reducing maternal mortality in other countries in the world. In Chile, higher education levels among women were a significant factor in the decline of maternal mortality. For every additional year of maternal education, there was a corresponding decrease in the MMR of 29.3 deaths per 100,000 live births. During the 50-year study period, the MMR decreased by 93.8 percent in parallel with a significant increase in the number of years of women's education (Koch et al 2012). In the Arab Republic of Egypt, the percentage of women having completed secondary/higher education almost doubled between 1992 and 2000, from 13 percent to 22 percent, while MMR over the same period was more than halved from 174 to 84 deaths per 100,000 live births (Gipson et al. 2005). Between 1952 and 1961, Malaysia doubled the female literacy rate from 17 percent to 32 percent and more than halved the MMR from 520 to 200 deaths per 100,000 live births (Pathmanathan et al. 2003). In Cambodia, which has seen reductions in maternal mortality since 2005, education efforts beginning in 1980 began showing clear improvements in literacy after 2001, including the narrowing the gender gap in primary education (Liljestrand and Sambath 2012).

Women's and girls' education levels combined with other important factors are associated with use of maternal and reproductive health (MRH) services in countries around the world. In a study in Indonesia, women who were more educated than their husbands were more likely to obtain prenatal care. Education enabled women to make decisions regarding their reproductive health care (Beegle, Frankenburg, and Thomas 2001). Women's education in a study of rural communities in Nigeria was a factor in uptake of maternal health service, though education alone was not a panacea (Nwakoby 1994). Maternal occupation, maternal education, religion, and the occupation of the husband all influence the number of antenatal visits, as well as whether delivery took place at a health facility or at home. In a study in Thailand, educational attainment at the secondary-school level was the most consistent predictor of maternal health service use in terms of immunizations, prenatal consultations, and assisted delivery. Although a rural-urban divide existed in the impact of secondary education—suggesting an economic dimension to the effects of education on women's health care use—the relationship between secondary school attainment and health care use was demonstrated across socioeconomic groups (Raghupathy 1996).

Transport and Communications

Transportation linkages, including the availability of vehicles, affordable travel, and reliable road infrastructure, are crucial to women's ability to access maternal health services and health care more generally throughout SAR (Babinard and Roberts 2006). Delays in reaching facilities offering maternal health services may be life threatening for pregnant women and are often due to the lack of infrastructure and difficulties in transport. Delays can be attributed to factors such as distance to health care centers, the availability and cost of public or private transport, the condition of roads, the navigability of terrain, and the safety of travel (Fiagbe, Asamoah, and Tabi Oduro 2012). In addition, many countries have not managed to sustain publically funded fleets of ambulances or other emergency vehicles (Babinard and Roberts 2006). Where access to transport is limited or unavailable, families encounter delays of several days while trying to amass the funds necessary to hire emergency transport, which often leaves them with significant financial burdens. Maternity patients continue to reach facilities on foot or by other means of travel that are unsafe, uncomfortable, or strenuous, thereby placing the mother and child at risk (Babinard and Roberts 2006; Fiagbe, Asamoah, and Tabi Oduro 2012). Difficulties with transport can also limit health workers' abilities to reach pregnant women in their communities. Globally, an estimated 75 percent of the women who die in the course of childbirth do so as a result of inadequate emergency transport (Babinard and Roberts 2006).

Box 7.1 Emergency Response System in Andhra Pradesh, India

The GVK-Emergency Management and Research Institute (GVK-EMRI) established a large-scale Emergency Response System in 2005 in the southern state of Andhra Pradesh. By 2012, it rapidly expanded its emergency response model to 11 Indian states. GVK-EMRI has modeled itself on the three paradigms of "Sense," "Reach," and "Care." It offers 24/7 emergency services for fire, police, and medical emergencies across all 23 districts of Andhra Pradesh. The state-subsidized first-response service is completely free for any user.

The largest beneficiary base for GVK-EMRI's services is pregnant mothers. While the primary objective of initiating the Emergency Response System was accident, trauma, and other medical emergencies, the main reason for ambulance dispatch in 2011 was pregnancy related. Pregnancy-related cases increased from 1.1 percent of the total cases in 2005 to 22.2 percent in 2011. Of these cases, perinatal cases accounted for 2.1 percent, and the remainder were normal deliveries. Many expectant mothers use the service for reliable free transport to the hospital for delivery. In rural areas, in many cases, ASHA workers accompany women to the hospital during a transfer for delivery.

Around 74 percent of the pregnancy cases handled by these services are from rural districts, 19 percent from urban areas, and 7 percent from tribal areas. The rural dependence probably reflects the importance of GVK-EMRI as an accessible and available maternal transport option in contrast to urban areas where other options may exist. The rural, urban, and tribal geographic distribution has remained around the same since 2009.

Source: Chauhan and Nagpal 2012.

Better transport and connectivity to the road network has a twofold significance for maternal survival. On the demand side, it increases uptake of maternal health services and provides a key link between the potential accessibility and actual use of services (Babinard and Roberts 2006). On the supply side, transport enables the supply chain for critical medical supplies, the health referral process, health workers' access to remote rural areas, and monitoring and supervision of maternal health services. Emergency response systems like the GVK-EMRI service in Andhra Pradesh, India, help to improve connectivity and transportation for pregnant women (see box 7.1).

In some SAR countries, improvements to rural road networks have led to higher demand for and uptake of maternal and general health services. In Bangladesh, 19,000 km of dirt roads, 32,000 km of paved roads, and 300 km of bridges were constructed between 2001 and 2010, greatly improving access to health facilities (El Arifeen et al. 2014). The Government of Bangladesh's Rural Roads and Markets Improvements and Maintenance Project-II (1997–2002) led to an increase in demand for health services in the designated project area. There was an annual growth of 23.7 percent in the total number of patients treated per month in health facilities compared to 17.5 percent in the control area (Bangladesh Institute of Development Studies 2009). Furthermore, the growth rate was greater for female patients than for men,

http://dx.doi.org/10.1596/978-1-4648-0963-7

suggesting that underdeveloped roads are a larger obstacle to women accessing health services than to men (Bangladesh Institute of Development Studies 2009). Likewise, the World Bank's Rural Transport Improvement Project in Bangladesh led to a 32 percent increase in health care service recipients in project areas with improved road infrastructure. The increase in health care use was particularly noticeable for women; their usage increased by 35 percent. In areas which did not benefit from the project, there was a 20 percent increase in health care service recipients and only a 3 percent increase in female recipients (World Bank 2013b).

Like transportation, communication networks are also important for maternal survival in SAR countries. They influence the efficiency of referral and health information systems, as well as the health system's ability to respond to emergencies. For example, between 2000 and 2010, Bangladesh went from 0.2 mobile phone subscriptions per 100 inhabitants to 46 subscriptions per 100 inhabitants, equating to approximately 66.6 million subscriptions, with two out of every three households owning a mobile phone (El Arifeen et al. 2014). During this same period, Bangladesh's MMR dropped from 322 deaths per 100,000 live births to 194, a decline attributed to greatly improved access to maternity services facilitated by changes within the health and non-health sectors, including communications (El Arifeen et al. 2014). Likewise, in Afghanistan and Sri Lanka, improvements in communications infrastructure as well as access to transportation have been linked to maternal mortality reductions (Rasooly et al 2014). As shown in figure 7.4, the increase in mobile cellular subscriptions was correlated with reduction in MMR.

Strengthening the transport and communication infrastructure has also been correlated with improved hospital referrals, reduced obstetric complications, and reduced MMR in countries in other regions. In Bo District, Sierra Leone, a project was implemented in 1992 to install a four-wheel drive

Figure 7.4 Correlation between Mobile Cellular Subscriptions and MMR, 2013

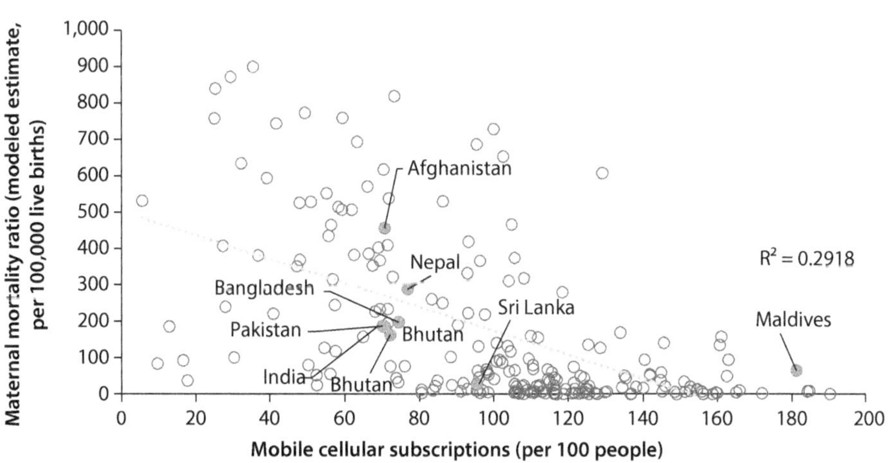

Source: World Bank 2015a.

vehicle at the government hospital and a small fleet of motorbikes at eight primary health units. A radio system unit was used to link the vehicles to the hospital and the primary health units. The project resulted in the number of women with major obstetric complications arriving at the hospital from the project area increasing from 0.9 to 2.6 per month, with the case fatality rate dropping in half, from 20 percent to 10 percent (Samai and Sengeh 1997). The project, however, was disrupted in 1994 by civil war. In Lesotho, Riders for Health provided motorcycles, ambulances, and four-wheel vehicles for health workers promoting reproductive, maternal, newborn, and child health (RMNCH). Outreach health workers conducted more than three times more health education meetings with women about family planning and other RMNCH topics each week after being mobilized on Riders for Health-managed motorcycles (Riders for Health; year unknown). In the Gambia, Riders for Health also managed 36 ambulances across the country, each based at a health center. These ambulances travelled over 760,000 km in their first year of operations, ensuring swift referral to hospitals in emergencies, including obstetric emergencies (Riders for Health; year unknown). In the Philippines, regional and rural/urban rates of MMR have been correlated with proximity to and density of road networks, market linkages, and ports. Such infrastructure provided improved access to services along with greater opportunities for employment and higher income (Collas-Monsod, Monsod, and Ducanes 2004). Likewise, maternal mortality reductions in Cambodia since 2005 occurred alongside improvements in the road and bridge network, which has facilitated access to health care (Liljestrand and Sambath 2012). Cellphone coverage has also expanded rapidly, increasing from 8 percent of households in 2005 to 58 percent in 2010 (Liljestrand and Sambath 2012). Access to a wider range of communications media has helped expose populations, even in remote areas, to better information on health-related topics, including maternal health.

The economic implications of inadequate transportation infrastructure disproportionately affects the poor in SAR and globally. In Bangladesh, transport was reported as patients' second most expensive item after medicines (Cockcroft, Milne, and Andersson 2001). Transport accounts for 28 percent of the total cost of using hospital services in Burkina Faso (Ensor and Cooper 2004). In a review of health-seeking responses to cost recovery, poor people in Tanzania traveled an average of over 60 km for care, whereas the non-poor traveled only 15 km. The findings in Kenya were similar (Newbrander, Collins, and Gilson 2000). The discrepancy is explained by the likelihood that the non-poor have their own means of transport and the poor travel farther to attend a facility where fees would be waived. At present, the degree to which equitable access to transportation is correlated with maternal mortality rates across wealth quintiles is poorly understood.

The impact of transport improvements is enhanced by community and educational assistance. Efforts in other regions to improve transport and communication combined with community support and education activities have been found to have a positive impact on the number of women receiving treatment for obstetric emergencies with consequent reductions in maternal death. This was demonstrated in projects in Uganda (Lalonde et al. 2003) and northwestern Tanzania (Ahluwalia et al. 2003). In both countries, community organizations played a crucial role in planning for emergencies when they occur, including preparing delivery plans, mobilizing resources through community funds, reducing transport costs, and strengthening referral chains.

Water and Sanitation

Water and sanitation are likely enablers of maternal survival in SAR and globally, though data on the linkage between water and sanitation and maternal health and MMR is limited. As shown in figure 7.5 and figure 7.6, improved water sources for rural population and improved sanitation were highly correlated to reduced MMR. There are several potential direct and indirect mechanisms through which poor water and sanitation can lead to adverse maternal health and possibly death (Benova, Cumming, and Campbell 2014). First, poor hygiene at the time of delivery at home or in facilities could lead to infection. Second, water storage encourages the breeding of mosquitoes that carry malaria and dengue, diseases that pose high risks to pregnant women. Malaria is a major contributing factor to maternal and infant mortality in malaria endemic areas. The disease exacerbates chronic health problems, which frequently become more acute during pregnancy, and it is associated with maternal anemia. Finally, the life course effect of repeated childhood infections from poor water and sanitation can result in stunting, maternal short stature, and increased risk of obstructed labor.

National level data on the relationship between water and sanitation and reductions in MMR is scant in the SAR countries and globally. In Bangladesh, the proportion of the population with access to clean water increased from

Figure 7.5 Correlation between Improved Water Source for Rural Population and MMR, 2013

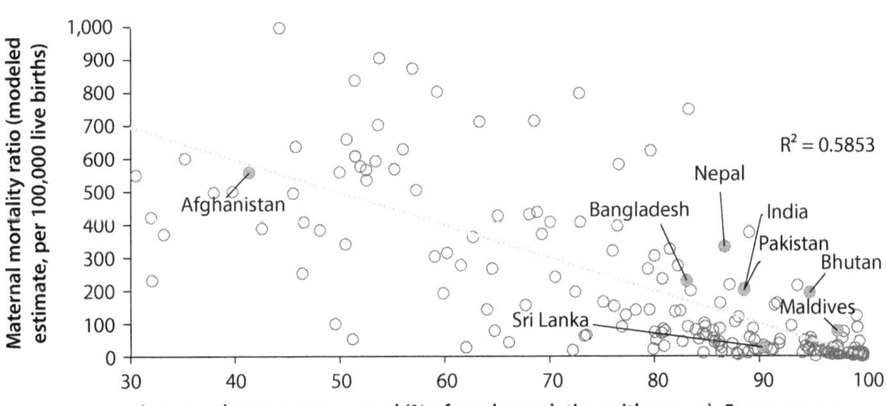

Source: World Bank 2015a.

Figure 7.6 Correlation between Improved Sanitation and MMR, 2013

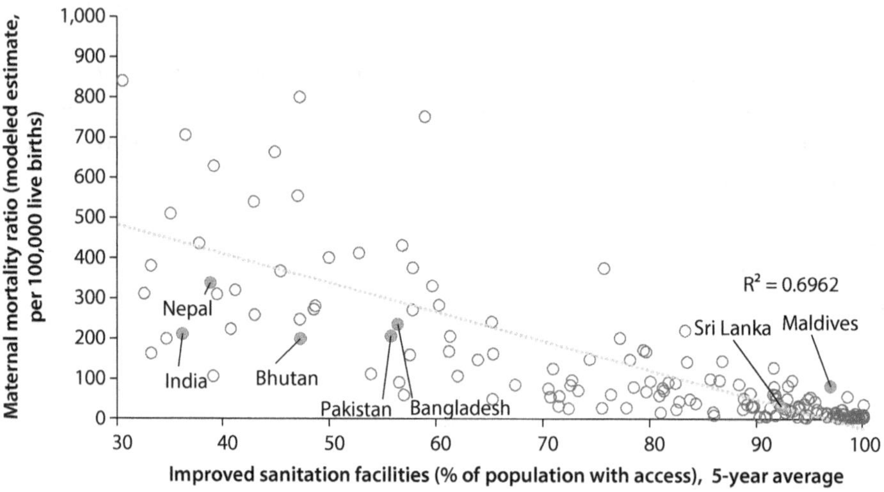

Source: World Bank 2015a.

76 percent in 1990 to 83 percent in 2011. The proportion of the population using an improved sanitation facility increased from 38 percent in 1990 to 55 percent in 2011 (World Bank 2013a). Rural access to improved water sources and sanitation facilities increased from 75 percent to 79 percent and from 34 percent to 55 percent, respectively, from 1990 to 2010 (United Nations Educational, Scientific, and Cultural Organization [UNESCO]). These improvements occurred at the same time as Bangladesh was reducing its MMR, but it is unclear how exactly these water and sanitation initiatives may have contributed to MMR declines. In Yunnan Province, China, access to clean drinking water was also positively correlated with lower MMR (Li et al. 2007). In Vietnam, which has successfully reduced maternal mortality by 70 percent between 1990 and 2009, there has been progress in increasing the proportion of the population using an improved drinking-water source and sanitation facility (Ministry of Health, Vietnam 2014). A multisectoral effort called the Rural Water Supply and Sanitation national target program, involving the Ministry of Agriculture and Rural Development and the Ministry of Health, began in 1998 and is now in its third phase. The percentage of the population with access to improved water sources increased from 58 percent to 95 percent between 1990 and 2012 and with access to improved sanitation facilities, increased from 37 percent to 75 percent in the same period (Ministry of Health Viet Nam 2014). Moreover, the gap between the rural and urban population with access to improved water sources has narrowed (Ministry of Health Viet Nam 2014). How these improvements have directly or indirectly contributed to Vietnam's progress on maternal mortality, however, is not fully understood.

More research is necessary to understand the relationship between water and sanitation and maternal mortality. While existing research has found an association between water and sanitation and maternal mortality, the number of studies

http://dx.doi.org/10.1596/978-1-4648-0963-7

is small and most do not explicitly examine water and sanitation as risk factors for maternal mortality. A systematic review of literature about the link between water and sanitation and maternal mortality called for closer collaboration between the water and sanitation and maternal health sectors, consideration of water and sanitation environments within maternal health strategies and programs, and more research on which specific causes of maternal mortality are associated with poor water and sanitation (Benova, Cumming, and Campbell 2014).

Nutrition

Poor nutrition is an underlying cause of maternal death in SAR countries. There is an association between obstructed labor and the short stature of mothers, which can result from poor nutritional status in childhood and adolescence. Severe anemia is also linked to maternal deaths, as it reduces women's ability to survive hemorrhage and is also associated with pregnancy-induced hypertension and sepsis. An estimated 42 percent of pregnant women globally have anemia; the majority of these women are in Africa and Asia (WHO 2008). Likewise, maternal depletion syndrome results from biological competition for nutrients during pregnancy, early pregnancies, poor maternal nutritional status at conception, and short intervals between pregnancies. The syndrome compounds preexisting maternal health deficiencies and contributes to poor MRH outcomes and poor fetal development (King 2003).

Efforts to improve nutrition for women of childbearing age and pregnant women have seen successes and challenges in SAR countries. In Nepal, the National Nutrition Program, part of the Department of Health Services, has a mission to improve the overall nutritional status of children and women of childbearing age and pregnant women. Between 1998 and 2006, the country reduced anemia among women of reproductive age by almost half, as well as improved overall maternal micronutrient status (Bhandari, Gordon, and Shakya 2011). A study in 2011 found that the percentage of anemic mothers, along with mean age at first birth, can account for 10 percent of the district variation in maternal mortality across the country (Hussein et al. 2011). In Tamil Nadu, India, part of the Dr. Muthulakshmi Reddy Memorial Maternity Assistance cash transfer scheme was to support improved nutrition among poor women and, especially, prevent anemia (Padmanaban, Raman, and Mavalanka 2009). Between 1998 and 2006, however, there was almost no reduction in maternal anemia, and rates remained between 53 percent and 56 percent. This suggests that targeted micronutrient support without a concomitant multisectoral effort to improve household food security and nutritional status may not be the best means by which to reduce nutritional factors contributing to maternal mortality.

National multisectoral strategies and policies to reduce malnutrition and micronutrient deficiencies are critical to improving maternal nutrition and nutrition-related mortality outcomes. Bangladesh had one of the highest rates of maternal and child malnutrition, including anemia, in the world, across a range of income quintiles, a rate that was strongly correlated with education levels of women (Faguet 2007). The integration of nutrition programs and alignment of policies, stakeholders, and donors across sectors has proven effective. The country managed to reduce the percentage of women with a body-mass index lower than 18·5 by 52 percent 1996–97 to 28 percent in 2011 (El Arifeen et al. 2014; Faguet 2007). Key to this achievement was the Bangladesh Integrated Nutrition Programme 1995–2002 (BINP), the first large-scale policy programme for nutrition in the country. The BINP targeted malnourished children and mothers for the delivery of community-based nutrition services, such as supplementary feeding, nutrition, education, and home gardening (Helen Keller International and IPHN 2001). Through the BINP, the government published the first significant nutrition policy document in 1997 called the National Plan of Action for Nutrition (NPAN). This document set out the country's goal to improve nutritional status and reduce malnutrition (BNNC 1997). The program led to a 5 percent reduction in malnutrition and a small increase in birth weights in the project areas (BNNC 1997). The project was then scaled up between 2002 and 2011 to the National Nutrition Programme (NNP). In 2007, the government also introduced the National Strategy for Anaemia Prevention and Control in Bangladesh, aimed at improving maternal, infant, and young child nutrition, incorporating specific measures, including micronutrient supplementation, dietary improvement, and food fortification to reduce anemia (Options Consultancy Services 2013). Through these efforts, Bangladesh has made some progress toward meeting the Millennium Development Goals (MDGs) related to nutrition, although the link to maternal health remains unclear and a significant proportion of the population falls below the minimum level of dietary energy consumption (Government of the People's Republic of Bangladesh 2014).

The link between nutritional interventions and maternal mortality reduction is not well documented in SAR or the global literature. Malaysia has prioritized the reduction of malnutrition since the 1940s and since the 1950s has ensured that the rural development initiatives, the rural health services program, and midwifery outreach included nutrition education (Pathmanathan et al. 2003). In Mexico, the PROGRESA program provides cash payments to low-income households to improve educational, health care, and nutritional behavior. By improving maternal nutrition, the program has successfully reduced the low birth weight of newborns (Gertler 2000). Furthermore, PROGRESA has empowered women's household decision-making and control over household resources, maximizing the likelihood of continued improvement in the nutritional status of families (Skoufias and McClafferty 2001). The relationship between programs such as these in Malaysia and Mexico and national progress on maternal mortality, however, has not been well measured. The contributory role played by nutritional interventions to maternal mortality reduction should be an area of further research.

Energy

Energy is an important enabler for the supply and uptake of maternal health services. Particularly during emergencies, facilities offering maternal health services rely on electricity for basic lighting, equipment sterilization, and power for essential equipment. Furthermore, households with electricity may have greater awareness of and be more likely to use maternal health services. The relationship of interventions in the energy section to maternal mortality reductions in countries, however, has not yet been shown in the literature.

In some SAR countries, electricity in health facilities is associated with an increased supply of maternal health services. For example, a study in India used health facility data from the DLHS 2007–2008 to explore the effects of supply-side factors on the volume of delivery care at Indian primary health centers (PHCs) (Kumar and Dansereau 2014). The study found that approximately 62 percent of PHCs had a regular supply of electricity and that access to electricity was significantly associated with an increased volume of delivery at PHCs.

Household electricity has been linked to greater knowledge of public health issues and uptake of maternal health and family planning services in SAR countries. Bangladesh's Rural Electrification Program improved awareness of public health issues in households benefitting from access to electricity than in those households that remain nonelectrified. More than half of the electrified households reported TV as their main source of knowledge (Barkat et al. 2002). Households with electricity were also more likely to use medically trained personnel for delivery than nonelectrified households: 36 percent and 23.1 percent, respectively (Barkat et al. 2002). They were also more likely to use ANC and postnatal care and seek treatment for maternal morbidity. Eighty percent of electrified households sought care from a medically trained professional for maternal morbidity occurring during pregnancy, at the time of delivery, and in the postpartum period, compared to between 50 percent and 60 percent from nonelectrified households (Barkat et al. 2002). Of poor women from electrified households, 79.2 percent sought care compared to 66.7 percent of richer women in nonelectrified villages (Barkat et al. 2002). Similarly, contraceptive use was higher among married women in electrified households, with 68 percent reporting using some form of contraceptive method. For women in households without electricity in electrified villages and women in the nonelectrified villages, the contraceptive prevalence rate (CPR) was slightly lower at 62.8 percent and 61.7 percent, respectively (Barkat et al. 2002). A socioeconomic dimension existed with household electricity and CPR. The poor electrified villages had a 65.7 percent CPR compared with 55 percent among the poor in nonelectrified villages. Almost a quarter of family planning users reported TV as an influential factor in family planning use (Barkat et al. 2002). There is evidence that electricity in the household positively motivates people through the medium of radio and TV to use reproductive and maternal health services. However, to what extent this is true elsewhere in SAR is unclear, as is the connection between rural electrification initiatives, household access to electricity, and overall maternal mortality decline.

http://dx.doi.org/10.1596/978-1-4648-0963-7

Interventions in the energy sector have been shown to be enablers for maternal health services in SAR and other countries, though data is limited. A study of maternal health in Uganda assessed health system factors associated with increased deliveries at 553 health facilities in 54 districts and found three key factors: running water, accommodation for staff, and electricity (Mbonye and Asimwe 2010). In Mongolia, energy-efficient design in a number of health facilities have sought to overcome the barrier to maternal health posed by the country's severe winters. These designs have led to a decrease in utility costs and an improvement in heating and facilitated the uptake of ANC and the willingness of women to use maternity waiting homes before giving birth (Mbonye and Asimwe 2010). Again, however, these findings relate electrification and energy efficiency to use of services rather than to maternal mortality reductions.

Conditional Cash Transfers

Conditional cash transfer (CCT) programs provide cash payments conditional on the use of some merit goods, services, or behaviors. CCT programs can be "narrow" or "broad." In a "narrow" sense, the aim of CCTs is to encourage the use of specific services, often for MCH. "Narrow" CCTs focusing on increasing service use are more common in South Asia than "broad" CCTs (see section "Health Care Financing" in chapter 5). In a "'broad' sense, the aim of CCTs is to reduce poverty, specifically targeting low-income groups. In this sense, CCTs can be considered multisectoral as the conditions or outcomes are not limited to the health sector. There are, however, CCTs in education that have an indirect link to maternal health as they affect delayed marriage. In Bangladesh, one such program is the Secondary School Assistance Program. This education program provided tuition and stipends to girls in low literacy areas throughout Bangladesh to attend secondary school up to grade 10. Conditions for receiving the stipends included maintaining satisfactory grades and agreement from parents to delay marriage for their daughters. As a result, enrollment tripled from 1.1 million in 1991 to 3.9 million in 2005. Secondary School Certificate pass rates also increased to 62.8 percent in 2008, up from 39 percent in 2001 (World Bank 2009). An impact study on the program found that it has led to an increase of 1.4 to 2.3 years in the age at marriage. It has also affected labor force participation with one additional year of education, leading to between 2.4 and 5.3 percent increase in the labor force participation of married women (Hong and Sarr 2012). Similarly, in Pakistan, the Female School Stipend Program (FSSP) aimed to increase female enrollment in middle schools and reduce gender gaps. Families of beneficiaries in 15 districts with the lowest literacy rates would be provided with quarterly subsidies of about US$10 on the condition that girls maintain an 80 percent attendance rate. In 2006, the FSSP would be extended to girls in high school. By 2010, the FSSP yielded positive results Enrollment increased significantly across all the cohorts, ranging from 11 to 32 percent. The program also has some statistically significant long-term results. Girls exposed to the program were more likely to marry 1.2–1.5 years later and have 0.3 fewer children (IEG 2011).

Broad-based CCTs that have both health and education conditions have largely been implemented in Latin America. Such programs include El Salvador's *Red Solidaria,* Guatemala's *Mi Familia Progresa,* and Mexico's *Opportunidades* (Glassman, Duran, and Koblinsky 2013). Mexico's *Opportunidades* program is an example of one of the few CCTs where the impact on maternal mortality was measured and found an 11 percent decline in maternal deaths between 1995 and 2002 (Murray et al. 2014).

Overall, systematic reviews have shown that CCTs have an impact on the use of maternity services. These reviews found that CCTs have increased antenatal visits by 8.4 percent (ranging from 8 percent in Mexico to 19 percent in Honduras), skilled attendance at birth by 12 percent (ranging from 4 percent in Guatemala to 37 percent in India), delivery at a health facility by 21 percent (ranging between 4 percent in Nepal and 43.5 percent in India), and tetanus toxoid vaccination by 8 percent (ranging from 4 percent in Honduras to 37 percent in Mexico), but there is little evidence regarding impact on maternal mortality or morbidity (Glassman, Duran, and Koblinsky 2013; Murray et al. 2014). They were less effective in improving outcomes as they mostly address demand-side and not supply-side barriers. Moreover, evidence on unconditional cash transfers was scanty (Murray et al. 2014).

Microcredit

Microcredit programs are often multisectoral in nature as they contribute to household income and women's empowerment and have shown positive impact on contraceptive use. In addition, microcredit programs often encourage education, nutrition, and small family norms, among other practices. Originating in Bangladesh, the Grameen Bank, for example, requires its borrowers to maintain small families as well as healthy sanitation practices as a part of the '16 Decisions' that borrowers commit to while participating in programs. Microcredit programs often target women and are active in an increasing number of countries, including India. They play a key role in creating economic opportunities and helping women lift their families out of poverty. Many studies have observed the impact of microcredit on income generation, alleviating poverty and empowerment. One study found that microcredit in Bangladesh reduces poverty (particularly extreme poverty), increases household consumption, and also has spillover effects for reducing village level poverty. About 40 percent in reductions of moderate rural poverty was attributed to microcredit (Khandker 2005). Regarding empowerment, a 2003 study found that microcredit in Bangladesh increases spousal communication and bargaining power, decision-making, and mobility (Pitt, Khandker, and Cartwright 2003). One study found that the presence of the Grameen Bank had a significant effect on women's empowerment within their families and a significant positive effect on the levels of contraceptive use and that participation in microcredit programs increases contraceptive use (Schuler, Hashemi, and Riley 1997). The percentage of married women aged below 50 years practicing contraception was higher in villages where the Grameen Bank

http://dx.doi.org/10.1596/978-1-4648-0963-7

was active (59 percent) than in comparison villages (43 percent) (Hashemi, Schuler, and Riley 1996). In another study, fertility declined 31 percent and an annual household per capita expenditure increased to Tk 786—the equivalent of about 14 percent of the moderate poverty line and 21 percent of the extreme poverty line among participating young women (Khandker, Koolwal, and Sinha 2008). This suggests that households are using credit in ways that increases the productivity of women's time with implications for fertility (Khandker, Koolwal, and Sinha 2008). Though the literature does not establish a direct causal relationship between microcredit and the use of other MRH services or maternal mortality reduction, it does suggest possible four pathways through which microcredit programs can affect health status: financing care in the event of health emergencies, financing health inputs such as improved nutrition, as a platform for health education, and by increasing social capital through group meetings and mutual support (Schurmann and Johnston 2007).

CHAPTER 8

Contextual Enablers

Key Messages

- The political, economic, demographic, and sociocultural contexts of countries can provide an enabling environment to reduce maternal mortality.
- Political enablers for maternal mortality reduction in South Asia Region (SAR) include peace and stability and political prioritization of and legislation for maternal and reproductive health issues.
- Reductions in maternal mortality have occurred concurrently with economic growth in most SAR countries and other countries.
- Reductions in maternal mortality in SAR countries have occurred concomitantly with declining fertility rates.
- Some sociocultural enablers such as women's autonomy, female employment, and greater gender equality have played a positive role in improving maternal health outcomes.

Introduction

Contextual factors in countries can enable or limit the overall impact of health systems and program drivers of maternal and reproductive health (MRH). Efforts to improve maternal survival are implemented in and interact with real-life contexts. Therefore, an understanding of these relationships is necessary. This chapter discusses political, economic, demographic, and sociocultural enablers that have contributed to maternal survival and improved reproductive health outcomes in SAR countries and elsewhere. These contextual enablers are primarily influenced at high decision-making levels and are often beyond the control of women and their families. They vary significantly across and within countries and require sustained attention from policymakers.

Political Enablers

Maternal mortality rates in a number of SAR countries are affected by the political context where health systems are operating and where MRH interventions are implemented. In Afghanistan, for example, years of war destroyed the

http://dx.doi.org/10.1596/978-1-4648-0963-7

infrastructure, economic development, and social services. The majority of districts lacked maternal and child health (MCH) services and most women delivered without a skilled birth attendant (SBA) (Rasooly et al. 2014). With the collapse of the Taliban regime in 2002, the country began to rebuild its economy and health system with the help of donors, which has led to improved health outcomes, including for mothers. In Pakistan, crisis with governance, proper allocation of funds to rural medical facilities, and the lack of strong political will to implement programs have all been cited as barriers to attaining maternal mortality goals (Mahmud et al. 2011).

Countries around the world have been affected by their political context. In the Philippines, provinces that have suffered from the decades-long Moro and Communist insurgencies have had poorer MCH outcomes than other provinces—as have provinces with higher rates of indigenous populations displaced by armed conflict, such as Mindanao (Collas-Monsod, Monsod, and Ducanes 2004). Additionally, provinces exhibiting higher rates of political dynasties—measured by the percentage of provincial officials related by blood and marriage—are also correlated with higher levels of poverty, lower per capita income, and slower progress in relation to the Philippines' Millennium Development Goal (MDG) targets (Collas-Monsod, Monsod, and Ducanes 2004). From 1975 to 1979, Cambodia experienced a period of genocide and breakdown of society and infrastructure under the Khmer Rouge. Peace since 1997 has stabilized the country and has allowed the government and development partners to scale up development efforts, including for maternal health (Liljestrand and Sambath 2012). Maternal mortality has fallen since 2005, from 472 deaths per 100,000 live births during 2000–2005 to 206 during 2006–2010 (Liljestrand and Sambath 2012).

Political prioritization of MRH is a key factor in reducing maternal mortality in SAR countries. Nepal formulated its National Safe Motherhood Plan in 1987, following the Nairobi Conference of Safe Motherhood (Karkee 2011). Subsequent developments included the Safe Motherhood and the Neonatal Long-Term Plan 2006–2017, the National Policy for Skilled Birth Attendants in 2006, and provision of a critical mandate for the Family Health and Child Health divisions of the Ministry of Health and Population (MOHP). The Safe Motherhood Program in Nepal has received substantial support from international development partners and has delivered significant achievements. The maternal mortality ratio (MMR) fell from 539 deaths per 100,000 live births in 1997 to 281 in 2006 (Barker et al. 2007a; Rath et al. 2007). In Bangladesh, there is strong political commitment to achieve the MDGs, especially those related to child and maternal health (Chowdhury et al. 2011). The national importance of population control has been emphasized since the country's First Five Year Plan launched after independence (Hasan, Reich, and Fink 2012). In 1976, the new government that came to power stated that rapid population growth was the most pressing problem for the country and launched the first National Population Policy, which viewed family planning as an integral component of development (Hasan, Reich, and Fink 2012). Population and family planning policies have been a consistent and significant

http://dx.doi.org/10.1596/978-1-4648-0963-7

component in Bangladesh's subsequent five-year development plans (Hasan, Reich, and Fink 2012). Bangladesh's commitment to family planning has resulted in two UN population awards: one to then President Hussain Muhammad Ershad in 1987 and the other in 2006 to Dr. Halida Hanum Akhter, the head of the Bangladesh Institute of Essential and Reproductive Health and Technologies.

In 2005, India's stagnating rates of maternal mortality resulted in a consensus among (Shiffman and Ved 2007) government officials and donors on a way forward to reduce the MMR. The consensus for action occurred within the context of a new government with social equity aims coming to power. The new government's agenda included a nationwide effort to expand health care access to the rural poor. These developments made maternal mortality a political priority in India. Even so, the experience of translating this political commitment into effective implementation has had mixed results. In Tamil Nadu State, the state government's long term "political commitment and proactive administration" toward maternal, newborn, and child health (MNCH) services have been cited as a key factor in the state's success compared to other states in India (Padmanaban, Raman, and Mavalankar 2009).

Political prioritization of MRH has been an important factor in countries around the world that have successfully reduced maternal mortality. In 2000, Rwanda's government recognized the importance of addressing MRH issues to reduce poverty (Bucagu et al. 2012). This prioritization was made in the context of a country with a population of 10.6 million (2010), of whom more than half are female (52 percent), young (65 percent under 25 years of age), living in rural areas (83 percent), and with a high total fertility rate (TFR 4.6) (Bucagu et al. 2012). In Honduras, a study found that activists and health authorities in the early 1990s generated political priority for safe motherhood initiatives after a survey demonstrated shockingly high rates of maternal mortality in the country (Shiffman, Stanton, and Salazar 2004).

Constitutional rights and legislation in a number of SAR countries have enabled maternal mortality reductions. In other countries, however, rights and legislation have been insufficiently enforced. Nepal's 2007 Interim Constitution introduced a rights-based framework, which included reproductive health as a citizen's right and an assurance that every citizen has the right to receive basic health services free of cost. Moreover, abortion was legalized in 2002 after 30 years of reform efforts (Thapa, Sharma, and Khatiwada 2014). Efforts to introduce the framework initially grew from government concerns about population growth but moved to a focus on reducing maternal morbidity and mortality and ensuring women's rights (Thapa, Sharma, and Khatiwada 2014). Safe abortion services are now available nationwide. However, women's awareness of the liberalization of the abortion law has been limited to wealthier and more educated women. Intensified efforts are required to educate disadvantaged women about the law, including where to access safe abortion services (Thapa, Sharma, and Khatiwada 2014).

In India, legislative controls for safe abortion in 1971, 1994, and 2002 have enabled a decline in abortion-related deaths, though problems remain with

http://dx.doi.org/10.1596/978-1-4648-0963-7

informal fees, service availability, quality of care, low levels of awareness of services, and social stigma (Siddhivinayak 2004). In Pakistan, legislative action through the Child Marriage Restraint Act prohibited child marriage in 1929. Under the Muslim Family Law Ordinance of 1961, the minimum age of marriage was raised to 16 years for females and 18 years for males. However, poor enforcement means that a high number of child marriages are among people below these ages. The law requires consent from both parties entering marriage—a mandatory signature or thumb impression of the bride and the signature of the groom or his representative on the agreement. Nonetheless, these measures have not prevented child marriages of girls because of nonregistration of marriages and the registrars' failure to always ensure compliance with the laws (Gah 2013).

According to the Pakistan DHS 2006–07, 13 percent of girls in the country are married by the time they are 15 years old and 40 percent by 18 years (Gah 2013). Inadequate enforcement of child marriage laws in Pakistan has meant continued risk of maternal mortality for Pakistan's girls from adolescent births. In India, the 73rd Amendment to the Constitution of India (1993) provided a legal framework for decentralization. This process, in theory, would allow local- or regional-level decision-making about maternal health, which is closer to the target population and more sensitive to their particular needs. However, decentralization in India has had mixed outcomes with no impact on the maternal mortality rate (Seshadri et al. 2015). The National Rural Health Mission (NRHM) has sought since 2005 to decentralize funders, functions, and functionaries to lower levels of government (Seshadri et al. 2015). A study in Karnataka State has found, however, that NRHM guidelines on decentralization are not always implemented on the ground and that capacity building at all levels of the health systems is required to ensure the empowerment of functionaries (Seshadri et al. 2015).

When laws are enforced and implemented, legislation in other countries has enabled maternal mortality reductions. In 1989, Romania had the highest recorded MMR in Europe, with 159 deaths per 100,000 live births. After the fall of the Nicolaie Ceausescu communist regime in December 1989, the new government immediately legalized abortion and eliminated restrictions on contraceptive use. In 1990, a dramatic decline in the MMR was apparent, down to 83 deaths per 100,000 live births (Hord et al. 1991). In Cambodia, abortion became legal in 1997, but access to safe abortion was limited until 2005 when government and partners increased their efforts to train doctors and midwives in public and private sectors. This led to a significant reduction in abortion-related maternal deaths between 2005 and 2009 (Liljestrand and Sambath 2012). In Mongolia, the liberalization of abortion laws led to high abortion rates of 230 to 1,000 live births in 2006. Rates remain high in Mongolia even though abortion is one of the few services not covered under a policy of free maternity services, and the quality of abortion care has been assessed as extremely low in the past (Hill, Dodd, and Dashdorj 2006).

Political enablers have shown to create a positive environment to reduce maternal mortality. Political enablers include peace and stability, political prioritization of MRH, and enforced legislation and constitutional rights. The importance of political factors is substantiated by a study that has shown that countries with higher scores on governance indicators—including government effectiveness, accountability, political stability, regulatory capacity, rule of law, and control over corruption—have been linked to lower rates of MMR (Kaufmann, Kraay, and Mastruzzi 2003). Further research on the specific links between effective governance and maternal mortality in SAR countries and elsewhere is needed.

Economic Enablers

Reductions in maternal mortality have occurred concomitantly with economic growth in most SAR countries. For example, while Nepal's maternal mortality rate was declining, its indicators were improving in most categories, according to the Human Development Index and Gender Empowerment Measure (Hussein et al. 2011). Bhutan's MMR has dropped from 900 deaths per 100,000 live births in 1990 to 120 in 2013 while its economy was growing, driven by hydropower, manufacturing, and domestic services. Bhutan's GDP grew from 8 percent in 2011–12 to 12.5 percent in 2012–13 (World Bank 2015a). Its per capita gross national income is one of the highest in SAR. It improved from US$730 in 2000 to US$2,070 in 2011 (World Bank 2015a). India's reductions in MMR since 1990 can be attributed in part to economic growth and the reduction of poverty, even though the country has struggled to achieve its maternal health goals (Rai and Tulchinsky 2015). As shown in figure 8.1, most SAR countries have achieved better maternal mortality reduction ratios than other countries at comparable income levels.

Figure 8.1 Correlation between MMR and Income Level, 2013

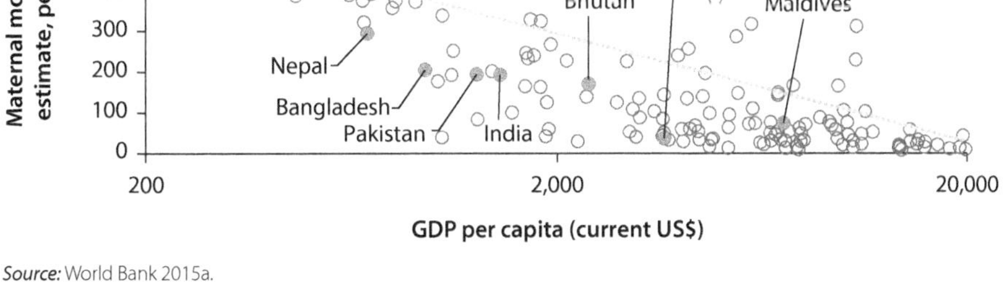

Maternal mortality ratio (modeled estimate, per 100,000 live births)

1,000
900
800
700
600
500
400
300
200
100
0

Afghanistan
Sri Lanka
$R^2 = 0.5051$
Bhutan
Maldives
Nepal
Bangladesh
Pakistan
India

200
2,000
20,000

GDP per capita (current US$)

Source: World Bank 2015a.

Other countries around the world have also shown a similar trend. As shown in figure 8.1, MMR tends to decrease as per capita GDP increases globally. A study assessing the relationship between economic factors and maternal mortality across several countries substantiated these findings. Countries with low MMR have higher GDP per capita (Adam and Franz-Vasdeki 2012). In Brazil, economic growth has been an enabling factor in the country's progress on maternal mortality by contributing to declining poverty rates and income inequality (Barros et al. 2010; Victora et al. 2011). Thailand's MMR began to decline in the 1960s but increased between 1997 and 2000 alongside an economic crisis. The MMR began to decline steadily after 2000 with Thailand's economic recovery and the government's introduction of universal health insurance coverage, the provincial Maternal and Child Health Board groups, the Healthy Thailand program, and the Saiyairak program (Acuin et al. 2011).

The full impact of economic growth on MMR may not be realized in countries with large inequities. Large inequities exist in India, for example. Rural areas in the poorest states of India have the highest MMR in the country (Montgomery et al. 2014). Moreover, women living in rural areas of poorer states in India recorded proportionately lower use of routine SBA and emergency obstetric care (EmOC) than women living in urban areas. This disparity in rural-urban health seeking did not occur in richer states, indicating the influence of the macroeconomic environment on MRH (Montgomery et al. 2014). Likewise, economic growth in China's Henan and Yunnan Provinces has contributed to increased government investment in health care more broadly and maternal health specifically. Economic growth has also led to rising income levels (Li et al. 2007). However, growth in China has not necessarily been equitably distributed and large differences in maternal health indicators can be seen when comparing provinces, regions within provinces, ethnic groups, wealth quintiles, and rural and urban areas (Li et al. 2007; You et al. 2012).

Demographic Enablers

At the same time that maternal mortality rates were falling in many SAR countries, fertility rates were also declining. In Bangladesh, for instance, the TFR fell from 3.2 to 2.5 between 2001 and 2010 while the country experienced a reduction in the MMR (Chowdhury et al. 2011) and a steady increase in the contraceptive prevalence rate (El Arifeen et al. 2014). In Afghanistan, decreases in the MMR occurred at the same time as a decline in the TFR from 6.3 in 2003 to 5.1 in 2010 (Rasooly et al. 2014). The major contributing factors in this reduction were the use of contraceptive methods and age at marriage, both of which were increasing in the same period (Rasooly et al. 2014). The increase in age at first marriage is a key factor in reducing the TFR and the risk of maternal mortality from adolescent births. Despite these promising trends in Afghanistan, sustained effort will be required for further improvement.

http://dx.doi.org/10.1596/978-1-4648-0963-7

In Nepal, during the same period of maternal mortality reductions, the TFR also declined. The most important contributing factor was the increase of the contraceptive prevalence rate (Bhandari, Gordon, and Shakya 2011; Malla et al. 2011). Though contraceptive use has increased from 24 percent in 1990, the rate of increase has stagnated between 44 percent and 50 percent since at least 2006 (MOHP Nepal, New ERA, and ICF International Inc. 2012). Fertility declined from approximately 4.6 births per woman in 1994 to 2.6 in 2011, with the greatest drop from 2001 to 2006 (Hussein et al. 2011). The age of marriage in Nepal is also rising among men and women. The percentage of women between 15 and 19 years of age who have not married rose to 71 percent in 2011 from 60 percent in 2001 (MOHP Nepal, New ERA, and ICF International Inc. 2012). Despite the recent increase in the marital age, the average age of marriage remains relatively low at 18 years. In India, factors contributing to the high number of maternal deaths in the country include poor coverage of contraceptive use, early age at marriage, and a high birth rate among adolescents (Rai and Tulchinsky 2015). Approximately 44.5 percent of women aged 20–24 years marry before their 18th birthday (Rai and Tulchinsky 2015). In Sri Lanka, the downward trend of the TFR began in the mid-1950s. This was initially due to an increase in women's age at marriage to 23.2 years in 2011, which was influenced by the impacts of the free education policy enacted in 1931 (Seneviratne and Rajapaksa 2000). This policy increased levels of female education and empowered women. Later reductions in fertility in Sri Lanka were due to increases in contraceptive use. These dynamics also mean that Sri Lanka has a low adolescent birth rate. In 2013, it was 17 births per 1,000 women aged 15–19 years (Seneviratne and Rajapaksa 2000).

Reductions in fertility rates in countries around the world have occurred alongside reductions in maternal mortality. In Malaysia, the TFR fell from 6.7 in 1957 to 3.2 in 1999, at the same time that the MMR was declining (Pathmanathan et al. 2003). TFR declined most steeply between 1960 and 1980, from 6.0 to 3.9, at the same time that the MMR fell from 282 to 63 maternal deaths per 100,000 live births (Pathmanathan et al. 2003). In Cambodia, the MMR declined from 472 deaths per 100,000 live births during 2000–2005 to 206 during 2006–2010 while fertility has also been decreasing (Liljestrand and Sambath 2012). This fertility reduction began following the post-Pol Pot baby boom in the 1980s and by 2010, reached a TFR of 3.0 (Liljestrand and Sambath 2012). The Islamic Republic of Iran, in 1960, had one of the highest estimated TFRs in the world at 7.0 (Moazzeni 2013). This fell to 1.8 in 2008 due to a number of family planning policies such as mandatory prenuptial education for couples including contraceptive counseling, endorsement of birth spacing and limiting family size to three, and encouragement of women to restrict childbearing from the ages of 16 to 35 (Moazzeni 2013). As shown in figure 8.2, MMR decline is strongly correlated with the decline in fertility rate globally. Most SAR countries, however, have higher levels of MMRs compared with countries that have comparable fertility rate levels.

http://dx.doi.org/10.1596/978-1-4648-0963-7

Figure 8.2 Correlation between MMR and Fertility Rate, 2013

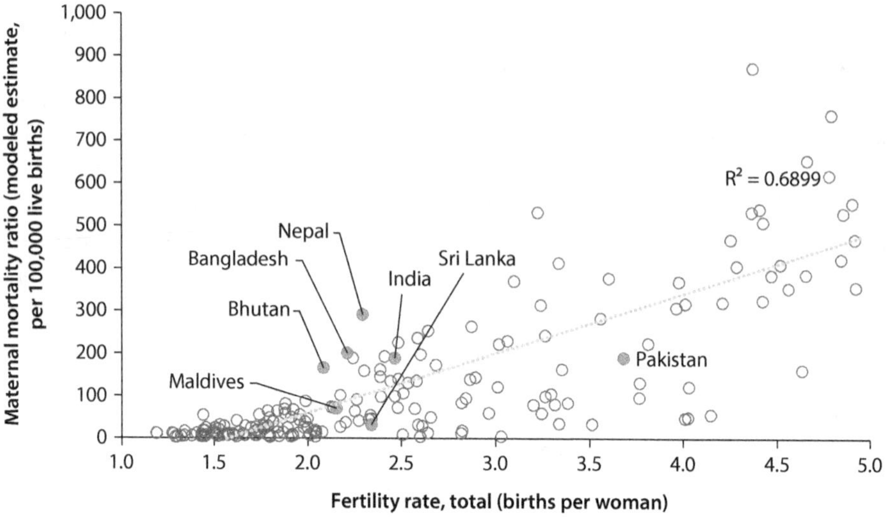

Source: World Bank 2015a.

Sociocultural Enablers

Cultural barriers in SAR, such as the caste system, impede marginalized women's demand for MRH services and are obstacles to further progress on reducing maternal mortality. In India, the social stratification that is enforced through the caste system remains strong and is one of the primary determinants of health status (Sanneving et al. 2013). For MRH in particular, studies show that the caste system functions as a barrier to use of reproductive health services and members of low-caste groups have poorer maternal health outcomes (Sanneving et al. 2013). The likelihood of receiving any type of antenatal care is lowest among women belonging to low-caste groups (Sanneving et al. 2013). Furthermore, only 18 percent of the births among these women are conducted at a health facility, compared to 51 percent among women who do not belong to lower castes (Sanneving et al. 2013). These patterns were also evident across numerous large studies undertaken in some of India's most populous states, including Jharkhand, Uttar Pradesh, and Rajasthan (Hazarika 2011; Iyengar et al. 2009; Maiti, Unisa, and Agrawal 2005; Saroha, Altarac, and Sibley 2008). In Nepal, women of a lower caste have been denied access to obstetric care due to social norms that give higher caste groups preferential access to resources (Karkee 2011; Rath et al. 2007). In Pakistan, women who belong to low-caste groups are more likely to deliver at home with the help of a relative or unskilled birth attendant (Mumtaz et al. 2014). They choose to deliver at home because of a combination of limited financial means and because of poor treatment by government health providers (Mumtaz et al. 2014). More studies are needed to understand how economic status, gender, and belonging to a marginalized group cause inequitable access to MRH services and act as barriers to further maternal mortality reductions, to provide insights on how to better design policy (Sanneving et al. 2013).

In India, an association has been shown between women's autonomy and higher use of prenatal, delivery, and postnatal care (Mistry, Galal, and Lu 2009). This effect varied by region in India, with the association highest in South India, which also had the highest self-reported women's autonomy (Mistry, Galal, and Lu 2009). The type of household has also been associated with access to MRH services, with increased access in families living in nuclear households, that is, households with husband, wife, and children, compared to joint households, that is, couples living together with parents of the husband (Sanneving et al. 2013). The quality of family relationships between husband and wife and between wives and in-laws was also a factor (Sanneving et al. 2013). The role of men and female in-laws, however, is not always negative. In urban Uttar Pradesh, India, households in which wives lived in their husbands' natal home or with their mothers-in-law were more likely to use modern family planning and institutional delivery than women who lived neither in the husbands' natal home nor with their mothers-in-law (Speizer et al. 2015).

In Bhutan, there is greater gender equality, and this has contributed to improved MRH and enabled maternal mortality reductions. Compared to other SAR countries, Bhutanese women enjoy relative equality of status with men. Gender equality is a proven significant factor contributing to improved MRH. Bhutanese women have equal or greater decision-making powers over reproduction, as well as over livelihood, and economic activities. They also have greater control and ownership of land and property. Within the household, cooking and childcare are shared equitably with men. There is no gender bias in access to or uptake of health care in Bhutan, with men and women practicing similar health behaviors. In most cases, Bhutanese women are the primary decision makers about contraceptive use, birth spacing, and motherhood. Most women also reported that contraceptives were easily available to them and that they experienced no unmet need.

In some SAR countries, women have had increasing employment opportunities, which may have an indirect link to maternal mortality. For example, Bangladesh has focused on providing opportunities to microcredit and formal sector employment for young women in urban and rural areas (Chowdhury et al. 2011). Studies have shown that women's employment can delay the age of marriage and child bearing. For example, a survey of garment factory workers in Bangladesh found that women's employment changed the average age of marriage from 16 to 20 years. The birth of the first child typically came a year after taking up employment, thus delaying the age at which mothers gave birth from 17 to 21 years (Naved, Ruchira, and Sajeda 1997).

CHAPTER 9

No Single Intervention Is Sufficient

In attempting to answer the question "What are the factors and interventions that led to this relative sharp maternal mortality ratio (MMR) decline in South Asia Region (SAR) against what is predicted by standard socioeconomic outcomes?" this study has examined six possible drivers and enablers that may have contributed to this achievement.

First, we examined the household drivers, including gender dynamics such as the role of men and female in-laws, access to information, women's education, and household income. We found that household factors are important drivers of MMR reduction and improved reproductive health outcomes—although they are often indirect drivers. Strategies and interventions that target traditional beliefs about gender roles, pregnancy and delivery, and men's involvement in maternal and reproductive health (MRH) can help overcome some demand-side barriers, as can involving the husbands' female family members, particularly the mothers-in-law. Improving households' access to information through Information, Education, and Communication (IEC)/behavior change communication (BCC), mass media, advocacy, and other campaigns can improve all relevant family members' knowledge of and attitudes and practices toward MRH and further encourage demand for services. Finally, women's education and household income have repeatedly been demonstrated to be vital household drivers of service uptake and MMR reduction. However, education and income are factors that cannot be addressed through health sector initiatives and affirm the need for multisectoral approaches to MRH. More importantly, household factors do not exist independent of the larger household context. While women's household status, education, and household income are variables that can be correlated with maternal mortality, these indicators alone do not explain why some SAR countries have achieved progress in decreasing their MMR. These indicators must be related to the broader political, economic, and social changes that influence them. For example, measurements of household income fail to account for whether or not women have access to that income or whether political and cultural assurances exist that enable women to retain or make decisions about household wealth. Similarly, changing rates of women's education or level of schooling alone do not account for the policy and social changes that have led families to prioritize girls' schooling.

Second, we examined the MRH programmatic interventions that may have improved access to and use of community and clinical MRH services across the continuum of care and MMR reduction in SAR. Key programs that have contributed to reducing maternal mortality include increasing family planning coverage, improving skilled birth attendance, increasing institutional delivery, and scaling up access to emergency obstetric care. Supportive interventions, such as those involving emergency transportation or maternity waiting homes, add value to programmatic interventions and improve access. Antenatal care (ANC) and access to safe abortion services have also been correlated with maternal mortality reduction in some countries. The success of the programmatic interventions is dependent on strong national health systems and is influenced by the political, social, and economic context in which they are implemented.

Third, we explored the broader health system inputs and how they may have improved women's access to and use of MRH services. The SAR countries, like many other countries around the world, have implemented initiatives to improve health financing. These include removal of user fees to reduce financial barriers to use, instituting performance-based financing (PBF) or results-based financing (RBF) to reduce quality barriers, and the introduction of demand-side interventions such as vouchers or cash-based incentives to remove financial barriers, generate demand, and increase uptake of MRH services. SAR countries have also increased the coverage and quality of health services to support improved MRH service delivery, though large disparities in quality of care in SAR persist and influence women's use of MRH services and further progress on MMR reduction. Efforts to professionalize the maternal health workforce have been made in SAR countries, which include hiring and training increasing numbers of midwives, other skilled birth attendants (SBAs), and doctors with obstetrics/gynecology specialization. Cadres of semiskilled volunteers and community workers have also been trained and deployed to fill the gap created by the shortage of skilled health professionals. In addition, SAR countries have tried to prioritize the delivery of the commodities. Moreover, many SAR countries have made investments in their national information systems, including MRH programs, and have implemented maternal death registration, facility-based and community-based verbal autopsy, and reviews and audits of maternal deaths and adverse events. Even SAR countries struggling to reach their MMR targets have made the important first step of laying the policy groundwork for MRH initiatives. Many countries have also instituted governance structures ensuring proper enforcement, accountability, and transparency.

Fourth, we examined the community-based interventions in SAR that may have worked to "create an enabling environment" to improve maternal survival and reproductive health outcomes. These interventions—such as deploying female community-based health workers recruited from and working in their communities, establishing participatory women's groups, and engaging community leaders—shift the focus from facility-based care to localized delivery of services involving community participation. Such schemes enable maternal survival by empowering communities to identify their own maternal health needs, interests, and preferences and allow the design of MRH services that are sensitive to the local context. They also offer the opportunity to engage multiple stakeholders, maximizing health care skills and resources in resource poor settings. To reach the most economically and socially marginalized women, community-based interventions to reduce maternal mortality must design equity-based strategies to identify these women and address the obstacles they face.

Fifth, experiences from SAR and other countries demonstrate that increasing maternal survival and improving reproductive health outcomes require the efforts of more than health sector interventions. Sustaining ongoing gains and making progress in public health—including MRH—will require mobilizing actions across sectors (Pierre-Louis et al. 2012). While evidence-based health sector interventions are critical for reducing maternal mortality, interventions in sectors outside of health—sometimes implemented through coordinated multisectoral action involving the health sector—are equally important for reaching maternal mortality targets. A minimum of 12 years of schooling for girls teaches them the importance of health and increases their receptivity to recommended health practices. Education also delays first marriage and first birth and decreases the risk of maternal mortality from adolescent births. By providing safe and adequate transportation and communication networks, health workers can better access remote and rural villages and mothers and families can better access health facilities, particularly during emergencies. Clean water and sanitation are basic goods that are critical to maintaining human health. Without them, progress in reducing maternal mortality may be limited, though the linkages are not yet fully understood. Proper nutrition is critical to a mother's health and survival; however, the role of nutritional interventions in reducing maternal mortality is not clear. The electrification of health facilities and households improves the efficiency and effectiveness of health facilities' maternal health services as well as the communication and health-seeking behaviors of mothers but further research is needed to show linkages with maternal mortality reductions. Conditional cash transfer (CCT) programs were found to be effective in increasing the use of MRH services and have less evident effect on outcomes while microcredit programs had an indirect effect through women's empowerment, income generation, and fertility reduction.

Finally, we explored the political, economic, demographic, and sociocultural factors that may enable or constrain improved MRH outcomes. These factors vary significantly by country and within countries. Therefore, each country context in SAR must be considered to make additional progress in maternal survival. SAR and other countries that have achieved maternal mortality reductions have been enabled by governments' political prioritization of MRH. Peace and stability, as well as legislation and its enforcement on MRH issues, have also been important factors. Economic growth has occurred alongside maternal mortality reductions in SAR countries, but the full impact of growth has not been realized in countries with large inequities. The economic and social status of women in SAR countries has progressed alongside maternal mortality reductions, but significant improvements are still required for further progress. Demographic dynamics such as fertility declines have occurred at the same time as MMR reductions, while factors such urbanization, urban-rural differences, and disparities for minority populations create challenges for many countries in SAR and elsewhere. The sociocultural context of gender hierarchies and the caste and class system in SAR countries are also key barriers to further progress in maternal mortality.

What Worked

This study has shown that MRH outcomes in SAR are affected by an array of drivers and enablers. Across the South Asian countries, numerous interventions are being implemented to improve women's access to equitable, effective, and quality MRH services. The evidence of the impact of these interventions varies widely. Figure 9.1 provides a schema of the pathways of the impact of those interventions on both maternal mortality reduction and increased use of MRH services together with the strength of evidence based mostly on the systematic reviews.

The most effective interventions that prevent maternal mortality are those that address the intra-partum stage—the point where most maternal deaths occur—and include improving skilled birth attendance coverage, increasing institutional delivery rates, and scaling up access to emergency obstetric care. These programmatic interventions have all directly contributed to reducing maternal mortality in SAR, which is not surprising given that 38 percent of maternal mortality causes are due to maternal hemorrhage, maternal sepsis, maternal hypertensive disorders, and obstructed labor and can be mainly addressed by these interventions. There is also adequate evidence that investing in **family planning** to increase contraceptive use also played a key role during the inter-partum phase by preventing unwanted pregnancies and thus averting the risk of maternal mortality in SAR countries. Two other interventions were correlated with maternal mortality reduction in some SAR countries: increased access to safe abortion and post-abortion services as well as ANC; however, the evidence that supports their effect is limited.

The levels of household income and women's education within the household were key drivers of maternal mortality reduction and the increased uptake of MRH services. Outside the programmatic interventions, only these two factors stand out as they were strongly correlated with improved MRH outcomes. Related to women's education within the household, completion of secondary education of girls, an education sector intervention, was also strongly correlated with improved MRH outcomes.

There is strong evidence that health financing schemes and CCTs were effective in increasing the uptake of MRH services in SAR countries and other regions. Both demand and supply-side schemes helped encourage women to use

http://dx.doi.org/10.1596/978-1-4648-0963-7

Figure 9.1 Pathways of Interventions and Factors that Improve MRH Service Use and Reduce Maternal Mortality

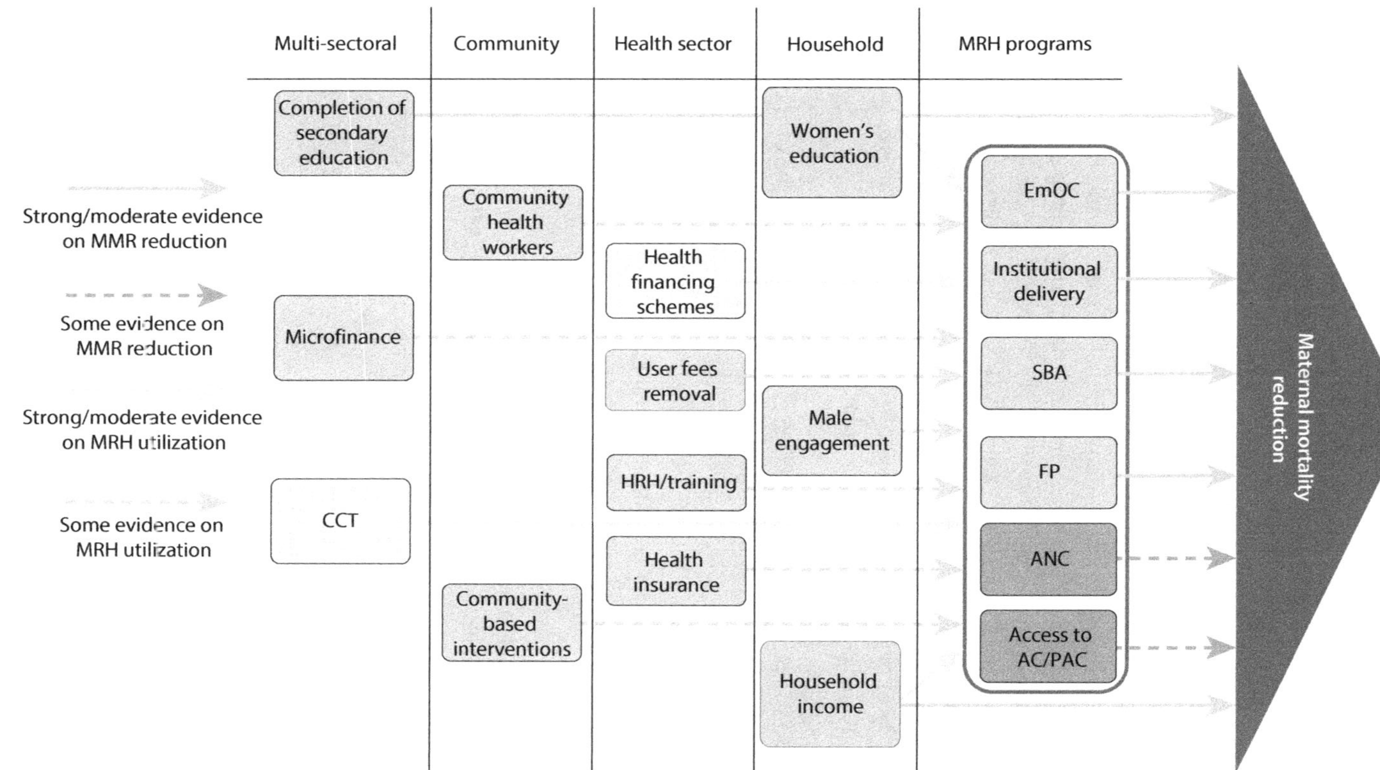

Note: AC = abortion care; ANC = antenatal care; CCT = conditional cash transfer; EmOC = emergency obstetric care; FP = family planning; MMR = maternal mortality ratio; MRH = maternal and reproductive health; PAC = post-abortion care; SBA = skilled birth attendant.

the services, reducing financial barriers to access services, reducing the burden of out-of-pocket expenditures, and incentivizing the providers, which contributed to the increased uptake of MRH services in many countries in SAR such as in the case of the *Janani Suraksha Yojana* program in India, the Safe Delivery Incentives Program (SDIP) in Nepal, the Maternal Health Voucher Scheme in Bangladesh, and the P4P scheme in Pakistan. CCT programs that provided cash payments conditional on the use of some merit goods, services, or behaviors were implemented in some SAR countries such as in the case of the Secondary School Assistance Program in Bangladesh and the Female School Stipend Program in Pakistan. The evidence of the effectiveness of the CCT programs however comes from the Latin America and the Caribbean region. CCT programs have long been a staple of development initiatives in Latin America and the Caribbean and the evidence of their effectiveness is drawn from rich, compelling, longitudinal data on the positive contribution of CCTs on MRH outcomes. This, however, does not mean that Latin America and the Caribbean had succeeded with CCTs and South Asian countries have not. It merely points to the fact that Latin America and the Caribbean has implemented these programs longer, that a greater body of evidence on their success in these countries exists, and that their governments have brought such programs at scale.

SAR countries have implemented several other interventions that may have contributed to increased use of MRH services but the evidence of their impact is limited. It is important to note, however, that these interventions, with the exception of male engagement, were not intended primarily to increase uptake of MRH services but had broader objectives. At the health sector level, training of health providers, removal of user fees, and expanding health insurance aimed at strengthening health systems, reducing financial barriers to overall use of services and expanding health coverage. Similarly, community-based interventions and mobilizing community health workers aimed at increasing the uptake of health services and not just MRH. Microcredit programs aimed at increasing poor household income and women's empowerment. Moving forward, MRH program managers should establish more linkages and harness the benefits of these interventions.

When examining drivers of change, what becomes most apparent is that very few of the factors examined are mutually exclusive. For example, the success of skilled birth attendance initiatives is partly dependent on Ministries of Health simultaneously carrying out training in emergency obstetric care (EmOC), improving rates of institutional delivery, and carrying out IEC and BCC campaigns to encourage women to use trained health care workers. Success has also been dependent on the government investing in, expanding, or creating cadres of health workers; locating sources of financing to pay such workers; and restructuring service delivery models. Any examination of SBA measures should recognize that such programs do not exist in a vacuum. Success often appears to depend less on rolling out discrete "interventions" than on building entire systems for managing both maternal health and health more generally. In this respect, interventions to improve MRH outcomes appear to be different than interventions for reducing child mortality in high mortality settings, in which simple targeted interventions

http://dx.doi.org/10.1596/978-1-4648-0963-7

like mass immunization campaigns or bed net distribution can deliver significant, large-scale, cost-effective results. For example, in Sub-Saharan Africa, Niger achieved a notable reduction in child mortality through such targeted interventions without any improvements to the overall health system and during adverse political, economic, and ecological conditions (Frost and Pratt 2014). With respect to MRH in SAR and elsewhere, the story is really one of simultaneous investment in systems, not just interventions. This finding accords with recent evidence emerging from systematic and narrative reviews of MRH interventions in low- and middle-income countries (LMICs), emphasizing that "no magic bullet intervention" exists for the reduction of maternal mortality, that clinical interventions are not sufficient, and that a comprehensive approach dependent on the context and the determinants of MRH in a setting is needed (Ross et al. 2005; Nyamtema, Urassa, and van Roosmalen 2011; and Pucher, Macdonnell, and Arulkumaran 2013). This finding points the way toward a broader understanding of how to more effectively address and finance MRH programs in the future.

Where More Evidence Is Needed

The cases and papers reviewed for this study point to the fact that there is rarely any discussion of true multisectoral interventions. There are discussions about health sector initiatives and initiatives outside the health sector that likely had the add-on benefit of improving MRH outcomes. However, in no instances did the literature suggest that true multisectoral action—that is partnership between and across sectors intentionally targeting MRH—contributed to improved MRH outcomes. The exception may have been for Bangladesh, where the expansion of road and bridge networks had the purpose of improving access to health services more generally (El Arifeen et al. 2014). Was the improvement of transportation networks in Bangladesh worked out through multisectoral collaboration, or did the ministries in charge of infrastructure development work independently of the health ministry on this initiative? This study suggests that multisectoral actions for MRH in SAR and other countries occur infrequently and that multisectoral action for MRH is not documented enough.

In addition to the information gap on multisectoral action, the literature on South Asia and worldwide is limited on the nutrition interventions that contribute to improved MRH outcomes. Other research has found that improvements to the nutritional status of women and children is one of the key contributing factors to successfully reducing national maternal mortality rates. Yet, the literature reviewed for this study—while suggesting that nutrition has played a role in MRH—has not carefully documented the linkage between nutrition and MMR. With the numerous current initiatives on nutrition through programs such as the Scaling Up Nutrition (SUN) movement and Feed the Future, it is hoped that a more sustained focus will result on how nutrition does (or does not) contribute to improved MRH outcomes, particularly nutrition's effect on reducing maternal mortality.

Similarly, there is lack of documentation on the role of the contextual factors as enablers for improving MRH outcomes. The analytical framework used in this

http://dx.doi.org/10.1596/978-1-4648-0963-7

study focuses on the political, economic, and sociocultural factors that "enable" improved MRH outcomes. However, the papers reviewed for this study more frequently demonstrate those factors to be "disabling" to MRH outcomes. Likewise, while the literature suggests that sociocultural and religious factors play an important part in the lack of uptake of MRH services in countries such as Nepal, Pakistan, Afghanistan, and India, the role that such factors play in improving MRH outcomes in those countries is also not very explicitly documented. In fact, this study points out that national MRH programs may prioritize and implement proven interventions and yet be undermined by the environment in which they are implemented. Notably, the case of Pakistan demonstrates that in spite of how diligently health professionals have worked to reduce maternal mortality through proven cost-effective reproductive and maternal health interventions, their efforts have been frequently undone by serious systemic issues within the health sector, as well as political conditions (Bhutta et al. 2013). A more comprehensive understanding of the contextual enablers that may contribute to overcoming non-financial, demand-side barriers to service use was lacking in the papers reviewed for this study. While the examined literature is better at describing how political, economic, and social contextual factors serve as barriers to improved MRH outcomes, it is not particularly informative on the role that contextual enablers play in this regard. There was a lack of contextual information and implementation process information available for maternal and reproductive health interventions (Yuan et al. 2014).

A critical gap in the literature is the lack of evidence on interventions that reduce inequity in maternal mortality and limited evidence on improved equity in other maternal and reproductive health outcomes. Even when interventions "enable" positive change for maternal health, they rarely do so consistently throughout a country, since rarely do all regions, ethnic groups, and wealth strata benefit equally from the political, economic, and sociocultural factors. A systematic review of effective interventions to reduce inequalities in maternal and child health (MCH) in LMICs did not find any looking at equity in maternal mortality. These studies covered five kinds of interventions: immunization campaigns, nutrition supplement programs, health care provision improvement interventions, demand-side interventions, and mixed interventions. The outcome indicators covered MCH outcomes. None of the included studies looked at equity in maternal mortality, adolescent birth rate, and unmet need for family planning. The included studies reported inequalities based on gender, income, education level, or comprehensive socioeconomic status. Stronger or moderate evidence showed that all kinds of included interventions may be more effective in improving maternal or child health for those from disadvantaged groups. The limited evidence showed that the interventions that were effective in reducing inequity included the improvement of health care delivery by outreach methods, using human resources in local areas or provided at the community level nearest to residents and the provision of financial or knowledge support to demand side (Yuan et al. 2014).

In this review, there was also lack of information on the cost and cost-effectiveness even for the effective interventions. In addition, to establish the "effectiveness"

http://dx.doi.org/10.1596/978-1-4648-0963-7

and impact of particular interventions, it is important for policymakers to know the associated costs of implementing these interventions and the cost-effectiveness of different alternatives. The search strings used for this study, however, did not explicitly seek to explore this aspect, so this finding should be interpreted with caution as a more expanded search may find otherwise.

What Made SAR Stand Out?

If SAR has successfully implemented effective interventions that other countries have also implemented, then what made SAR stand out? Several factors emerge.

Government commitment to family planning and reproductive health was strong. In attempting to dissect the factors that may have made SAR stand out, it may be necessary to examine the countries that had the highest decline in maternal mortality: India, Bangladesh and Pakistan. Governments in these three countries were committed to population control in the mid- and late-1960s but the programmatic strategies were labelled as coercive and top down by civil society in the buildup to the International Conference on Population and Development in 1994. However, the government commitment remained but expanded the strategies to more comprehensive MRH and child health programs to be more acceptable to the civil society and nongovernmental organizations (NGOs) after the International Conference on Population and Development. Also, the donors, who initially supported family planning programs, expanded their support to the more comprehensive package of services. In essence, the government commitment never faltered—their main goal moved from population control to fertility control and transition and then to child survival and maternal survival. The programs, with support from donors, also evolved to fit this strategy, from family planning service, information, and education to programs to enhance maternal survival—ANC, skilled attendance at birth, institutional deliveries, and so on. Also, generally in SAR, health—and more specifically population—was always a non-partisan issue and also largely politically secular. Though the government commitment was necessary, it was not sufficient and had to be complemented.

The NGOs played a key role in complementing the government's commitment to improved MRH outcomes. As indicated in chapter 5, SAR had low public spending on health, high out-of-pocket expenditures, and generally inequitable access to public health services; yet, it achieved this remarkable decline in MMR. A key ingredient in complementing the government commitment was the strong role that the NGOs played, particularly in the family planning programs and, to a certain extent, later in the MRH programs. Bangladesh is a case in point where NGOs played a critical role in the social sectors—trying out alternate modes of service delivery and innovations for enhancing knowledge and awareness. In Pakistan, the growth of the NGO sector growth has been due to the donors' financing strategy, PAYMAN, and similar programs implemented largely through the NGOs. In India, the role of NGOs was limited in service delivery (except in HIV/AIDS programs) but civil society has been active in making the public service providers more accountable.

http://dx.doi.org/10.1596/978-1-4648-0963-7

SAR implemented many of these interventions simultaneously; thus, there was an increased synergy and effectiveness. A systematic review of 54 programs integrating multiple interventions in 23 LMICs, including Bangladesh, India, Nepal, and Pakistan, were more likely to have significant positive impacts on maternal outcomes. Training in EmOC; placement of care providers; refurbishment of existing health facility infrastructure; and improved supply of drugs, consumables, and equipment for obstetric care were the most frequently integrated interventions in these programs. Statistically significant reduction of 55 percent in MMR and 40 percent in case fatality rate were reported as well as an increase of 71 percent in births in EmOC facilities and 75 percent in caesarean sections. The programs in the SAR countries had a higher impact (odds ratio) on maternal mortality compared to the other LMICs in the study (Nyamtema, Urassa, and van Roosmalen 2011). In addition to implementing a comprehensive package of services, SAR has been a center of innovative interventions such as oral rehydration salt therapy, community-based distribution, and microcredit.

The contextual factors may have also played a critical role in improving MRH outcomes in SAR. For instance, the countries achieving the most dramatic progress in reducing their MMR have also progressed in an array of economic and social development indicators—beyond those specific to MRH. Some countries such as Nepal, Bangladesh, and Sri Lanka have been more successful than others in reducing their MMR. This is partly because in all three countries, health and non-health sector factors have played a role in contributing to maternal mortality reduction and improved MRH outcomes. Moreover, while the success in these countries has sometimes been due to intentional decision-making by national policymakers, in many instances, maternal health has also benefitted from broader political, economic, and social change (Frost and Pratt 2015). For example, there was a significant increase in access to information and to mobile phones, especially in countries like India, Bangladesh, and Pakistan. Also, poverty reduction in SAR was 63 percent between 1990 and 2013, which is the second highest after East Asia and the Pacific region, and may have played a role in the microfinance programs started in SAR and has also contributed to women's empowerment and increased household income levels among the poor.

The Way Forward

The global community is now moving toward implementing a new sustainable development agenda to end poverty by 2030. The Millennium Development Goals (MDGs) have provided a platform for governments, donors, and researchers to rally around and to focus their efforts and resources in a concerted way toward achieving them. MDG 5 on maternal health, one of the nine MDGs, received adequate attention and resources, which led to significant improvements in many countries. Building on the MDGs, a new set of 17 ambitious Sustainable Development Goals (SDGs) and targets now form the base of the international development agenda (United Nations 2015b). The shaping and adoption of the SDGs was coupled by a corresponding effort to mobilize

http://dx.doi.org/10.1596/978-1-4648-0963-7

adequate resources at the Third International Conference on Financing for Development (United Nations 2015c). The global health community capitalized on these efforts to secure financial resources through the Global Financing Facility in Support of Every Woman and Every Child (World Bank 2015c). In SAR, both India and Bangladesh will benefit from this Global Financing Facility and this will constitute an opportunity to accelerate progress toward the MRH-related SDGs. In parallel, many countries have committed to achieving Universal Health Coverage, which aims at ensuring that all people have access to the services they need, without the risk of incurring financial ruin by paying for them (WHO 2012). However, there is no room for complacency in striving to achieve the SDG-related MRH targets.

Securing adequate funding for MRH will become increasingly challenging for several reasons. First, only two of the 169 SDG targets are related to MRH and include reducing the MMR and increasing access to sexual and reproductive health services.[1] Therefore, governments will be struggling to mobilize resources among different competing sectors and targets at the national level. Second, most donor countries are facing an uphill challenge to recover from the recent global economic crisis, which will greatly affect the financial and technical resources that they can make available to support the global development agenda. Third, countries in SAR, such as India and Bangladesh, have experienced significant economic growth in recent years. They may therefore soon achieve middle-income status with the risk of losing access to donor grants and concessional financing (Salvado and Waltz 2014).

A confluence of interrelated factors requires the judicious use of available and potential financial and technical resources in support of MRH programs. First and foremost, it will require the use of "available" evidence, knowledge, and data about proven interventions to design effective MRH programs at the outset. Given the limited evidence on what mix of interventions works and how they work to improve MRH in LMICS, it is imperative to generate new evidence and knowledge to improve the effectiveness and efficiency of policies, programs, and interventions within real-world settings to improve MRH outcomes in SAR and worldwide. The GREAT (Guideline development, Research priorities, Evidence synthesis, Applicability of evidence, Transfer of knowledge) Project[2] led by the World Health Organization (WHO) advocates that the "Expansion of sexual and reproductive health care services is firmly linked to the capacity of health systems to adopt evidence-based practices, in both clinical practice and organization and implementation of interventions. A key priority therefore has to be the transfer of evidence based knowledge to health systems along with well- researched and synthesized knowledge about ways of implementing interventions." The "Implementation Research and Delivery Science" initiative—supported by the WHO, USAID, and the World Bank—is a platform that calls for embedding research within the process of implementation that should be led by policymakers or program implementers, address multiple barriers to implementation, engage different stakeholders, use a multidisciplinary approach, and support a culture of continuous learning and adaptation (Alliance for Health Policy and Systems Research 2015). Because no single intervention alone will increase the effectiveness of MRH programs, it is essential to develop a mix of synergistic interventions in the health and non-health sector to accelerate progress toward achieving the MRH targets of the new global sustainable development agenda.

Notes

1. The MRH targets are SDG 3.1: reduce the global maternal mortality ratio to less than 70 per 100,000 live births by 2030 and SDG 3.7: ensure universal access to sexual and reproductive health care services, including for family planning, information, and education and the integration of reproductive health into national strategies and programs by 2030.
2. See http://www.who.int/reproductivehealth/topics/best_practices/Great_Project_2010.pdf?ua=1 for more information about the GREAT Project.

http://dx.doi.org/10.1596/978-1-4648-0963-7

APPENDIX A

The Different Conceptual Frameworks for Maternal Health Outcomes

Several frameworks have been developed to relate maternal mortality and other maternal and reproductive health outcomes to different causes and factors. The frameworks presented in this section seek to highlight all potential factors associated with maternal mortality and morbidity and to explain how they affect maternal and reproductive health.

"The Three Delay Model" explains direct factors that can cause maternal deaths (Thaddeus and Maine 1994). The model identifies the following three common delays in accessing quality maternal care by women and households.

- Delay One: **Recognizing Danger Signs and Deciding to Seek Care** are influenced by a woman's knowledge of pregnancy-related health risks and by her ability to access the resources of her family and community. Poor families in communities with limited information and resources tend to delay decision-making or make inappropriate choices when complications arise.
- Delay Two: **Reaching Appropriate Care** is exacerbated for poor rural women and their families, who tend to face higher and less predictable costs of emergency transportation because of distance and poor infrastructure.
- Delay Three: **Receiving Care at Health Facilities** is influenced by economic status, discrimination based on gender or ethnic prejudice, and availability of providers. Poor families often have to borrow money to pay up front when complications arise. Frequently, households do not have ready access to sufficient cash in time, and often, credit is withheld for needed supplies, medications, and services (Lule et al. 2005).

The "Ecological Model" explains how decisions about seeking maternal and reproductive health care and how care is being provided may be affected by individual and social environmental factors (McLeroy et al. 1988).

http://dx.doi.org/10.1596/978-1-4648-0963-7

This model assumes that appropriate changes in the social environment will produce changes in individuals, and that supporting individuals in the population is essential to implement environmental changes. The model identifies five domains:

- **Intrapersonal factors:** Characteristics of the individual such as knowledge, attitudes, behavior, self-concept, skills, and developmental history
- **Interpersonal processes and primary groups:** Formal and informal social networks and social support systems, including households and extended family structures
- **Institutional factors:** Social institutions with organizational characteristics and formal (and informal) rules and regulations for operations
- **Community:** Relationships among organizations, institutions, and informational networks within defined boundaries
- **Public policy:** Local, state, national, and global laws and policies

In addition to influencing individual behavior to make better decisions, United Nations Children's Fund (UNICEF) proposed a "Conceptual framework for maternal and neonatal mortality and morbidity," which postulates that health outcomes are also determined by interrelated factors encompassing nutrition, water, sanitation and hygiene, health care services and healthy behaviors, and disease control, among others. These factors are defined as proximate (individual); underlying (household, community, and district); and basic (societal). Factors at one level influence other levels (UNICEF 2009). This framework is devised to be useful in assessing and analyzing the causes of maternal and newborn mortality and morbidity and in planning effective actions to enhance maternal and neonatal health.

Another way to consider systemic effects on maternal and reproductive health (MRH) is to conceptualize five "control knobs" or inputs, including financing, payment, organization, regulation, and communication (Roberts et al. 2004) is another way to consider systemic effects on MRH. These inputs feed into specific interventions, which combine governance-based, infrastructural, resource-based, cultural, and demographic factors. These factors all affect maternal and reproductive health as well as other health outcomes.

Improving MRH outcomes would require the mobilization of financial resources in the most effective way, which can be achieved through multisectoral response in "four pillars," according to the "UK's Framework for Results for improving reproductive, maternal and newborn health in the developing world." The four pillars are empowering women and girls to make healthy reproductive choices, removing barriers that prevent access to services, expanding the supply of quality services, and enhancing accountability (DfID 2010).

Finally, a range of multisectoral factors may influence improvements in maternal and reproductive health outcomes including government policies and actions, health systems, other sectors such as education and transport, household and community behaviors, and cultural norms. However, improvement

Figure A.1 Pathways to Improved Maternal Health Outcomes

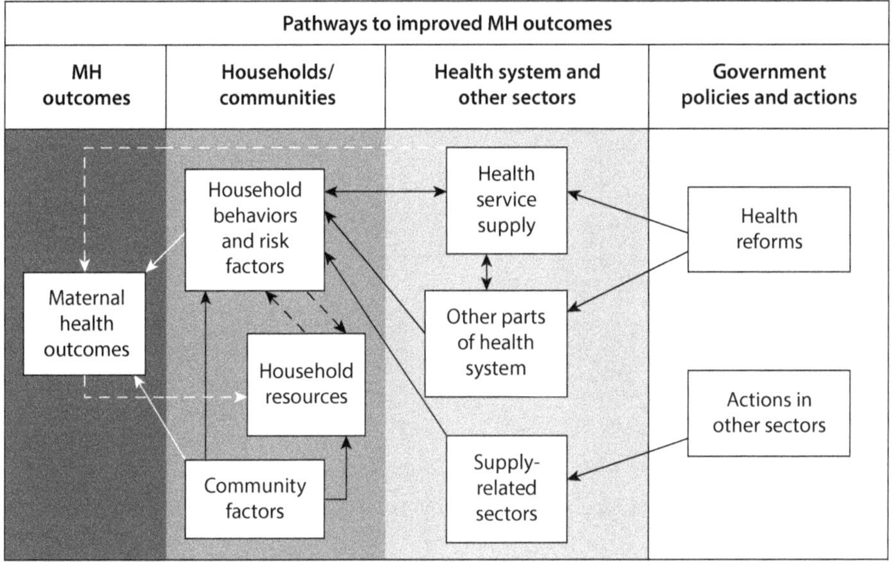

Source: PRSP Sourcebook, Claeson et al. 2001.

can occur through various pathways. The "Pathways to Improved Maternal Health Outcomes" conceptualizes the interconnectedness of variables that affect health outcomes and helps identify risk factors and interventions at the different levels of the system—all of which affect maternal health outcomes (Claeson et al. 2001). This framework identifies direct and indirect pathways to improved MRH outcomes through three levels: households/communities, the health system and other sectors, and government policies and actions. In figure A.1, the solid lines link the predominant pathways through which various factors influence maternal health outcomes. The dashed lines represent some of the secondary linkages that also need to be considered.

In summary, improving maternal survival and reproductive health outcomes requires strategic efforts that address forces from within and outside the health system. It is also important to consider factors at the household and community levels, as well as within the health system. A range of multisectoral factors, as well as factors at play at various levels, such as global, country, community, and home, influence maternal health outcomes.

APPENDIX B

Structured Literature Review on Maternal Mortality

We conducted a literature review to understand the factors that explain the significant reductions in maternal mortality in South Asian countries. What lessons can be learned from a close examination of their progress? What is the context of countries' successes and remaining challenges? How do the experiences of reducing maternal mortality in South Asia compare with those of countries outside the region? This narrative review of the literature examines these questions and identifies the drivers and enablers that explain the progress in reducing maternal mortality in South Asian countries.

This narrative review used a structured literature review strategy. It assessed a subset of articles from a larger literature review on child and maternal mortality. This broader literature review drew from English language articles, reports, and other literature focused on the reduction of maternal and child mortality at the country level in the 139 countries that the World Bank designated in 2015 as LMICs.[1] The cut-off date for all literature included was May 1, 2015. No specific start date was selected to include as broad a time frame as possible. Databases searched were PubMed, World Bank e-library, SSRN, JStor, EconLit, Lilacs, and the Google Scholar search engine. Several search strategies for this broader literature review were employed using key words, combinations and MeSH such as 'maternal mortality', 'millennium development goal', 'on track', 'success', 'progress' 'factors', and the names of each of the 139 LMICs. The search strategy did not include study design filters to capture all information of potential interest in the review. Additional published and grey literature was identified through a PMNCH Endnote Web database for the Success Factors study series and a purposeful search of Google and bibliographies of papers retrieved.

In two phases, we reviewed the abstracts and full text of the papers in the broader literature review in two phases and assessed them for inclusion based on six exclusion criteria.[2]

1. The document does not focus on at least one of the 139 LMICs and cross-country comparisons must include at least one LMIC.

2. The document does not study the factors that explain changes in maternal mortality rates, for example, death of a woman while pregnant or within 42 days of termination of pregnancy, from any cause related to or aggravated by the pregnancy or its management.
3. The document solely attributes the country's progress to a single factor—for example, female education—instead of analyzing a range of factors and the broader country context. The focus in the literature review on papers that analyze multiple factors, instead of single factors, allows a broader understanding of country context and how countries were able to reduce maternal mortality.
4. The document has a subnational, that is, district-level focus, rather than a national-level or comparative national focus. The exception would be documents with a state-level focus in large federally administered countries such as India, China, and Brazil.
5. The document is a duplicate version of another report or study that is published elsewhere, for example, a working paper that then gets published in a peer-reviewed journal.
6. The document is conceptual, an advocacy piece, a commentary, or a textbook that does not include national-level empirical data.

Given these exclusion criteria, a number of well-known papers related to maternal mortality have been left out of this review since those papers focus predominantly on the causes of mortality instead of the key interventions and their steps or investments that particular countries have taken to achieve results.

We conducted a thematic analysis of all included papers in NVivo using deductive and inductive coding to identify factors that explain maternal mortality reductions, with a particular focus on countries in South Asia. For deductive coding, codes were drawn from the 'Drivers and Enablers Framework for Improving Maternal and Reproductive Health Outcomes'. Inductive coding involved identifying additional themes in the studies that were not found in the analytical framework. Please refer to figure B.1 for the literature review flow chart.

Search Strings

In the broader literature review on child and maternal mortality, four search strings were used:

- (("Infant Mortality/trends" [MeSH]) OR ("Child Mortality/trends" [MeSH]) OR ("Maternal Mortality/trends" [MeSH])) AND ("Millennium development goal" OR "MDG")
- (("Infant Mortality/trends" [MeSH]) OR ("Child Mortality/trends" [MeSH]) OR ("Maternal Mortality/trends" [MeSH])) AND ("Millennium development goal" OR "MDG") AND ("on track" OR "progress" OR "success")
- (("Infant Mortality/trends" [MeSH]) OR ("Child Mortality/trends" [MeSH]) OR ("Maternal Mortality/trends" [MeSH])) AND ("Millennium development goal" OR "MDG") AND ("factors")

http://dx.doi.org/10.1596/978-1-4648-0963-7

- (("Infant Mortality/trends" [MeSH]) OR ("Child Mortality/trends" [MeSH]) OR ("Maternal Mortality/trends" [MeSH]) AND ("Millennium development goal" OR "MDG") AND ("Malawi" [MeSH]) – LMICs

The following table shows documents retrieved per sources and search strings:

Source/Search string	*Documents retrieved*
A. DATABASES	
Pubmed	
(("Infant Mortality/trends" [MeSH]) OR ("Child Mortality/trends" [MeSH]) OR ("Maternal Mortality/trends" [MeSH])) AND ("Millennium development goal" OR "MDG") (filters on English language and dates)	163
World Bank e-library	
(("Infant Mortality/trends" [MeSH]) OR ("Child Mortality/trends" [MeSH]) OR ("Maternal Mortality/trends" [MeSH])) AND ("Millennium development goal" OR "MDG") AND ("on track" OR "progress" OR "success")	10
SSRN	
((Infant Mortality) OR (Maternal Mortality) OR (Child Mortality)) AND ("Millennium development goal" OR "MDG") in all years	27
EconLit	
((Infant Mortality) OR (Maternal Mortality) OR (Child Mortality)) AND ("Millennium development goal" OR "MDG")	34
Google Scholar	
(("Infant Mortality/trends") OR ("Child Mortality/trends") OR ("Maternal Mortality/trends")) AND ("Millennium development goal" OR "MDG")	250
J-Stor	
1. ((Infant Mortality) OR (Child Mortality) OR (Maternal Mortality)) AND ("Millennium development goal" OR "MDG")	378
2. (("Infant Mortality) OR ("Child Mortality) OR ("Maternal Mortality)) AND ("Millennium development goal" OR "MDG") AND ("Millennium development goal" OR "MDG") AND ("on track" OR "progress" OR "success")	328
3. ((Infant Mortality) OR (Child Mortality) OR (Maternal Mortality)) AND ("Millennium development goal" OR "MDG") AND ("factors")	283
Lilacs	
(("Infant Mortality") OR ("Child Mortality") OR ("Maternal Mortality") AND ("Millennium development goal" OR "MDG") AND ("on track" OR "progress" OR "success") – filtered for English language AND just Lilacs database	2
Documents retrieved from databases	*1,475*
B. OTHER SOURCES	
Grey literature	
Purposeful search of PMNCH portal, MeasureDHS, WHO, UNICEF, and UNFPA websites using key words: "child mortality," "infant mortality," "maternal mortality," "trends," "progress," "success," "decline"	16
PMNCH Endnote Web database	
Purposeful search of the PMNCH Endnote Web Database and retrieved documents not already identified that mentioned "mortality" or "child survival" or "MDG 4" or "MDG 5"	105
Bibliographic searches	
Documents retrieved from searches of bibliographies of retrieved papers	25
Documents retrieved from other sources	*146*
TOTAL NUMBER OF DOCUMENTS RETRIEVED	**1,621**

http://dx.doi.org/10.1596/978-1-4648-0963-7

Figure B.1 Literature Review Flow Chart

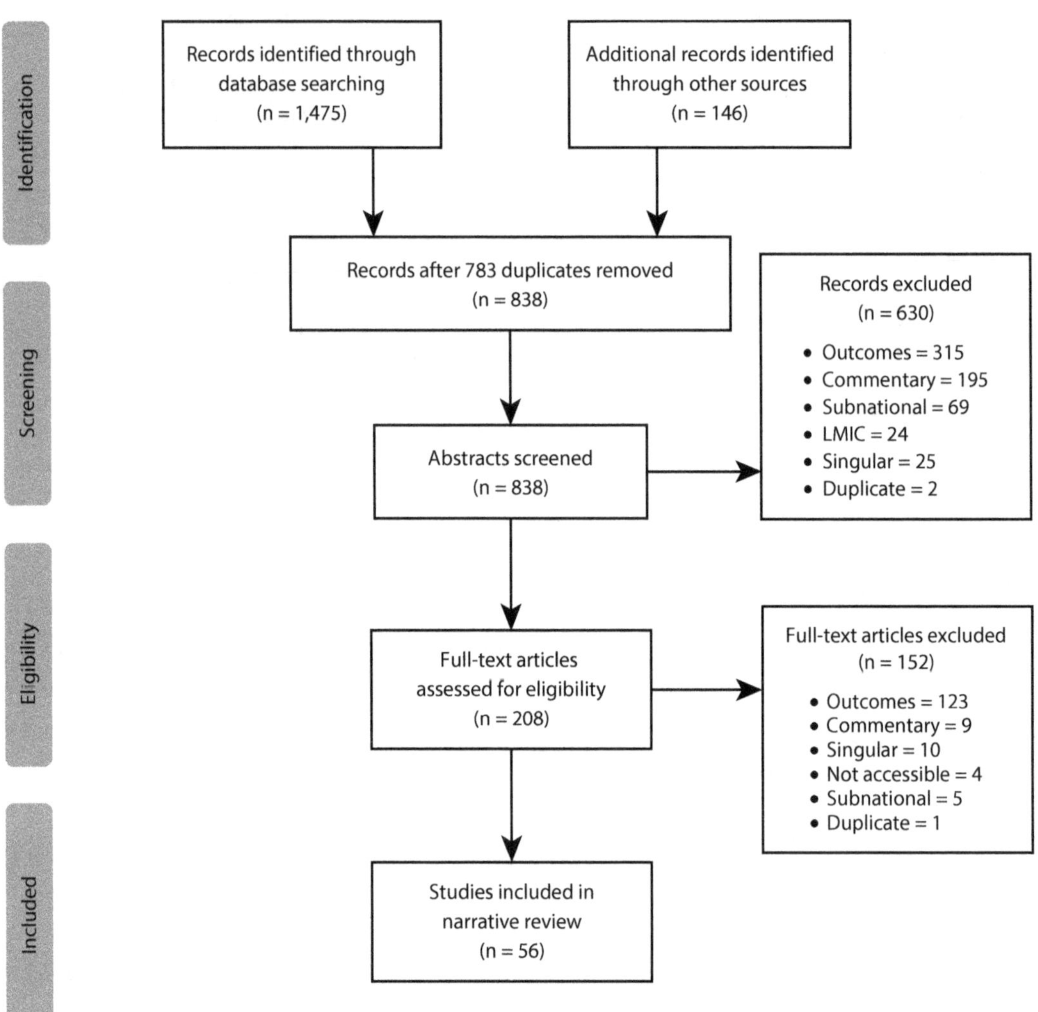

The following table shows the final papers included in the maternal mortality literature review.

No.	*Reference*	*Country*	*Low- or middle-income*	*Year of publication*	*Years covered by the study*
1.	Abdesslam 2011	Morocco	Lower-middle-income	2011	1980–2011
2.	Accorsi et al. 2010	Ethiopia	Low-income	2010	1990–2005
3.	Acuin et al. 2011	Multi-country: Southeast Asia	Low- and middle-income	2011	1990–2008
4.	Adogu 2014	Nigeria	Lower-middle-income	2014	2009–2013
5.	Amibor 2013	Haiti	Low-income	2013	1990–2013
6.	Bankole 2007	Nigeria	Lower-middle-income	2007	1993–2003
7.	Barker 2007a.	Nepal	Low-income	2007	1997–2006

table continues next page

http://dx.doi.org/10.1596/978-1-4648-0963-7

No.	Reference	Country	Low- or middle-income	Year of publication	Years covered by the study
8.	Barros et al. 2010	Brazil	Upper-middle-income	2010	1997–2007
9.	Bhandari, Gordon, and Shakya 2011	Nepal	Low-income	2011	1996–2006
10.	Bhutta et al. 2013; 381	Pakistan	Lower-middle-income	2013	1987-2011
11.	Bucagu et al. 2012	Rwanda	Low-income	2012	2000–2010
12.	Campbell et al. 2005	Egypt, Arab Rep.	Lower-middle-income	2005	1992–2000
13.	Chatterjee and Paily 2011	India	Lower-middle-income	2011	1992–2008
14.	Chowdhury et al. 2009b	Bangladesh	Low-income	2007	1976–2005
15.	Chowdhury et al. 2011	Bangladesh	Low-income	2011	1990–2011
16.	Collas-Monsod, Monsod, and Ducanes 2004	Philippines	Lower-middle-income	2004	1990–2000
17.	Countdown Coverage Writing Group et al. 2008	Multi-country	Low- and middle-income	2008	1990–2006
18.	Danel 1999	Honduras	Lower-middle-income	1999	1990–1997
19.	El Arifeen et al. 2014	Bangladesh	Low-income	2014	2001–2010
20.	Faguet 2007	Bangladesh	Low-income	2007	1986–2001
21.	Gipson et al. 2005	Egypt, Arab Rep.	Lower-middle-income	2005	1992/93–2000
22.	Hazarika 2012	India	Lower-middle-income	2012	1990–2008; 1960–2008
23.	Hill, Dodd, and Dashdorj 2006	Mongolia	Lower-middle-income	2006	1994–2004
24.	Hord et al. 1991	Romania	Upper-middle-income	1991	1989–1990
25.	Hussein et al. 2011	Nepal	Low-income	2011	1996–2008
26.	Islam 2011	Multi-country: Southeast Asia	Low- and middle-income	2011	1990–2011
27.	Jafarey et al. 2008	Pakistan	Lower-middle-income	2008	1990–2008
28.	Jain 2011	India, Pakistan, Bangladesh	Low- and middle-income	2011	1990-2008
29.	Janes and Chuluundorj 2004	Mongolia	Lower-middle-income	2004	1990–1999
30.	Karkee 2011	Nepal	Low-income	2011	1996–2005
31.	Koblinsky 2003.	Multi-country	Low- and middle-income	2003	1980–2000
32.	Koblinsky et al. 2008.	Bangladesh	Low-income	2008	1985–2003
33.	Li et al. 2007	China (Yunnan)	Upper-middle-income	2007	1994–2005
34.	Liljestrand and Sambath 2012	Cambodia	Low-income	2012	2000–2010
35.	Mahmud et al. 2011	Pakistan	Lower-middle income	2011	1990–2011
36.	Malik and Kayan 2014	Pakistan	Lower-middle income	2014	1990–2010
37.	Malla et al. 2011	Nepal	Low-income	2011	1990–2011
38.	Moazzeni 2013	Iran, Islamic Rep.	Upper-middle-income	2013	1975–2008
39.	Du et al. 2015	China	Upper-middle-income	2015	1996–2009
40.	Nnamuchi 2015	Nigeria	Lower-middle income	2015	1990–2015
41.	Padmanaban, Raman, and Mavalankar 2009	India	Lower-middle-income	2007	1993–2007
42.	Pathmanathan et al. 2003	Malaysia and Sri Lanka	Upper- and lower-middle income	2003	1947–1970
43.	Qiu et al. 2010	China (Zheijiang)	Upper-middle-income	2010	1988–2008
44.	Rai and Tulchinsky 2015	India	Lower-middle-income	2015	1990–2015
45.	Rasooly et al. 2014.	Afghanistan	Low-income	2014	2002–2010

table continues next page

http://dx.doi.org/10.1596/978-1-4648-0963-7

No.	Reference	Country	Low- or middle-income	Year of publication	Years covered by the study
46.	Rath et al. 2007	Nepal	Low-income	2007	1997–2004
47.	Scopaz, Eckermann, and Clarke 2011	Lao PDR	Lower-middle-income	2011	1990–2008
48.	Senanayake et al. 2011	Sri Lanka	Lower-middle-income	2011	1990–2011
49.	Seneviratne and Rajapaksa 2000	Sri Lanka	Lower-middle-income	2000	1881–1995
50.	Shiffman, Stanton, and Salazar 2004	Honduras	Lower-middle-income	2004	1990–1997
51.	Shiffman and Ved 2007	India	Lower-middle-income	2007	1987–2005
52.	Thomsen et al. 2011	China, India, Indonesia, Vietnam	Low- and middle-income	2011	1990–2011
53.	Van Lerberghe et al. 2014	Burkina Faso, Cambodia, Indonesia, Morocco	Low- and lower-middle-income	2014	1990–2014
54.	Victora et al. 2011	Brazil	Upper-middle-income	2011	1997–2007
55.	You et al. 2012	China	Upper-middle-income	2012	1996–2009
56.	Zere et al. 2010	Namibia	Upper-middle-income	2010	1991/2000–1998/2007

Notes

1. The list of 139 countries can be found at http://data.worldbank.org/about/country-and-lending-groups.
2. The criteria were drawn from similar literature reviews, such as in Mays et al. (forthcoming).

APPENDIX C

Literature Review of Systematic Reviews on Maternal and Reproductive Health

We conducted search for systematic reviews and meta-analyses related to MRH and the interventions that may have had an impact on maternal mortality reduction and/or improved MRH outcomes using the potential interventions in the "drivers and enablers" analytical framework.

Below are the databases that were searched, the search strings used, and the articles that were retrieved. A total of 215 articles were retrieved.

http://dx.doi.org/10.1596/978-1-4648-0963-7

	Search criteria	*Number of articles found with the criteria*
PubMed	((((("maternal mortality"[Title/Abstract] OR "maternal survival"[Title/Abstract] OR "maternal health"[Title/Abstract]) AND "family planning"[All Fields]) OR contraceptives[Title/Abstract]) OR antenatal care[Title/Abstract]) OR "conditional cash transfers"[Title/Abstract]) AND systematic review[Title] AND ("meta-analysis"[Publication Type] OR "meta-analysis as topic"[MeSH Terms] OR "meta-analysis"[All Fields]) AND (hasabstract[text] AND "2005/10/25"[PDAT]:"2015/10/22"[PDAT])	58
Cochrane Database of Systematic Reviews	("maternal mortality" OR "maternal survival" OR "Reproductive Health") in Title, Abstract, Keywords or "maternal health" in Title, Abstract, Keywords and ("antenatal care" OR "family planning" OR "conditional cash transfers" OR "antenatal care") in Title, Abstract, Keywords or "institutional delivery" in Title, Abstract, Keywords and "meta-analysis" in Record Title)	53
	"pregnancy and childbirth" AND "Antenatal care"	1
	"pregnancy and childbirth" AND "Basic care during pregnancy"	7
	"pregnancy and childbirth" AND "institutional delivery"	5
HEALTH EVIDENCE	("Maternal mortality" OR "Maternal survival" OR "Maternal health") AND ("skilled birth attendance" OR "antenatal care" OR "family planning" OR "institutional delivery" OR "emergency obstetric care") OR "conditional cash transfers" OR "antenatal care") in Title, Abstract, Keywords.	22
	("Maternal mortality" OR "Maternal survival" OR "Maternal health" OR "skilled birth attendance" OR "antenatal care" OR "family planning" OR "institutional delivery" OR "emergency obstetric care") AND ("training of health workers" OR "Training of health providers" OR "health financing schemes" OR "conditional cash transfers" in Title, Abstract, Keywords.	13
Medline	("Maternal mortality" OR "Maternal survival" OR "Maternal health") AND ti(("systematic review" OR "systematic literature review" OR "structured literature review")) AND (Political OR "Economic development" OR "Social development" OR multisectoral OR "multi sectoral" OR multi-sectoral OR education OR transportation OR community OR NGO OR "civil society" OR "non-governmental organization" OR "non-governmental organization" OR "health sector" OR "health system" OR "service delivery" OR "service coverage" OR "health financing" OR "results-based financing" OR "demand-side financing" OR access OR "human resources" OR program OR programme OR "emergency obstetric care" OR contraceptives OR "institutional delivery" OR "skilled birth attendants" OR "community midwives" OR household OR income OR "women's status" OR "role of men")	56

http://dx.doi.org/10.1596/978-1-4648-0963-7

After removing the duplicates and reviewing the abstracts, only 42 articles were found relevant to study and are presented in the table below.

No.	*Reference*
1	Alison, Peterson, and Hatt 2013
2	Benova, Cumming, and Campbell 2014
3	Berhan and Berhan. 2014b
4	Berhan and Berhan 2014a
5	Betrán et al. 2005
6	Brown, Allen, and Torkelson 2013
7	Bucagu et al. 2012
8	Byrne et al. 2014
9	Carroli, Rooney, and Villar 2001
10	Dzakpasu, Powell-Jackson, and Campbell 2014
11	Gil-González, Carrasco-Portiño, and Ruiz 2006
12	Gilmore and McAuliffe 2013
13	Glassman, Duran, and Koblinsky 2013
14	Gopalan et al. 2014
15	Holmer et al. 2015
16	Hussein et al. 2012
17	IEG 2014
18	Kidney et al. 2009
19	Knight, Self, and Kennedy 2013
20	Langlois et al. 2013
21	Lassi and Bhutta 2015
22	Lassi et al. 2013
23	Marston et al. 2013
24	Moyer and Mustafa 2013
25	Moyer, Dako-Gyeke, and Adanu 2013
26	Murray et al. 2014
27	Ni Bhuinneain and McCarthy 2015
28	Nwolise et al. 2015
29	Nyamtema, Urassa, and van Roosmalen 2011
30	Piane and Clinton 2014
31	Piane 2009
32	Pyone, Sorensen, and Tellier 2012
33	Sibley, Sipe, and Barry 2012
34	Soubeiga et al. 2014
35	Sutcliffe et al. 2013
36	van Lonkhuijzen, Stekelenburg, and van Roosmalen 2012
37	Vieira et al. 2012
38	Whitworth and Dowswell 2009
39	Wilson et al. 2013
40	Yargawa and Leonardi-Bee 2015
41	Yuan et al. 2014

Bibliography

Abdesslam, B. 2011. "Social Determinants of Reproductive Health in Morocco." *African Journal of Reproductive Health* 15 (2): 57–66.

Accorsi, S., N. K. Bilal, P. Farese, and V. Racalbuto. 2010. "Countdown to 2015: Comparing Progress towards the Achievement of the Health Millennium Development Goals in Ethiopia and other Sub-Saharan African Countries." *Transactions of the Royal Society of Tropical Medicine and Hygiene* 104 (5): 336–42.

Acuin, C. S., G. L. Khor, T. Liabsuetrakul, E. L. Achadi, T. T. Htay, R. Firestone, and Z. A. Bhutta. 2011."Maternal, Neonatal, and Child Health in Southeast Asia: Towards Greater Regional collaboration." *The Lancet* 377: 516–25.

Adam, T., and J. Franz-Vasdeki. 2012. "A Quantitative Mapping of Trends in Reductions of Maternal and Child Mortality in the High Mortality-burden Countdown to 2015 Countries [Partnership for Maternal, Newborn & Child Health and partners Technical Paper]." Background paper for Success Factors to Reduce Preventable Maternal and Child Deaths Study in Cortez et al. 2014, Geneva, Switzerland.

Adogu, P. 2014. "Midwifery and Midwives Service Scheme: A Panacea for Improvement of Some Maternal and Neonatal Indices in Nigeria—A Brief Review." *Open Journal of Obstetrics and Gynecology* 2014, 4, 343–348.

Afzal, M., G. Cometto, and S. M. Rosskam. 2011. "The Global Health Workforce Alliance: Increasing Momentum for Health Workforce Development." *Revista Peruana de Medicina Experimental y Salud Pública* 28 (2): 298–306.

Aggarwal, A. 2010. "Impact Evaluation of India' s 'Yeshasvini' Community-Based Health Insurance Programme. *Health Economics* 19 (Suppl 1): 5–35.

Aggarwal, R., and A. Thind. 2011. "Effect of Maternal Education on Choice of Location for Delivery among Indian Women." *National Medical Journal of India* 24 (6): 328–34.

Agha, S. 2011. "Impact of a Maternal Health Voucher Scheme on Institutional Delivery among Low Income Women in Pakistan." *Reproductive Health* 8 (10). http://www.reproductive-health-journal.com/content/8/1/10.

Agha, S., and T. W. Carton. 2011. "Determinants of Institutional Delivery in Rural Jhang, Pakistan." *International Journal for Equity in Health* 10 (31).

Ahluwalia, I. B., T. Schmid, M. Kouletio, and O. Kanenda. 2003. "An Evaluation of a Community-Based Approach to Safe Motherhood in Northwestern Tanzania."

http://dx.doi.org/10.1596/978-1-4648-0963-7

International Journal of Gynecology & Obstetrics 82 (2): 231–40. doi:10.1016/S0020-7292(03)00081-X.

Ahmed, S., Q. Li, L. Liu, and A. O. Tsui. 2012. "Maternal Deaths Averted by Contraceptive Use: An Analysis of 172 Countries." *The Lancet* 380 (9837): 111–25. http://www.jhsph.edu/departments/population-family-and-reproductive-health/_docs/faculty-in-the-news-saifuddin-july-2012.pdf.

Ahmed, T., and S. M. Jakaria. 2009. "Community-Based Skilled Birth Attendants in Bangladesh: Attending Deliveries at Home." *Reproductive Health Matters* 17 (33): 45–50. doi:10.1016/S0968-8080(09)33446-1.

Alison, B., L. A. Peterson, and L. E. Hatt. 2013. "Effect of Health Insurance on the Use and provision of Maternal Health Services and Maternal and Neonatal Health Outcomes: A Systematic Review." *Journal of Health, Population, and Nutrition* 31 (4 Suppl 2): 81–105. http://search.proquest.com/professional/docview/1543048471?accountid=41588.

Alliance for Health Policy and Systems Research. 2015. "Advancing Implementation Research and Delivery Science." Accessed at http://www.who.int/alliance-hpsr/projects/irds/en/.

Al Sabir, A., M. A. Alam, S. Mohammed, R. Ubaidur, and M. E. Khan. 2004. *Integration of Reproductive Health Services for Men in Health and Family Welfare Centers in Bangladesh*. Dhaka: NIPORT.

Amibor, P. 2013. "What Will it Take to Maintain the Maternal and Child Health Gains Made in Haiti Prior to the 2010 Earthquake? An Analysis of Past Progress, Trends, and the Prospects for the Realization of the United Nations Millennium Development Goals 4 and 5." *Maternal and Child Health Journal* 17: 1339–45.

Anwar, I., H. Y. Nababan, S. Mostari, A. Rahman, and J. A. M. Khan. 2014. "Trends and Inequities in Use of Maternal Health Care Services in Bangladesh, 1991–2011." *PLoS One* 10 (3): e0120309.

APHI/MoPH (Afghan Public Health Institute, Ministry of Public Health, Afghanistan), CSO (Central Statistics Organization), ICF Macro, IIHMR (Indian Institute of Health Management Research), and WHO/EMRO (World Health Organization Regional Office for the Eastern Mediterranean). 2011. *Afghanistan Mortality Survey 2010*. APHI/MoPH, CSO, ICF Macro, IIHMR, and WHO/EMRO, Calverton, MD.

Azad, K., S. Barnett, B. Banerjee, S. Shaha, K. Khan, AR Rego, S. Barua, D. Flatman, C. Pagel, A. Prost, M. Ellis, A. Costello. 2010. "Effect of Scaling up Women's Groups on Birth Outcomes in Three Rural Districts in Bangladesh: A Cluster-Randomised Controlled Trial." *The Lancet* 375 (9721): 1193–202.

Babinard, J., and P. Roberts. 2006. "Maternal and Child Mortality Development Goals: What Can the Transport Sector Do?" Transport Paper TP-12, World Bank and Transport Sector Board, Washington, DC. http://www-wds.worldbank.org/external/default/WDSContentServer/WDSP/IB/2006/09/19/000160016_20060919131433/Rendered/PDF/373660tp120Mat1development01PUBLIC1.pdf.

Bajpai, N., and R. H. Dholakia. 2011. "Improving the Performance of Accredited Social Health Activists in India." Working Paper No. 1, Columbia Global Centers South Asia, May. http://globalcenters.columbia.edu/files/cgc/pictures/Improving_the_Performance_of_ASHAs_in_India_CGCSA_Working_Paper_1.pdf.

Bangladesh Institute of Development Studies. 2009. *Long-run Socio-Economic Impact Study of Rural Roads and Markets Improvement & Maintenance Project-II*. Dhaka: BID.

Bankole, A., G. Sedgh, F. Okonofua, C. Imarhiagbe, R. Hussain, and others. 2007. *Barriers to Safe Motherhood in Nigeria*. Guttmacher Institute.

Barkat, A., S. H. Khan, M. Rahman, S. Zaman, A. Poddar, S. Halim, N. N. Ratna, M. Majid, A. K. M. Maksud, A. Karim, and S. Islam. 2002. *Economic and Social Impact Evaluation Study of the Rural Electrification Program in Bangladesh*. Dhaka: Human Development Research Centre, NRECA International Ltd., and USAID. http://www.hdrc-bd.com/admin_panel/images/notice/1387698662.4a.%20%20economic%20and%20social%20impact%20evaluation%20study%20of%20rural%20electrification%20program%20in%20bangladesh.pdf.

Barker, C., E. Bird, A. Pradhan, and G. Shakya. 2007a. "Support to the Safe Motherhood Programme in Nepal: An Integrated Approach." *Reproductive Health Matters* 15: 81–90.

Barker, G., C. Ricardo, and M. Nascimento. 2007b. *Engaging Men and Boys in Changing Gender-Based Inequity in Health: Evidence from Programme Interventions*. Geneva: WHO. www.who.int/gender/documents/Engaging_men_boys.pdf.

Barros, F. C., A. Matijasevich, J. H. Requejo, E. Giugliani, A. G. Maranhao, C. A. Monteiro, A. J. Barros, F. Bustreo, M. Merialdi, and C. G. Victora. 2010. "Recent Trends in Maternal, Newborn, and Child Health in Brazil: Progress toward Millennium Development Goals 4 and 5." *American Journal of Public Health* 100: 1877–89.

Bartlett, L., A. LeFevre, H. Gibson, J. Rahmanzai, K. Viswanathan, K. Yari, L. Steinhardt, M. Azimy, N. Ansari, N. Assefi, P. Manalai, P. Azfar, R. Callaghan, and S. Turkmani. 2011. *Evaluation of the Pre-Service Midwifery Education Program in Afghanistan*. Kabul: Jhpiego; Baltimore, MD: Health Services Support Project.

Bashir, H., S. Kazmi, R. Eichler, A. Beith, and E. Brown. 2009. *Pay for Performance: Improving Maternal Health Services in Pakistan. P4P Case Studies–Pakistan*. Bethesda, MD: Abt Associates Inc. https://www.hfgproject.org/wp-content/uploads/2015/02/Pay-for-Performance-Improving-Maternal-Health-Services-in-Pakistan.pdf.

Basinga, P., P.J. Gertler, A. Binagwaho, A.L.B. Soucat, J. Sturdy, C.M.J. Vermeersch. 2011. "Effect on Maternal and Child Health Services in Rwanda of Payment to Primary Health-care Providers for Performance: An Impact Evaluation." *The Lancet* 377 (9775): 1421–28.

Beegle, K., E. Frankenburg, and D. Thomas. 2001. "Bargaining Power within Couples and Use of Prenatal and Delivery Care in Indonesia." *Studies in Family Planning* 32 (11): 130–46.

Béhague, D. P., and K. T. Storeng. 2008. "Collapsing the Vertical–Horizontal Divide: An Ethnographic Study of Evidence-Based Policymaking in Maternal Health." *American Journal of Public Health* 98 (4): 644–49. doi:10.2105/AJPH.2007.123117.

Benderly, B. L. 2010. *Getting Health Results in Afghanistan*. The World Bank. https://www.rbfhealth.org/sites/rbf/files/RBF_FEATURE_GettingHealthResultsAfghanistan.pdf.

Benova, L., O. Cumming, and O. M. R. Campbell. 2014. "Systematic Review and Meta-analysis: Association between Water and Sanitation Environment and Maternal Mortality." *Tropical Medicine & International Health* 19 (4): 368–87. http://search.proquest.com/professional/docview/1496842739?accountid=41588.

Bergeson-Lockwood, J., E. L. Madsen, and J. Bernstein. 2010. *Maternal Health Supplies in Bangladesh*. Washington, DC: Population Action International.

Berhan, Y., and A. Berhan. 2014a. "Skilled Health Personnel Attended Delivery as a Proxy Indicator for Maternal and Perinatal Mortality: A Systematic Review." *Ethiopian Journal of Health Sciences* 24 (September): 69–80.

———. 2014b. "Antenatal Care as a Means of Increasing Birth in the Health Facility and Reducing Maternal Mortality: A Systematic Review." *Ethiopian Journal of Health Sciences* 24 (September): 93–104. http://search.proquest.com/professional/docview/1634935998?accountid=41588.

Betrán, A. P., D. Wojdyla, S. F. Posner, and A. M. Gülmezoglu. 2005. "National Estimates for Maternal Mortality: An Analysis Based on the WHO Systematic Review of Maternal Mortality and Morbidity." *BMC Public Health* 5 (December): 131. http://search.proquest.com/professional/docview/590076702?accountid=41588.

Bhandari, A., M. Gordon, and G. Shakya. 2011. "Reducing Maternal Mortality in Nepal." *BJOG: An International Journal of Obstetrics and Gynaecology* 118 (Suppl 2): 26–30. doi:10.1111/j.1471-0528.2011.03109.x.

Bhat, R., D. V. Mavalankar, P. V. Singh, and S. Neelu Singh. 2009. "Maternal Healthcare Financing: Gujarat's Chiranjeevi Scheme and Its Beneficiaries." *Journal of Health and Popular Nutrition* 27 (2): 249–58.

Bhutta, Z. A., A. Hafeez, A. Rizvi, N. Ali, A. Khan, F. Ahmad, S. Bhutta, T. Hazir, A. Zaidi, and S. N. Jafarey.2013. "Reproductive, Maternal, Newborn, and Child Health in Pakistan: Challenges and Opportunities." *The Lancet* 381 (9884): 2207–18. doi:10.1016/S0140-6736(12)61999-0.

Bhutta, Z. A., and Z. S. Lassi. 2010. "Empowering Communities for Maternal and Newborn Health." *The Lancet* 375 (9721): 1142–44.

Bhutta, Z. A., Z. A. Memon, S. Soofi, M. S. Salat, S. Cousens, and J. Martines. 2008. "Implementing Community-Based Perinatal Care: Results from a Pilot Study in Rural Pakistan." *Bulletin of the World Health Organization* 86 (6): 452–59.

Bjorkman, M., and J. Svensson. 2009. "Power to the People: Evidence from a Randomized Field Experiment on Community-Based Monitoring in Uganda." *Quarterly Journal of Economics* 124 (2): 735–69.

BNNC (Bangladesh National Nutrition Council). 1997. *Bangladesh National Plan of Action for Nutrition (NPAN)*. Dhaka: Ministry of Health and Family Welfare, Dhaka.

Bongaarts, J., J. Cleland, J. W. Townsend, J. T. Bertrand, and G. M. Das. 2012. *Family Planning Programs in the 21st Century: Rationale and Design*. New York: Population Council.

Brinkerhoff, D. W. 2004. "Accountability and Health Systems: Toward Conceptual Clarity and Policy Relevance." *Health Policy and Planning* 19 (6): 371–79. doi:10.1093/heapol/czh052.

Brown, G., L. Allen, and A. Torkelson. 2013. "Direct Patient Interventions that can Reduce Maternal Mortality in Developing Countries: A Systematic Review." *Family Medicine* 45 (8) (September): 550–57. http://search.proquest.com/professional/docview/1442315692?accountid=41588

Bryce, J., B. Daelmans, A. Dwivedi, V. Fauveau, J. E. Lawn, E. Mason, H. Newby, A. Shankar, A. Starrs, and T. Wardlaw. 2008. "Countdown to 2015 for Maternal, Newborn, and Child Survival: The 2008 Report on Tracking Coverage of Interventions." *The Lancet* 371: 1247–58.

Bucagu, M., J. M. Kagubare, P. Basinga, F. Ngabo, B. K. Timmons, and A. C. Lee. 2012. "Impact of Health Systems Strengthening on Coverage of Maternal Health Services in Rwanda, 2000–2010: A Systematic Review." *Reproductive Health Matters* 20: 50–61. http://search.proquest.com/professional/docview/1024775574?accountid=41588.

Byrne, A., A. Hodge, E. Jimenez-Soto, and A Morgan. 2014. "What Works? Strategies to Increase Reproductive, Maternal and Child Health in Difficult to Access Mountainous

Locations: A Systematic Literature Review." *PLoS One* 9 (2): e87683. http://search.proquest.com/professional/docview/1494768389?accountid=41588.

Caldwell, B. K. 2005. "Factors Affecting Female Age at Marriage in South Asia: Contrasts between Sri Lanka and Bangladesh." *Asian Population Studies* 1 (3): 283–301.

Callen, M., E. Berman, S. A. Hasanaian, S. Gulzar, and Y. Khan. 2013. "The Political Economy of Health Worker Absence: Experimental Evidence from Pakistan." Policy brief 6011. International Growth Centre, London School of Economics. http://www.theigc.org/wp-content/uploads/2015/02/Callen-Et-Al-2013-Policy-Brief.pdf.

Campbell, O., R. Gipson, A. H. Issa, N. Matta, B. El Deeb, A. El Mohandes, A. Alwen, and E. Mansour. 2005. "National Maternal Mortality Ratio in Egypt Halved between 1992–93 and 2000." *Bulletin of the World Health Organization* 83: 462–71.

Carroli, G., C. Rooney, and J. Villar. 2001. "How Effective is Antenatal Care in Preventing Maternal Mortality and Serious Morbidity? An Overview of the Evidence. *Journal of Paediatric and Perinatal Epidemiology* 15 (Suppl S1): 1–42. doi:10.1046/j.1365-3016.2001.0150s1001.x.

Chatterjee, A., and V. P. Paily. 2011. "Achieving Millennium Development Goals 4 and 5 in India." *BJOG: An International Journal of Obstetrics and Gynecology* 118 (Suppl 2): 47–59.

Chauhan, K. T., and S. Nagpal. 2012. "Case Study on the Emergency Response System." Unpublished paper, World Bank, Washington, DC.

Chowdhury, M. E., R. Botlero, M. Koblinsky, S. K. Saha, G. Dieltiens, and C. Ronsmans. 2009b. "Determinants of Reduction in Maternal Mortality in Matlab, Bangladesh: A 30-Year Cohort Study." *The Lancet* 370 (9595): 1320–28.

Chowdhury, S., L. A. Banu, T. A. Chowdhury, S. Rubayet, and S. Khatoon. 2011. "Achieving Millennium Development Goals 4 and 5 in Bangladesh." *BJOG: an International Journal of Obstetrics and Gynaecology* 118 (Suppl 2): 36–46.

Chowdhury, S., S. A. Hossain, and A. Halim. 2009a. "Assessment of Quality of Care in Maternal and Newborn Health Services Available in Public Health Care Facilities in Bangladesh." *Bangladesh Medical Research Council Bulletin* 35 (2): 53–6.

Claeson, M., C. Griffin, T. Johnston, M. McLachlan, A. Soucat, A. Wagstaff, and A. Yazbeck. 2001. "Poverty-Reduction and the Health Sector." HNP Discussion Paper Series. Washington, DC: World Bank.

Cockcroft, A., L. Pearson, C. Hamel, and N. Andersson. 2011. "Reproductive and Sexual Health in the Maldives: An Analysis of Data from Two Cross-Sectional Surveys." *BMC Health Services Research* 11 (Suppl 2): 56.

Cockcroft, A., D. Milne, and N. Andersson. 2001. *Health and Population Sector Programme, 1998–2003*. Ottawa: CIET-Canada; Bangladesh, Ministry of Health and Family Welfare, Government of the People's Republic of Bangladesh in Merrick, "Maternal-Neonatal Health (MNH) and Poverty."

Coffey, P. S., J. Sharma, K. C. Gargi, D. Neupane, P. Dawson, and Y. V. Pradhan. 2012. "Feasibility and Acceptability of Gentamicin in the Uniject Prefilled Injection System for Community-Based Treatment of Possible Neonatal Sepsis: The Experience of Female Community Health Volunteers in Nepal." *Journal of Perinatology* 32 (12): 959–65. doi:10.1038/jp.2012.20.

Cohen, R. L., Y. N. Alfonso, T. Adam, S. Kuruvilla, J. Schweitzer, and D. Bishai. 2014. "Country Progress towards the Millennium Development Goals: Adjusting for

Socioeconomic Factors Reveals Greater Progress and New Challenges." *Globalization and Health* 10 (67).

Colbourn, T., B. Nambiar, A. Bondo, C. Makwenda, E. Tsetekani, A. Makonda-Ridley, M. Msukwa, P. Barker, U. Kotagal, C. Williams, R. Davies, D. Webb, D. Flatman, S. Lewycka, M. Rosato, F. Kachale, C. Mwansambo, and A. Costello. 2013. "Effects of Quality Improvement in Health Facilities and Community Mobilization through Women's Groups on Maternal, Neonatal and Perinatal Mortality in Three Districts of Malawi: MaiKhanda, a Cluster Randomized Controlled Effectiveness Trial." *International Health*.

Collas-Monsod, S., T. Monsod, and G. Ducanes. 2004. "Philippines' Progress towards the Millennium Development Goals: Geographical and Political Correlates of Subnational Outcomes." *Journal of Human Development* 5: 121–49.

Condo, J., C. Mugeni, B. Naughton, K. Hall, M. A. Tuazon, A. Omwega, F. Nwaigwe, P. Drobac, Z. Hyder, F. Ngabo, and A. Binagwaho. 2014. "Rwanda's Evolving Community Health Worker System: A Qualitative Assessment of Client and Provider Perspectives." *Human Resources for Health* 12 (1): 71.

Cortez, R., S. Saadat, S. Chowdhury, and I. Sarker. 2014. "Maternal and Child Survival: Findings from Five Countries' Experience in Addressing Maternal and Child Health Challenges." HNP Discussion Paper 91294, World Bank, Washington, DC.

Countdown Coverage Writing Group, Countdown to 2015 Core Group, J. Bryce, B. Daelmans, A. Dwivedi, V. Fauveau, J. E. Lawn, E. Mason, H. Newby, A. Shankar, A. Starrs and, T. Wardlaw. 2008. "Countdown to 2015 for Maternal, Newborn, and Child Survival: The 2008 Report on Tracking Coverage of Interventions." *The Lancet* 371 (9620): 1247–58.

Countdown to 2015: Maternal Newborn and Child Survival. 2012. *Country Case Study: Zambia: Zambia Countdown Leads to Improved Polices and Actions for Meeting the Health-Related Millennium Development Goals*. Geneva: PMNCH. http://www.countdown2015mnch.org/documents/2012Report/Zambia_CD_case_study%20_final_0612.pdf.

Currie, S., P. Azfar, and R. C. Fowler. 2007. "A Bold New Beginning for Midwifery in Afghanistan." *Midwifery* 23 (3): 226–34.

Danel, I. 1999. *Maternal Mortality Reduction in Honduras 1990–1997: A Case Study*. Washington, DC. World Bank.

Das, M. B. 2008. "Whispers to Voices: Gender and Social Transformation in Bangladesh." Bangladesh Development Series Paper No. 22. March 2008, World Bank, Washington, DC.

DCS (Department of Census and Statistics) and MOH (Ministry of Healthcare and Nutrition). 2009. *Sri Lanka Demographic and Health Survey 2006–07*. DCS and MOH, Colombo.

de Brauw, A., and A. Peterman. 2011. "Can Conditional Cash Transfers Improve Maternal Health and Birth Outcomes? Evidence from El Salvador's Comunidades Solidarias Rurales." In IFPRI Discussion Paper 2011, International Food Policy Research Institute. p. 36.

Deussom, R., W. Jaskiewicz, S. Dwyer, and K. Tulenko. 2012. "Holding Health Workers Accountable: Governance Approaches to Reducing Absenteeism." IntraHealth International Technical Brief No. 3, May 2012. http://www.intrahealth.org/page/new-publication-on-health-worker-absenteeism.

Devadasan N., B. Criel, W. Van Damme, S. Manoharan, P. S. Sarma, P. Van der Stuyft. 2010. "Community Health Insurance in Gudalur, India, Increases Access to Hospital Care." *Health Policy Plan* 25: 145–54.

DfID (Department for International Development, Government of United Kingdom). 2010. "Choices for Women: Planned Pregnancies, Safe Births and Healthy Newborns the UK's Framework for Results for Improving Reproductive, Maternal and Newborn Health in the Developing World." https://www.gov.uk/government/uploads/system/uploads/attachment_data/file/67640/RMNH-framework-for-results.pdf.

DGHS (Directorate General of Health Services Bangladesh) and United Nations Population Fund Bangladesh. 2011. *Evaluation of the Community Based Skilled Birth Attendant (CSBA) Programme-Bangladesh.* Government of the People's Republic of Bangladesh: Directorate General of Health Services, Ministry of Health and Family Welfare.

Dongre, A., and A. Kapur. 2013. "How is Janani Suraksha Yojana Performing in Backward Districts of India?" *Economic and Political Weekly* 48 (42): 53–9.

Du, Q., W. Lian, O. Naess, E. Bjertness, B. N. Kumar, and S. H. Shi. 2015. "The Trends in Maternal Mortality between 1996 and 2009 in Guizhou, China: Ethnic Differences and Associated Factors." *Journal of Huazhong University of Science and Technology Medical sciences = Hua zhong ke ji da xue xue bao Yi xue Ying De wen ban = Huazhong keji daxue xuebao Yixue Yingdewen ban* 35: 140–46.

Dzakpasu, S., T. Powell-Jackson, and O. M. R. Campbell. 2014. "Impact of User Fees on Maternal Health Service Utilization and Related Health Outcomes: A Systematic Review." *Health Policy and Planning* 29 (2): 137–50. http://search.proquest.com/professional/docview/1283511020?accountid=41588.

El Arifeen, S., K. Hill, K. Z. Ahsan, K. Jamil, Q. Nahar, and P. K. Streatfield. 2014. "Maternal Mortality in Bangladesh: A Countdown to 2015 Country Case Study." *The Lancet* 384: 1366–74.

El-Saharty, S., N. Ohno, I. Sarker, and F. Secci. 2014. *Knowledge Notes. Health Nutrition and Population*. South Asia: Maternal and Reproductive Health at a Glance. Washington, DC: World Bank Group.

Ensor, T., S. Clapham, and D. P. Prasai. 2009. "What Drives Health Policy Formulation: Insights from the Nepal Maternity Incentive Scheme?" *Health Policy* 90 (2–3): 247–53. doi:10.1016/j.healthpol.2008.06.009.

Ensor, T., and S. Cooper. 2004. "Overcoming Barriers to Health Service Access: Influencing the Demand Side." *Health Policy and Planning* 19 (2): 69–79.

Exavery, A., A. M. Kanté, M. Njozi, K. Tani, H. V. Doctor, A. Hingora, and J. F. Phillips. 2014. "Access to Institutional Delivery Care and Reasons for Home Delivery in Three Districts of Tanzania." *International Journal of Equity in Health* 13 (1): 48.

Faguet, J. P. 2007. "To the MDGs and Beyond: Accountability and Institutional Innovation in Bangladesh." Bangladesh Development Series Paper No. 14, January. World Bank, Washington, DC.

Family Health Bureau. 2015. *Technical Units*. http://fhb.health.gov.lk/web/index.php?option=com_content&view=article&id=11&Itemid=130&lang=en.

Farmer, P. E., C. T. Nutt, C. M. Wagner, C. Sekabaraga, T. Nuthulaganti, J. L. Weigel, D. B. Farmer, A. Habinshuti, S. D. Mugeni, J. C. Karasi, and P. C. Drobac. 2013. "Reduced Premature Mortality in Rwanda: Lessons from Success." *BMJ* 346.

Fiagbe, P., D. Asamoah, and F. T. Oduro. 2012. "Assessing the Role of Transport in the Achievement of Maternal Mortality Reduction in Ghana." *International Journal of Business and Management* 7 (5): 256–68. doi:10.5539/ijbm.v7n5p256.

Fikree, F. F., A. M. Mir, and I. U. Haq. 2006. "She may Reach a Facility But Will Still Die! An Analysis of Quality of Public Sector Maternal Health Services, District Multan, Pakistan." *Journal of the Pakistan Medical Association* 56 (4): 156–63.

Frost, L., and B. A. Pratt. 2012. "Promising Mechanisms to Strengthen Domestic Financing for Women's and Children's Health." Background Paper for Meeting on Value for Money, Sustainability and Accountability in the Health Sector: A High Level Dialogue between Ministers of Finance and Health. Tunis, July 4–5. PMNCH, Geneva. http://www.who.int/pmnch/media/news/2012/20120705_domestic_financing_mechanisms.pdf.

———. 2014. *A Review of the Literature on Factors Contributing to the Reduction of Maternal and Child Mortality in Low-Income and Middle-Income Countries: An Evidence Synthesis for the Success Factors Study Series*. Geneva: PMNCH. http://www.who.int/pmnch/knowledge/publications/qualitative_evidence_synthesis.pdf.

———. 2015. *A Review of the Literature on Factors Contributing to the Reductions of Maternal Mortality in South Asia*. Global Health Insights. Background report.

Gah, S. 2013. *Women's Resource Centre Pakistan. Submission on child, early and forced marriage*. http://www.wluml.org/resource/child-early-and-forced-marriage-pakistan-submission-ohchr.

George, A. 2003. "Using Accountability to Improve Reproductive Health Care." *Reproductive Health Matters* 11 (21): 161–70.

Gertler, P. J. 2000. *Final Report: The Impact of PROGRESA on Health*. Washington, DC: International Food Policy Research Institute.

GHWA. 2008. *Case Study: Pakistan's Lady Health Worker Programme*. GHWA Task Force on Scaling Up Education and Training for Health. Geneva: WHO.

———. 2010. *Ethiopia's Human Resources for Health Programme: Country Case Study*. Geneva: WHO. http://www.who.int/workforcealliance/knowledge/case_studies/Ethiopia.pdf.

Gil-González, D., M. Carrasco-Portiño, and M. T. Ruiz. 2006. "Knowledge Gaps in Scientific Literature on Maternal Mortality: A Systematic Review." *Bulletin of the World Health Organization* 84 (11): 903–09. http://search.proquest.com/professional/docview/599942601?accountid=41588.

Gilmore, B., and E. McAuliffe. 2013. "Effectiveness of Community Health Workers Delivering Preventive Interventions for Maternal and Child Health in Low- and Middle-income Countries: A Systematic Review." *BMC Public Health* 13 (September): 847. http://search.proquest.com/professional/docview/1432928186?accountid=41588.

Gipson, R., M. A. El, O. Campbell, A. H. Issa, N. Matta, and E. Mansour. 2005. "The Trend of Maternal Mortality in Egypt from 1992–2000: An Emphasis on Regional Differences." *Maternal and Child Health Journal* 9: 71–82.

Glassman, A., D. Duran, and M. Koblinsky. 2013. "Impact of Conditional Cash Transfers on Maternal and Newborn Health." CGD Policy Paper 019, Center for Global Development, Washington, DC. www.cgdev.org/publication/impact-conditional-cash.

Goli, S., R. Doshi, and A. Perianayagam. 2013. "Pathways of Economic Inequalities in Maternal and Child Health in Urban India: A Decomposition Analysis." *PLoS One* 8 (3): e58573. doi:10.1371/journal.pone.0058573.

Goodburn, E., and O. Campbell. 2001. "Reducing Maternal Mortality in the Developing World: Sector-Wide Approaches May be the Key." *BJM* 322: 912–20. http://documents.worldbank.org/curated/en/2009/06/16403660/reducing-maternal-mortality-strengthening-world-bank-response.

Gopalan, S. S., S. Mohanty, and A. Das. 2012. "Assessing Community Health Workers' Performance Motivation: A Mixed-Methods Approach on India's Accredited Social Health Activists (ASHA) Programme." *BMJ Open* 2 (5): e001557.

Gopalan, S. S., R. Mutasa, J. Friedman, and A. Das. 2014. "Health Sector Demand-side Financial Incentives in Low- and Middle-income Countries: A Systematic Review on Demand- and Supply-side Effects." *Social Science & Medicine* 100 (January): 72–83. http://search.proquest.com/professional/docview/1507127700?accountid=41588

Government of the Islamic Republic of Afghanistan. 2011. *Strategic Plan for the Ministry of Public Health 2011–2015*. Kabul: Ministry of Public Health.

Government of Nepal. 2007. *An Analytical Report on National Survey of Female Community Health Volunteers of Nepal*. https://www.dhsprogram.com/pubs/pdf/FR181/FCHV_Nepal2007.pdf.

———. 2010. *Nepal Health Sector Programme-2 Implementation Plan: 2010–2015*. Kathmandu: Ministry of Health and Population. http://www.nhssp.org.np/health_policy/Consolidated%20NHSP-2%20IP%20092812%20QA.pdf.

———. 2014. *Evaluation of Postpartum Hemorrhage Prevention Program in Nepal*. Kathmandu: Department of Health Services, Ministry of Population and Development. http://dohs.gov.np/wp-content/uploads/chd/SafeMotherhood/Evaluation_PPH_Prevention_19_January_2014_EN.pdf.

———. 2015. *Family Health Division*. Kathmandu: Ministry of Health and Population Department of Health Services. http://dohs.gov.np/divisions/family-health-division/.

Government of the People's Republic of Bangladesh. 2014. "Millennium Development Goals: Bangladesh Country Report 2013". General Economic Division, Bangladesh Planning Commission.

Greene, M. E., M. Mehta, J. Pulerwitz, D. Wulf, A. Bankole, and S. Singh. 2006. "Involving Men in Reproductive Health: Contributions to Development." Background paper prepared for the United Nations Millennium Project, The Millennium Project, New York. http://www.unmillenniumproject.org/documents/Greene_et_al-final.pdf.

Greene, M. E., and C. Ostrowski. Undated. *Delivering Solutions: Advancing Dialogue to Improve Maternal Health*. http://www.wilsoncenter.org/sites/default/files/Deliverying%20Solutions%20for%20Maternal%20Health%20Report.pdf.

Hanson, K., and T. Powell-Jackson. 2010. "Financial Incentives for Maternal Health: Impact Evaluation of a National Programme in Nepal." Social Science Research Network, Rochester, NY. http://papers.ssrn.com/sol3/papers.cfm?abstract_id=1582863.

Hasan, R., M. Reich, and G. Fink. 2012. "Agenda Setting of Population in Bangladesh and West Bengal and Impact of Fertility." Paper presented at the Population Association of America 2012 Annual Meeting, San Francisco, CA May 3–5. http://paa2012.princeton.edu/papers/121206.

Hashemi, S., S. Schuler, and A. Riley. 1996. "Rural Credit Programs and Women's Empowerment in Bangladesh." *World Development* 24 (4): 635–53.

Hazarika, I. 2011. "Factors that Determine the Use of Skilled Care during Delivery in India: Implications for Achievement of MDG-5 Targets." *Maternal Child Health Journal* 15 (8): 1381–88.

———. 2012. "India at the Crossroads of Millennium Development Goals 4 and 5." *Asia-Pacific Journal of Public Health* 24 (3): 450–63.

Health Partners International. 2013. *Mobilising Access to Maternal Health Services in Zambia*. http://www.healthpartners-int.co.uk/our_projects/documents/MAMaZ_EOP_SINGLE_LOW_000.pdf.

Helen Keller International and IPHN (Institute of Public Health Nutrition). 2001. *National Surveillance Project: Evaluating National Nutrition Programs in Bangladesh: The Role of the Nutritional Surveillance Project.* Bulletin No. 5. Dhaka: Helen Keller International.

Henderson, J. T., M. Puri, M. Blum, C. C. Harper, A. Rana, G. Gurung, N. Pradhan, K. Regmi, K. Malla, S. Sharma, D. Grossman, L. Bajracharya, I. Satyal, S. Acharya, P. Lamichhane, and P. D. Darney. 2013. "Effects of Abortion Legalization in Nepal, 2001–2010." *PLoS One* 8 (5): e64775. doi:10.1371/journal.pone.0064775.

Hill, P. S., R. Dodd, and K. Dashdorj. 2006. "Health Sector Reform and Sexual and Reproductive Health Services in Mongolia." *Reproductive Health Matters* 14: 91–100.

Hirve, S. 2004. *Abortion Policy in India – Lacunae and Future Challenges.* Abortion Assessment Project India. Mumbai: CEHAT. http://www.cehat.org/go/uploads/AapIndia/hirve.pdf.

Holmer, H., K. Oyerinde, J. G. Meara, R. Gillies, J. Liljestrand, and L. Hagander. 2015. "The Global Met Need for Emergency Obstetric Care: A Systematic Review." doi:10.1111/1471-0528.13230.

Hong, S. Y., and L. R. Sarr. 2012. *Long-term Impacts of the Free Tuition and Female Stipend Programs on Education Attainment, Age of Marriage, and Married Women's Labor Market Participation in Bangladesh.* Washington, DC: World Bank. http://documents.worldbank.org/curated/en/2012/10/18257128/long-term-impacts-free-tuition-female-stipend-programs-education-attainment-age-marriage-married-womens-labor-market-participation-bangladesh.

Hord, C., H. P. David, F. Donnay, and M. Wolf. 1991. "Reproductive Health in Romania: Reversing the Ceausescu Legacy." *Studies in Family Planning* 22: 231–40.

Hornik, R., and E. McAnany. 2001. "Mass Media and Fertility Change." In *Diffusion Processes and Fertility Transition*, edited by J. B. Casterline, 208–39. Washington, DC: National Academy Press.

Hotchkiss, D., D. Godha, and M. Do. 2014. "Expansion in the Private Sector Provision of Institutional Delivery Services and Horizontal Equity: Evidence from Nepal and Bangladesh." *Health Policy and Planning* 29: i12–19. doi:10.1093/heapol/czt062.

Hou, X., and N. Ma. 2013. "The Effect of Women's Decision-Making Power on Maternal Health Services Uptake: Evidence from Pakistan." *Health Policy and Planning* 28 (2): 176–84.

Hounton, S., P. Byass, and B. Brahima. 2009. "Towards Reduction of Maternal and Perinatal Mortality in Rural Burkina Faso: Communities are not Empty Vessels." *Global Health Action* 2.

Huber, D., N. Saeedi, and A. K. Samadi. 2010. "Achieving Success with Family Planning in Rural Afghanistan." *Bulletin of the World Health Organization* 88: 227–31.

Hussein, J., J. Bell, M. Dar Iang, N. Mesko, J. Amery, and W. Graham. 2011. "An Appraisal of the Maternal Mortality Decline in Nepal." *PLoS One* 6 (5): e19898. doi:10.1371/journal.pone.0019898.

Hussein, J., L. Kanguru, M. Astin, and S. Munjanja. 2012. "The Effectiveness of Emergency Obstetric Referral Interventions in Developing Country Settings: A Systematic Review." *PLoS Medicine* 9 (7): e1001264. http://search.proquest.com/professional/docview/1038888599?accountid=41588

Hyoju, S. K., C. S. Agrawal, P. K. Pokhrel, and S. Agrawal. 2011. "Transfer of Clinical Breast Examination Skills to Female Community Health Volunteers in Nepal." *Asian Pacific Journal of Cancer Prevention* 12 (12): 3353–56.

IEG (Independent Evaluation Group). 2011. *Do Conditional Cash Transfers Lead to Medium-Term Impacts? Evidence from a Female School Stipend Program in Pakistan.* Washington, DC: World Bank.

———. 2014. *Delivery the Millennium Development Goals to Reduce Maternal and Child Mortality: A Systematic Review of Impact Evaluation Evidence.* Washington, DC: World Bank.

iERG. 2013. *MAMaZ Case Study: iERG Report 2013.* http://www.who.int/woman_child_accountability/ierg/reports/23_Quigley_MAMaZ.pdf.

IHP+ (International Health Partners). 2015. *IHP+ Partners.* www.internationalhealthpartnership.net/en/ihp-partners/.

IHP+Results. 2015. *Progress in the International Health Partnership and Related Initiatives (IHP+): 2014 Annual Performance Report.* Reet, Belgium: Hera. http://www.internationalhealthpartnership.net/fileadmin/uploads/ihp/Result_2014/Documents/IHP_report-ENG-WEB_v2.PDF.

IIPS (International Institute for Population Sciences) and Macro International. 2007. *National Family Health Survey (NFHS-3), 2005–06: India.* Volume I. IIPS, Mumbai.

IIPS (International Institute for Population Sciences). 2009. *District Level Household and Facility Survey—DLHS-3, State Factsheets, 2009.* India. Mumbai: IIPS.

IIPS and Macro International. 2007a. *National Family Health Survey (NFHS-3), 2005–06. India: Volume I.* Mumbai: IIPS.

———. 2007b. *National Family Health Survey (NFHS-3), 2005–06, India: Key Findings.* Mumbai: IIPS. http://dhsprogram.com/pubs/pdf/SR128/SR128.pdf.

Ishikawa, K. 1990. *Introduction to Quality Control.* Tokyo: 3A Corporation.

Islam, M. 2011. "Progress t owards Achieving Millennium Development Goal 5 in South-East Asia." *Bangladesh Journal of Obstetrics & Gynaecology* 118 (s2): 6–11.

Islam, M. T., M. M. Hossain, M. A. Islam, and Y. A. Haque. 2005. "Improvement of Coverage and Utilization of EmOC Services in Southwestern Bangladesh." *International Journal of Gynecology and Obstetrics* 91: 298–305. doi:10.1016/j.ijgo.2005.06.029.

Islam, N., M. T. Islam, and Y. Yoshimura. 2014. "Practices and Determinants of Delivery by Skilled Birth Attendants in Bangladesh." *Reproductive Health* 11 (86). http://www.reproductive-health-journal.com/content/11/1/86.

Iyengar, K., S. D. Iyengar, V. Suhalka, and K. Dashora. 2009. "Pregnancy-Related Deaths in Rural Rajasthan, India: Exploring Causes, Context, and Care-seeking through Verbal Autopsy." *Journal of Health, Population, and Nutrition* 27: 293–302.

Jafarey S, I. Kamal, A. F. Qureshi, and F. Fikree. 2008. "Safe Motherhood in Pakistan." *International Journal of Gynecology & Obstetrics* 102 (2): 179–85.

Jain, A. K. 2011. "Measuring the Effect of Fertility Decline on the Maternal Mortality Ratio." *Studies in Family Planning* 42 (2): 247–60.

Janes, C. R., and O. Chuluundorj. 2004. "Free Markets and Dead Mothers: The Social Ecology of Maternal Mortality in Post-Socialist Mongolia." *Medical Anthropology Quarterly* 18 (2): 230–57.

Jensen, R., and E. Oster. 2009. "The Power of TV: Cable Television and Women's Status in India." *Quarterly Journal of Economics* 124 (3): 1057–94.

Johnston, H. B., E. Oliveras, S. Akhtar, and D. G. Walker. 2010. "Health Systems Costs of Menstrual Regulation and Care for Abortion Complications." *International Perspectives on Sexual and Reproductive Health* 36 (4). https://www.questia.com/library/journal/1G1-250217667/health-system-costs-of-menstrual-regulation-and-care.

Johnson, K. 2001. "Media and Social Change: The Modernizing Influences of Television in Rural India." *Media, Culture and Society* 23: 147–69.

Kabagenyi, A., P. Ndugga, S. O. Wandera, and B. Kwagala. 2014. "Modern Contraceptive Use among Sexually Active Men in Uganda: Does Discussion with a Health Worker Matter?" *BMC Public Health* 14: 286.

Kabeer, N. 2006. "Poverty, Social Exclusion and the MDGs: The Challenge of 'Durable Inequalities' in the Asian context." *IDS Bulletin* 37 (3): 64–78.

Kamran, I., K. Mumraiz, and Z. Tasneem. 2014. *Involving Men in Reproductive and Fertility Issues: Insights from Punjab*. Washington, DC: World Bank. http://hdl.handle.net/10986/17541.

Kannan, R. 2013. "More People Opting for Private Healthcare." *The Hindu*. http://www.thehindu.com/sci-tech/health/more-people-opting-for-private-healthcare/article4967288.ece.

Karkee, R. 2011. "How did Nepal Reduce the Maternal Mortality? A Result from Analysing the Determinants of Maternal Mortality." *Journal of the Nepal Medical Association* 52 (186): 88–94.

Kassebaum, N. J., A. Bertozzi-Villa, M. S. Coggeshall, K. A. Shackelford, C. Steiner, K. R. Heuton, D. Gonzalez-Medina, R. Barber, C. Huynh, et al. 2014. "Global, Regional, and National Levels and Causes of Maternal Mortality during 1990–2013: A Systematic Analysis for the Global Burden of Disease Study 2013." *The Lancet* 384 (9947): 980–1004. doi:10.1016/S0140-6736(14)60696-6.

Kaufmann, D., A. Kraay, and M. Mastruzzi. 2003. *Government Matters III: Governance Indicators for 1996–2002*. Washington, DC: World Bank.

Khan, M. E., G. Darmstadt, U. K. Tarigopula, D. Ganju, and F. Donnay. 2012. *Shaping Demand and Practices to Improve Family Health Outcomes: Designing a Behavior Change Communication Strategy in India, Volume I: Uttar Pradesh, Volume II: Bihar.* New Delhi: SAGE Publications.

Khan, M. E., and P. Panda. 2004. "Involving Men in Reproductive Health in India: Policies, Programs and Achievements." *The Journal of Family Welfare* 50: 57–70. http://medind.nic.in/jah/t04/s1/jaht04s1p57g.pdf.

Khandker, S. R. 2005. *Microfinance and Poverty: Evidence using Panel Data from Bangladesh.* Published by Oxford University Press on behalf of the World Bank. © World Bank. https://openknowledge.worldbank.org/handle/10986/16478 License: CC BY-NC-ND 3.0 IGO.

Khandker, S. R., G. Koolwal, and N. Sinha. 2008. "Benefits of Improving Young Women's Labor Market Opportunities: Evidence from Group-Based Credit Programs in Rural

Bangladesh." Background paper for Adolescent Girls Initiative. World Bank, Washington, DC.

Kidney, E., H. R. Winter, K. S. Khan, A. M. Gülmezoglu, C. A. Meads, J. J. Deeks, and C. Macarthur. 2009. "Systematic Review of Effect of Community-Level Interventions to Reduce Maternal Mortality." *BMC Pregnancy and Childbirth* 9 (1): 2. http://search.proquest.com/professional/docview/602724882?accountid=41588.

Kim, Y. M., N. Ansari, A. Kols, H. Tappis, S. Currie, P. Zainullah, P. Bailey, J. van Roosmalen, and J. Stekelenburg. 2013. "Prevention and management of severe pre-eclampsia/eclampsia in Afghanistan." *BMC Pregnancy and Childbirth* 13 (186). doi:10.1186/1471-2393-13-186.

Kimuna, S. R., and D. J. Adamchak.2001. "Gender Relations: Husband–Wife Fertility and Family Planning Decisions in Kenya." *Journal of Biosocial Science* 33: 13–23.

King, J. C. 2003. "The Risk of Maternal Nutritional Depletion and Poor Outcomes Increases in Early or Closely Spaced Pregnancies." *Journal of Nutrition* 133 (5 Suppl 2): 1732S36S.

Kingdom of Bhutan. 2014. *Human Resources for Health Country Profile Bhutan*. Thimpu: Human Resource Division, Ministry of Health.

Knight, H., A. Self, and S. H. Kennedy.2013. "Why Are Women Dying When They Reach Hospital on Time? A Systematic Review of the 'Third Delay'." *PLoS One* 8 (5): e63846. http://search.proquest.com/professional/docview/1355289639?accountid=41588.

Koblinsky, M., I. Anwar, M. K. Mridha, M. E. Chowdhury, and Roslin Botlero. 2008. "Reducing Maternal Mortality and Improving Maternal Health: Bangladesh and MDG 5." *Journal of Health, Population and Nutrition* 26 (3): 280–294. doi:10.3329/jhpn.v26i3.1896.

Koblinsky, M. A., 2003. *Reducing Maternal ortality: Learning from Bolivia, China, Egypt, Honduras, Indonesia, Jamaica, and Zimbabwe*. Washington, DC: World Bank.

Koch, E., J. Thorp, M. Bravo, S. Gatica, C. X. Romero, H. Aguilera, and I. Ahlers. 2012. "Women's Education Level, Maternal Health Facilities, Abortion Legislation and Maternal Deaths: A Natural Experiment in Chile from 1957 to 2007." *PLoS One* 7 (5): e36613. doi:10.1371/journal.pone.0036613.

Kumar, S., and E. Dansereau. 2014. "Supply-Side Barriers to Maternity-Care in India: A Facility-Based Analysis." *PLoS One* 9 (8): e103927. doi:10.1371/journal.pone.0103927.

Kuruvilla, S., J. Schweitzer, D. Bishai, S. Chowdhury, D. Caramani, L. Frost, A. de Francisco, R. Cortez, B. Daelmans, T. Adam, R. Cohen, Y. N. Alfonso, J. Franz, S. Saadaat, B. A. Pratt, B. Eugster, S. Bandali, P. Venkatachalam, R. Hinton, J. Murray, S. Arscott-Mills, I. Sarkar, S. Jack, H. Axelson, B. Maliqi, R. Lakshminarayanan, T. Jacobs, E. Mason, A. Ghaffar, N. Mays, C. Presern, and F. Bustreo. 2014. "Success Factors for Women's and Children's Health: Multisector Action Accelerates Country Progress." *Bulletin of the World Health Organization*. New York. (Earlier manuscript BLT-2014-138131 used.)

Lalonde, A. B., P. Okong, A. Mugasa, and L. Perron. 2003. "The FIGO Save the Mothers Initiative: The Uganda-Canada Collaboration." *International Journal of Gynecology & Obstetrics* 80 (2): 204–12. doi:10.1016/S0020-7292(02)00389-2.

Langlois, E., M. Miszkurka, D. Ziegler, I. Karp, and M. V. Zunzunegui. 2013. "Protocol for a Systematic Review on Inequalities in Postnatal Care Services Utilization in Low- and

Middle-income Countries." *Systematic Reviews* 2 (July): 55. http://search.proquest.com/professional/docview/1398572139?accountid=41588.

Lassi, Z. S., and Z. A. Bhutta. 2015. "Community Based Intervention Packages for Reducing Maternal and Neonatal Morbidity and Mortality and Improving Neonatal Outcomes." *Cochrane Database of Systematic Reviews 2015* 23 (3): CD007754. http://summaries.cochrane.org/CD007754/PREG_community-based-intervention-packages-for-preventing-maternal-and-newborn-illness-and-death-and-improving-neonatal-outcomes#sthash.hcC8vzAU.dpuf.

Lassi, Z. S., G. Cometto, L. Huicho, and Z. A. Bhutta. 2013. "Quality of Care Provided by Mid-level Health Workers: Systematic Review and Meta-analysis." *Bulletin of the World Health Organization* 91 (11): 824–33I. http://search.proquest.com/professional/docview/1469385260?accountid=41588.

Leone, T., K. S. James, and S. S. Padmadas. 2013. "The Burden of Maternal Health Care Expenditure in India: Multilevel Analysis of National Data." *Maternal Health Journal* 17 (9): 1622–30. doi:10.1007/s10995-012-1174-9.

Lewycka, S., C. Mwansambo, M. Rosato, P. Kazembe, T. Phiri, A. Mganga, H. Chapota, F. Malamba, E. Kainja, M. L. Newell, G. Greco, A. M. Pulkki-Brännström, J. Skordis-Worrall, S. Vergnano, D. Osrin D, and A. Costello. 2013. "Effect of Women's Groups and Volunteer Peer Counselling on Rates of Mortality, Morbidity, and Health Behaviours in Mothers and Children in Rural Malawi (MaiMwana): A Factorial, Cluster-Randomised Controlled Trial." *The Lancet* 381 (9879): 1721–35.

Li, J., C. Luo, R. Deng, P. Jacoby, and N. de Klerk. 2007. "Maternal Mortality in Yunnan, China: Recent Trends and Associated Factors." *BJOG: An International Journal of Obstetrics and Gynecology* 114: 865–74.

Liljestrand, J., and I. Pathmanathan. 2004. "Reducing Maternal Mortality: Can we Derive Policy Guidance from Developing Country Experiences?" *Journal of Public Health Policy* 25 (3–4): 299–314.

Liljestrand, J., and M. R. Sambath. 2012. "Socio-Economic Improvements and Health System Strengthening of Maternity Care are Contributing to Maternal Mortality Reduction in Cambodia." *Reproductive Health Matters* 20 (39): 62–72.

Lim, S., L. Dandona, J. Hoisington, S. James, M. Hogan, and E. Gakidou. 2010. "India's Janani Suraksha Yojana, A Conditional Cash Transfer Programme to Increase Births in Health Facilities: An Impact Evaluation." *The Lancet* 375 (9730): 5–11.

Lule, E., N. Oomman, J. Epp, D. Huntington, G. N. V. Ramanad, and J. E. Rosen. 2005. "Achieving the Millennium Development Goal of Improving Maternal Health: Determinants, Interventions and Challenges." HNP Discussion Paper, World Bank, Washington, DC.

Mahmud, G., F. Zaman, S. Jafarey, R. L. Khan, R. Sohail, and S. Fatima. 2011. "Achieving Millennium Development Goals 4 and 5 in Pakistan." *BJOG: an International Journal of Obstetrics and Gynaecology* 118 (Suppl 2): 69–77.

Maiti S., S. Unisa, and P. K. Agrawal. 2005. "Health Care and Health among Tribal Women in Jharkhand: A Situational Analysis." *Studies of Tribes and Tribals* 3 (1): 37–46.

Majrooh, M. A., S. Hasnain, J. Akram, A. Siddiqui, and Z. Ali Memon. 2014. "Coverage and Quality of Antenatal Care Provided at Primary Health Care Facilities in the 'Punjab' Province of 'Pakistan." *PLoS One* 9 (11): e113390. doi:10.1371/journal.pone.0113390.

Malik, M. F., and M. A. Kayan. 2014. "Issues of Maternal Health in Pakistan: Trends towards Millennium Development Goal 5." *The Journal of the Pakistan Medical Association (JPMA)* 64: 690–93.

Malla, D. S., K. Giri, C. Karki, and P. Chaudhary. 2011. "Achieving Millennium Development Goals 4 and 5 in Nepal." *BJOG: an International Journal of Obstetrics and Gynaecology* 118 (Suppl 2): 60–8.

Manandhar, D. S., D. Osrin, B. P. Shrestha, N. Mesko, J. Morrison, K. M. Tumbahangphe, S. Tamang, S.Thapa, D. Shrestha, B. Thapa, J. R. Shrestha, A. Wade, J. Borghi, H. Standing, M. Manandhar, and A. M. de L Costello. 2004. "Effect of a Participatory Intervention with Women's Groups on Birth Outcomes in Nepal: Cluster-Randomised Controlled Trial." *The Lancet* 364 (9438): 970–79.

Mangeni, J. N., A. Mwangi, S. Mbugua, and V. Mukthar. 2013. "Male Involvement in Maternal Health Care as a Determinant of Utilization of Skilled Birth Attendants in Kenya." DHS Working Paper, ICF International, Calverton, MD.

Mangham-Jefferies, L., M. Bereket, J. Russell, and A. Bekele. 2014. "How do Health Extension Workers in Ethiopia Allocate their Time?" *Human Resources for Health* 14: 12.

Marie Stopes International. 2008. *Perceptions and Realities Yemeni Men and Women and Contraception: Key Findings from a Knowledge, Attitudes and Practices Survey and Peer Ethnographic Evaluation Research Study Yemen.* London: Marie Stopes International.

Marston, C., A. Renedo, C. R. McGowan, and A. Portela. 2013. "Effects of Community Participation on Improving Uptake of Skilled Care for Maternal and Newborn Health: A Systematic Review." *PLoS One* 8 (2): e55012. http://search.proquest.com/professional/docview/1346763593?accountid=41588.

Maternal Mortality Estimation Inter-Agency Group. 2013. Bangladesh. Geneva: WHO. http://www.who.int/gho/maternal_health/countries/bgd.pdf.

———. 2014. *Maternal Mortality 1990–2013 Bhutan.* Geneva: WHO. www.who.int/gho/maternal_health/countries/btn.pdf.

Mays, N., J. Erwin, P. R. De Lay, and E. J. Beck. Forthcoming. "Understanding Country Responses to their HIV Epidemics: An Exploratory Qualitative Comparative Analysis." Manuscript in Preparation.

Mbonye, A. K., and J. B. Asimwe. 2010. "Factors Associated with Skilled Attendance at Delivery in Uganda: Results from a National Health Facility Survey." *International Journal of Adolescent Medicine and Health* 22 (2): 249–56.

McAlister, C., and T. Baskett. 2006. "Female Education and Maternal Mortality: A Worldwide Survey." *Journal of Obstetrics and Gynaecology Canada* 28 (11): 983–90.

McCaw-Binns, A., S. F. Alexander, J. L. Lindo, C. Escoffery, K. Spence, and others. 2007. "Epidemiologic Transition in Maternal Mortality and Morbidity: New Challenges for Jamaica." *International Journal of Gynaecology and Obstetrics: the Official Organ of the International Federation of Gynaecology and Obstetrics* 96: 226–32.

McLeroy, K. R., D. Bibeau, A. Steckler, and K. Glanz. 1988. "An Ecological Perspective on Health Promotion Programs." *Health Education Quarterly* 15: 351–77.

Medical Statistics Unit. 2008. *Sri Lanka: Health at a Glance.* Volume 1. Colombo: Ministry of Healthcare and Nutrition.

Medhanyie, A., M. Spigt, Y. Kifle, N. Schaay, D. Sanders, R. Blanco, D. GeertJan and Y. Berhane. 2012. "The Role of Health Extension Workers in Improving Utilization of

Maternal Health Services in Rural Areas in Ethiopia: A Cross Sectional Study." *BMC Health Services Research* 12 (1): 352.

Middleton, J., G. Shabbir, H. Qureshi, F. Ud Din, V. Vargas, and A. Asif. 2012. *Mid-term Evaluation of the National Maternal and Child Health Programme in Pakistan: Findings and Recommendations. September 26*. Islamabad: Technical Resource Facility.

Ministry of Health and Family Welfare. 2004. *Annual Report 2003–2004*. New Delhi: Ministry of Health and Family Welfare, Government of India.

———. 2010. *Rural Health Statistics in India*. New Delhi: Ministry of Health and Family Welfare, Government of India.

Ministry of Health Viet Nam, PMNCH, WHO, World Bank, Alliance for Health Policy and Systems Research (AHPSR) and Participants in the Viet Nam Multi-Stakeholder Policy Review. 2014. *Success Factors for Women's and Children's Health: Viet Nam*.

Mistry, R., O. Galal, and M. Lu. 2009. "Women's Autonomy and Pregnancy Care in Rural India: A Contextual Analysis." *Social Science & Medicine* 69 (6): 926–33.

Moazzeni, M. S. 2013. "Maternal Mortality in the Islamic Republic of Iran: On Track and in Transition." *Maternal and Child Health Journal* 17: 577–80.

MOHF (Ministry of Health and Family) and ICF Macro. 2010. *Maldives Demographic and Health Survey 2009*. MOHF and ICF Macro, Calverton, MD.

MOHP (Ministry of Health and Population), New ERA, and ICF International Inc. 2012. *Nepal Demographic and Health Survey 2011*. MOHP, Kathmandu; New ERA, Nepal; and ICF International, Calverton, MD.

MOHP (Ministry of Health and Population) [Nepal], New ERA, and ICF International Inc. 2012. *Nepal Demographic and Health Survey 2011*. Kathmandu, Nepal: Ministry of Health and Population, New ERA, and ICF International, Calverton, MD.

Montgomery, A. L., U. Ram, R. Kumar, and P. Jha. 2014. "Maternal Mortality in India: Causes and Healthcare Service Use Based on a Nationally Representative Survey." *PLoS One* 9 (1): e83331. doi:10.1371/journal.pone.0083331.

Moyer, C. A., and A. Mustafa. 2013. "Drivers and Deterrents of Facility Delivery in Sub-Saharan Africa: A Systematic Review." *Reproductive Health* 10 (August): 40. http://search.proquest.com/professional/docview/1426922672?accountid=41588.

Moyer, C. A., P. Dako-Gyeke, and R. M. Adanu. 2013. "Facility-Based Delivery and Maternal and Early Neonatal Mortality in Sub-Saharan Africa: A Regional Review of the Literature." *African Journal of Reproductive Health September* 17 (3): 30–43.

Mridha, M. K., I. Anwar, and M. Koblinksy. 2009. "Public-sector Maternal Health Programmes and Services for Rural Bangladesh." *Journal of Health Population and Nutrition* 27 (2): 124–38.

Muldoon, K. A., L. P. Galway, M. Nakajima, S. Kanters, R. S. Hogg, E. Bendavid, and E. J. Mills. 2011. "Health System Determinants of Infant, Child and Maternal Mortality: A Cross-sectional Study of UN Member Countries." *Globalization and Health* 7: 42. doi:10.1186/1744-8603-7-42.

Mullany, B. C. 2005. "Barriers to and Attitudes toward Promoting Husbands' Involvement in Maternal Health in Katmandu, Nepal." *Social Science and Medicine* 62 (11): 2798–809.

Mullany, B. S., S. Becker, and M. J. Hindin. 2007. "The Impact of Including Husbands in Antenatal Health Education Services on Maternal Health Practices in Urban Nepal: Results from a Randomized Controlled Trial." *Health Education Research* 22 (2): 166–76.

Mumtaz, Z., and S. Salway. 2009. "Understanding Gendered Influences on Women's Reproductive Health in Pakistan: Moving beyond the Autonomy Paradigm." *Social Science & Medicine* 68: 1349–56.

Mumtaz, Z., S. Salway, A. Bhatti, L. Shanner, S. Zaman, L. Laing, and G. T. H. Ellison. 2014. "Improving Maternal Health in Pakistan: Toward a Deeper Understanding of the Social Determinants of Poor Women's Access to Maternal Health Services." *American Journal of Public Health* 104 (S1): S17–24.

Munsur, A. M., A. Atia, and K. Kawahara. 2010. "Relationship between Educational Attainment and Maternal Health Care Utilization in Bangladesh: Evidence from the 2005 Bangladesh Income and Expenditure Survey." *Research Journal of Medical Sciences* 4 (1): 33–7. doi:10.3923/rjmsci.2010.33.37.

Murray, S. F., B. M. Hunter, R. Bisht, T. Ensor, and D. Bick. 2014. "Effects of Demand-Side Financing on Utilisation, Experiences and Outcomes of Maternity Care in Low- and Middle-income Countries: A Systematic Review." *BMC Pregnancy and Childbirth* 14:30. http://search.proquest.com/professional/docview/1490607872?accountid=41588.

Nag, M. 1992. "Family Planning Success Stories in Bangladesh and India." Policy Research Working Paper WPS 1041, World Bank, Washington, DC.

Nasreen, H., S. M. Ahmed, H. A. Begum, and K. Afsana. 2007. *Maternal, Neonatal and Child Health Programmes in Bangladesh: Review of Good Practices and Lessons Learned.* BRAC.

Nasreen, H. E., M. Leppard, M. Al Mamun, M. Billah, S. K. Mistry, M. Rahman, and P. Nicholls. 2012. "Men's Knowledge and Awareness of Maternal, Neonatal, and Child Health Care in Rural Bangladesh: A Comparative Cross Sectional Study." *Reproductive Health* 9 (18). http://www.reproductive-health-journal.com/content/9/1/18.

National Statistics Bureau. 2011. *Bhutan Multiple Indicator Survey.* National Statistics Bureau, Thimphu, Bhutan.

National Statistics Bureau. 2011. *Bhutan Multiple Indicator Survey 2010.* New York: UNICEF; New York: UNFPA. http://www.aidsdatahub.org/sites/default/files/documents/MICS_Bhutan_2010.pdf.

Naved, T., M. N. Ruchira, and A. Sajeda. 1997. "Female Labor Migration and its Implication for Marriage and Child Bearing in Bangladesh". Paper presented at Population Council Workshop on Adolescence and Marriage among Female Garments workers of Dhaka, BIDS Dhaka, May 15. Cited in P. Paul-Majumder and A. Begum. 2000. "The Gender Imbalances in the Export Oriented Garment Industry in Bangladesh." Policy Research Report on Gender and Development Working Paper Series 12, World Bank, Washington, DC. http://siteresources.worldbank.org/INTGENDER/Resources/trademajumder.pdf.

Nayar, K. R. 2007. "Social Exclusion, Caste and Health: A Review Based on the Social Determinants of Health Framework." *Indian Journal of Medical Research* 126 (4): 355–63.

Newbrander, W., D. Collins, and L. Gilson. 2000. *Ensuring Equal Access to Health Services: User Fee Systems and the Poor.* Management Sciences for Health, 187 p.

Nguyen, H. T. H., L. Hatt, M. Islam, N. L. Sloan, J. Chowdhury, J. O. Schmidt, A. Hossain, and H. Wang. 2012. "Encouraging Maternal Health Service Utilization: An Evaluation of the Bangladesh Voucher Program." *Social Science & Medicine* 74 (7): 989–96.

Ni Bhuinneain, G. M., and F. P. McCarthy. 2015. "A Systematic Review of Essential Obstetric and Newborn Care Capacity Building in Rural Sub-Saharan Africa." *BJOG: An International Journal of Obstetrics and Gynaecology* 122 (2): 174–82. http://search.proquest.com/professional/docview/1640943455?accountid=41588.

NIPORT (National Institute of Population Research and Training) MEASURE Evaluation, and icddr,b. 2012. *Bangladesh Maternal Mortality and Health Care Survey 2010*. Dhaka: NIPORT.

NIPORT (National Institute of Population Research and Training), Mitra and Associates, and ICF International. 2013. *Bangladesh Demographic and Health Survey 2011*. NIPORT, Dhaka; Mitra and Associates, Bangladesh; and ICF International, Calverton, MD.

NIPORT, Mitra and Associates, and ICF International. 2013. *Bangladesh Demographic and Health Survey 2011*. Dhaka, Bangladesh and Calverton, MD, USA: NIPORT, Mitra and Associates, and ICF International.

NIPS (National Institute of Population Studies) and ICF International. 2013. *Pakistan Demographic and Health Survey 2012–13*. NIPS, Islamabad; ICF International, Calverton, MD.

Nnamuchi, O. 2015. "Maternal Health and Millennium Development Goal (MDG) 5 in Nigeria: Any Catalytic Role for Human Rights?" *Journal of Law and Medicine* 34.

NRHM (National Rural Health Mission). 2012. *Minutes of the Fifteenth Meeting of the Empowered Program Committee*. October 4.

Nwakoby, B. N. 1994. "Use of Obstetric Services in Rural Nigeria." *Journal of the Royal Society of Health* 114 (3): 132–36. doi:10.1177/146642409411400304.

Nwolise, C. H., J. Hussein, L. Kanguru, J. Bell, and P. Patel. 2015. "The Effectiveness of Community-Based Loan Funds for Transport during Obstetric Emergencies in Developing Countries: A Systematic Review." *Health Policy and Planning* 30 (7): 946–55. http://search.proquest.com/professional/docview/1555049653?accountid=41588.

Nyamtema, A. S., D. P. Urassa, and J. van Roosmalen. 2011. "Maternal Health Interventions in Resource Limited Countries: A Systematic Review of Packages, Impacts and Factors for Change." *BMC Pregnancy and Childbirth* 11 (April): 30. http://search.proquest.com/professional/docview/862681990?accountid=41588.

Olenik, L. 2000. "Women's Exposure to Mass Media Is Linked to Attitudes toward Contraception in Pakistan, India and Bangladesh." *International Family Planning Perspectives* 26 (1): 48–50.

Options Consultancy Services/Evidence for Action, Cambridge Economic Policy Associates, and the Partnership for Maternal, Newborn and Child Health. 2013. "Success Factors for Women's and Children's Health: Country Specific Review of Data and Literature on 10 Fast-Track Countries' Progress towards MDGs 4 and 5." Background paper, WHO, Geneva.

Oxford Policy Management. 2009. *External Evaluation of the National Programme for Family Planning and Primary Health Care: Lady Health Worker Programme, Management Review*. http://www.opml.co.uk/sites/default/files/Lady%20Health%20Worker%20Programme%20-%204th%20Evaluation%20-%20Summary%20of%20Results.pdf.

Padmanaban, P., P. S. Raman, and D. V. Mavalankar. 2009. "Innovations and Challenges in Reducing Maternal Mortality in Tamil Nadu, India." *Journal of Health, Population, and Nutrition* 27: 202–19.

Pathmanathan, I., J. Liljestrand, J. M. Martins, L. C. Rajapaksa, C. Lissner, A. de Silva, S. Selvaraju, and P. J. Singh. 2003. *Investing in Maternal Health: Learning from Malaysia and Sri Lanka. Health, Nutrition, and Population Series.* Washington, DC: World Bank. http://documents.worldbank.org/curated/en/2003/12/8188495/investing-maternal-health-learning-malaysia-sri-lanka.

Piane, G. M. 2009. "Evidence-Based Practices to Reduce Maternal Mortality: A Systematic Review." *Journal of Public Health* (Oxford, England) 31 (1): 26–31. http://search.proquest.com/professional/docview/602763089?accountid=41588.

Piane, G. M., and E. A. Clinton. 2014. "Maternal Mortality Interventions: A Systematic Review." *Open Journal of Preventive Medicine* 4 (9): 699–707. http://search.proquest.com/professional/docview/1614281136?accountid=41588.

Pierre-Louis, A. M., S. El-Saharty, A. Stanciole, O. Jonas, F. B. Pascual, R. Oelrichs, M. Meiro-Lorenz, T. Villafan, F. Lavadensz, and M. Rock. 2012. "Connecting Sectors and Systems for Health Results". Public Health Policy Note, The World Bank, Washington, DC. http://www-wds.worldbank.org/external/default/WDSContentServer/WDSP/IB/2013/03/14/000442464_20130314150659/Rendered/PDF/756500REPLACEM0ublic0Health02012013.pdf.

Pitt, M. M., S. R. Khandker, and J. Cartwright. 2003. *Does Micro-Credit Empower Women: Evidence from Bangladesh.* Washington, DC: World Bank. https://openknowledge.worldbank.org/handle/10986/19162 License: CC BY 3.0 IGO.

Planning Commission. 2008. "Health and Family Welfare and AYUSH." In *Eleventh Five-Year Plan, 2007–2012, Volume II,* edited by Planning Commission, 57–127. New Delhi: Planning Commission, Government of India. http://www.planningcommission.nic.in/plans/planrel/fiveyr/11th/11_v2/11th_vol2.pdf.

Prost A., T., Colbourn, N. Seward, K. Azad, A. Coomarasamy, A. Copas, T. A. Houweling, E. Fottrell, A. Kuddus, S. Lewycka, C. MacArthur, D. Manandhar, J. Morrison, C. Mwansambo, N. Nair, B. Nambiar, D. Osrin, C. Pagel, T. Phiri, A. M. Pulkki-Brännström, M. Rosato, J. Skordis-Worrall, N. Saville, N. S. More, B. Shrestha, P. Tripathy, A. Wilson, and A. Costello. 2013. "Women's Groups Practising Participatory Learning and Action to Improve Maternal and Newborn Health in Low-resource Settings: A Systematic Review and Meta-analysis." *The Lancet* 381 (9879): 1736–46.

Pubudu de Silva, A. 2011. *The Contribution of Public Health Midwives to Better Health in Rural Communities in Sri Lanka.* Case Study for the Second Global Forum on Human Resources for Health, Bangkok, Thailand, January 25–29.

Pucher, P. H., M. Macdonnell, and S. Arulkumaran. 2013. "Global Lessons on Transforming Strategy into Action to Save Mothers' Lives." *International Journal of Gynaecology and Obstetrics: the Official Organ of the International Federation of Gynaecology and Obstetrics* 123: 167–72.

Pyone, T., B. L. Sorensen, and S. Tellier. 2012. "Childbirth Attendance Strategies and their Impact on Maternal Mortality and Morbidity in Low-income Settings: A Systematic Review." *Acta Obstetricia et Gynecologica Scandinavica* 91 (9): 1029–37. http://search.proquest.com/professional/docview/1013892730?accountid=41588.

Qiu, L., J. Lin, Y. Ma, W. Wu, L. Qiu, A. Zhou, W. Shi, A. Lee, and C. Binns. 2010. "Improving the Maternal Mortality Ratio in Zhejiang Province, China, 1988–2008." *Midwifery* 26 (5): 544–48.

Raghupathy, S. 1996. "Education and the Use of Maternal Health Care in Thailand." *Social Science and Medicine* 43 (4): 459–71. doi:10.1016/0277-9536(95)00411-4.

Rahman, M., M. T. Islam, M. G. Mostofa, and M. S. Reza. 2015. "Men's Role in Women's Antenatal Health Status: Evidence from Rural Rajshahi, Bangladesh." *Asia Pacific Journal of Public Health* 27 (2): 1182–92. doi:10.1177/1010539512437693.

Rai, R. K., and T. H. Tulchinsky. 2015. "Addressing the Sluggish Progress in Reducing Maternal Mortality in India." *Asia-Pacific Journal of Public Health/Asia-Pacific Academic Consortium for Public Health* 27: NP1161–1169.

Rajbhandari, S., S. Hodgins, H. Sanghvi, R. McPherson, Y. V. Pradhan, and A. H. Baqui; Misoprostol Study Group. 2010. "Expanding Uterotonics Protection Following Childbirth through Community-Based Misoprostol: Operations Research Study in Nepal." *International Journal of Gynecology and Obstetrics* 108 (3): 282–88. doi: 10.1016/j.ijgo.2009.11.006.

Rammohan, A., N. Awofeso, and M. C. Robitaille. 2012. "Addressing Female Iron-Deficiency Anaemia in India: Is Vegetarianism the Major Obstacle?" *ISRN Public Health* 2012.

Randive, B., V. Diwan, and A. De Costa. 2013. "India's Conditional Cash Transfer Programme (the JSY) to Promote Institutional Birth: Is there an Association between Institutional Birth Proportion and Maternal Mortality?" *PLoS One* 8 (6): e67452. doi:10.1371/journal.pone.0067452. http://www.plosone.org/article/info%3Adoi%2F10.1371%2Fjournal.pone.0067452#abstract0.

Rannan-Eliya, R. P., G. Kasthuri, and S. De Alwis. 2012. *Impact of Maternal and Child Health Private Expenditure on Poverty and Inequity: Maternal and Child Health Expenditure in Bangladesh. Technical Report* C. Mandaluyong City, Philippines: Asian Development Bank.

Rasooly, M. H., P. Govindasamy, A. Aqil, S. Rutstein, F. Arnold, B. Noormal, A. Way, S. Brock, and A. Shadoul. 2014. "Success in Reducing Maternal and Child Mortality in Afghanistan." *Global Public Health* 9 (Suppl 1): S29–42.

Rath, A. D., I. Basnett, M. Cole, H. N. Subedi, D. Thomas, and S. F. Murray. 2007. "Improving Emergency Obstetric Care in a Context of Very High Maternal Mortality: The Nepal Safer Motherhood Project 1997–2004." *Reproductive Health Matters* 15 (30).

Registrar General of India and Centre for Global Health Research. 2006. *Maternal Mortality in India, 1997–2003: Trends, Causes and Risk Factors*. New Delhi: Registrar General of India.

Retherford, R. D., and V. Mishra. 1997. "Media Exposure Increases Contraceptive Use." *National Family Health Survey Bulletin* 7. Honolulu: International Institute for Population Sciences, Mumbai and East-West Center Program on Population.

Ricardo, C., M. Nascimento, V. Fonseca, and M. Segundo. 2010. *Program H and Program M: Engaging Young Men and Empowering Young Women to Promote Gender Equality and Health*. PAHO Best Practices in Gender and Health. Washington, DC: PAHO.

Riders for Health. Year unknown. "The Role of Riders for Health's Managed-transport Systems in Promoting Maternal, Newborn and Child Health (MNCH)." https://riders-live-cms.s3.amazonaws.com/OurImpact/Riders%20for%20Health-%20Support%20for%20MNCH.pdf.

Roberts, M., W. Hsia, P. Berman, and M. R. Reich. 2004. *Getting Health Reform Right: A Guide to Improving Performance and Equity*. Oxford: Oxford University Press.

Robinson, W. 1978. "Family Planning in Pakistan 1955–1977: A Review." *The Pakistan Development Review* 17 (2): 233–47. http://www.pide.org.pk/pdf/PDR/1978/Volume2/233-247.pdf.

Robinson, W. C., and J. A. Ross, eds. 2007. *The Global Family Planning Revolution: Three Decades of Population Policies and Programs*. Washington, DC: World Bank.

Royal Government of Bhutan. 2015. *Program Profiles*. Thimpu: Ministry of Health. http://www.health.gov.bt/about/program-profiles/.

———. 2011. *SAARC Development Goals: Mid-Term Review Report 2011*. Gross National Happiness Commission. Bhutan: The Royal Government of Bhutan. http://www.gnhc.gov.bt/wp-content/uploads/2011/12/SAARC-DEVELOPMENT-GOALS-BHUTAN.pdf.

Ross, L., P. Simkhada, and W. C. Smith. 2005. "Evaluating Effectiveness of Complex Interventions Aimed at Reducing Maternal Mortality in Developing Countries." *Journal of Public Health* 27 (4): 331–37.

Rusa, L., J. D. D. Ngirabega, W. Janssen, S. Van Bastelaere, D. Porignon, and W. Vandenbulcke. 2009. "Performance-Based Financing for Better Quality of Services in Rwandan Health Centres: Three-year Experience." *Tropical Medicine & International Health* 14 (7): 830–37.

Saadat, S., R. Cortez, A. Voetberg, S. Chowdhury, and S. Intissar. 2014. *Achieving MDGS 4 and 5: Nepal Progress on Maternal and Child Health*. Health, Nutrition and Population Global Practice Knowledge Brief. Washington, DC: World Bank Group. http://documents.worldbank.org/curated/en/2014/08/20351558/achieving-mdgs-4-5-nepal-progress-maternal-child-health.

Saffron, K., L. Say, J. P. Souza, C. J. Hogue, D. L. Calles, A. M. Gülmezoglu, and R. Raine. 2011. "The Relationship between Maternal Education and Mortality among Women Giving Birth in Health Care Institutions: Analysis of the Cross Sectional WHO Global Survey on Maternal and Perinatal Health." *BMC Public Health* 11: 606. doi:10.1186/1471-2458-11-606.

Salvado, R. C., and J. Waltz. 2014. "Aid Eligibility and Income per Capita: A Sudden Stop for MICs?" DPAF Working Paper, Bill & Melinda Gates Foundation, Seattle, USA.

Samai, O., and P. Sengeh. 1997. "Facilitating Emergency Obstetric Care through Transportation and Communication, Bo, Sierra Leone." *International Journal of International Gynecology and Obstetrics* 59 (Suppl 2): S157–64.

Samandari, G., M. Wolf, I. Basnett, A. Hyman, and K. Andersen. 2012. "Implementation of Legal Abortion in Nepal: A Model for Rapid Scale-Up of High-Quality Care." *Reproductive Health* 9 (7). http://www.reproductive-health-journal.com/content/9/1/7.

Sanneving, L., N. Trygg, D. Saxena, D. Mavalankar, and S. Thomsen. 2013. "Inequity in India: the Case of Maternal and Reproductive Health." *Global Health Beyond 2015* 6 (19145). doi:10.3402/gha.v6i0.19145.

Sarfraz, M., and S. Hamid. 2014. "Challenges in Delivery of Skilled Maternal Care – Experiences of Community Midwives in Pakistan." *BMC Pregnancy and Childbirth* 14 (1): 59.

Saroha, E., M. Altarac, and L. M. Sibley. 2008. "Caste and Maternal Health Care Service Use among Rural Hindu Women in Maitha, Uttar Pradesh, India." *Journal of Midwifery and Women's Health* 53 (5): e41–7. doi:10.1016/j.jmwh.2008.05.002.

Schuler, S., S. Hashemi, and A. Riley. 1997. "The Influence of Changing Roles and Status in Bangladesh's Fertility Transition: Evidence from a Study of Credit Programs and Contraceptive Use." *World Development* 25 (4): 563–75.

Schurmann, A. T., and H. B. Johnston. 2007. "The Group-lending Model and Social Closure: Microcredit, Exclusion, and Health in Bangladesh." *Journal of Health, Population, and Nutrition* 27 (4): 518–27. ISSN 1606–0997.

Schwarz, D., R. Sharma, C. Bashyal, R. Schwarz, A. Baruwal, G. Karelas, B. Basnet, N. Khadka, J. Brady, Z. Silver, J. Mukherjee, J. Andrews, and D. Smith-Rohrberg Maru. 2014. "Strengthening Nepal's Female Community Health Volunteer Network: A Qualitative Study of Experiences at Two Years." *BMC Health Services Research* 14 (473). http://www.biomedcentral.com/1472-6963/14/473.

Scopaz, A., L. Eckermann, and M. Clarke. 2011. "Maternal Health in Lao PDR: Repositioning the Goal Posts." *Journal of the Asia Pacific Economy* 16 (4): 597–611.

Senanayake, H., M. Goonewardene, A. Ranatunga, R. Hattotuwa, S. Amarasekera, and I. Amarasinghe. 2011. "Achieving Millennium Development Goals 4 and 5 in Sri Lanka." *BJOG: An International Journal of Obstetrics and Gynecology* 118 (Suppl 2): 78–87. doi:10.1111/j.1471-0528.2011.03115.x.

Seneviratne, H. R., and L. C. Rajapaksa. 2000. "Safe Motherhood in Sri Lanka: A 100-year March." *International Journal of Gynaecology and Obstetrics: the Official Organ of the International Federation of Gynaecology and Obstetrics* 70: 113–24.

Seshadri, S. R., S. Parab, S. Kotte, N. Latha, and K. Subbiah. 2015. "Decentralization and Decision Space in the Health Sector: A Case Study from Karnataka, India." Health Policy Plan.

Shankar and Reddy. 2012. "Anaemia in Pregnancy Still a Major Cause of Morbidity and Mortality: Insights from Koppal District, Karnataka, India." *Reproductive Health Matters* 20 (40).

Sharma, S. 2005. *Formal and Informal Fees for Maternal Health Care Services in Five Countries: Policies, Practices, and Perspectives*. Washington, DC: USAID.

Sharma, S. K., Y. Sawangdee, and B. Sirirassamee. 2007. "Access to Health: Women's Status and Utilization of Maternal Health Services in Nepal." *Journal of Biosocial Science* 39 (5): 671–92.

Shefner-Rogers, C. L., and S. Sood. 2004. "Involving Husbands in Safe Motherhood: Effects of the SUAMI SIAGA Campaign in Indonesia." *Journal of Health Communication* 9 (3): 233–58. doi:10.1080/10810730490447075.

Sheikh, B., and J. Hatcher. 2004. "Health Seeking Behaviour and Health Service Utilization in Pakistan: Challenging the Policy Makers." *Journal of Public Health* 27 (1): 49–54. doi:10.1093/pubmed/fdh207.

Shiffman, J. 2007. "Generating Political Priority for Maternal Mortality Reduction in 5 Developing Countries." *American Journal of Public Health* 97 (5): 796.

Shiffman, J., and R. R. Ved. 2007. "The state of Political Priority for Safe Motherhood in India. *BJOG: an International Journal of Obstetrics and Gynaecology* 114: 785–90.

Shiffman, J., C. Stanton, and A. P. Salazar. 2004. "The Emergence of Political Priority for Safe Motherhood in Honduras." *Health Policy and Planning* 19: 380–90.

Shukla, A. 2012. "Community-Based Monitoring of Health Services in Maharashtra, India." www.sathicehat.org/uploads/CurrentProjects/CBM_Report_June10_ Final.pdf.

Sibley, L. M., T. A. Sipe, and D. Barry. 2012. "Traditional Birth Attendant Training for Improving Health Behaviours and Pregnancy Outcomes." *Cochrane Database of Systematic Reviews* 2012 (10): CD006759. http://onlinelibrary.wiley.com/enhanced /doi/10.1002/14651858.CD005460.pub3

Siddhivinayak, H. 2004. *Abortion Policy in India – Lacunae and Future Challenges*. Abortion Assessment Project India, Mumbai: CEHAT and Healthwatch.

Sikder, S. S., A. B. Labrique, H. Ali, A. A. Hanif, R. D. Klemm, S. Mehra, K. P. West, Jr., and P. Christine. 2015. "Availability of Emergency Obstetric Care (EmOC) among Public and Private Health Facilities in Rural Northwest Bangladesh." *BMC Public Health* 15 (36). doi:10.1186/s12889-015-1405-2.

Singh, D., M. Lample, and J. Earnest. 2014. "The Involvement of Men in Maternal Health Care: Cross-Sectional, Pilot Case Studies from Maligita and Kibibi, Uganda." *Reproductive Health* 11 (68). doi:10.1186/1742-4755-11-68.

Singh, K. K., S. S. Bloom, and A. O. Tsui. 1998. "Husbands' Reproductive Health Knowledge, Attitudes, and Behaviour in Uttar Pradesh, India." *Studies in Family Planning* 29 (4): 388–99.

Singhal, A., D. Sharma, M. Papa, and K. Witte. 2003. "Air Cover and Ground Mobilization: Integrating Entertainment-Education Broadcasts with Community Service Delivery in India. In *Entertainment-Education and Social Change: History, Research, and Practice*, edited by A. Singhal, M. J. Cody, E. M. Rogers, and M. Sabido, 351–376. New York: Routledge.

Skoufias, E., and B. McClafferty. 2001. "Is PROGRESA Working? Summary of the Results of an Evaluation by IFPRI." FCND Discussion Paper 118, International Food Policy Research Institute, Washington, DC.

Soubeiga, D., L. Gauvin, M. A. Hatem, and M. Johri. 2014. "Birth Preparedness and Complication Readiness (BPCR) Interventions to Reduce Maternal and Neonatal Mortality in Developing Countries: Systematic Review and Meta-analysis." *BMC Pregnancy and Childbirth* 14 (April): 129. http://search.proquest.com/professional/docview/1513691086?accountid=41588.

Speizer, I. S., P. Lance, R. Verma, and A. Benson. 2015. "Descriptive Study of the Role of Household Type and Household Composition on Women's Reproductive Health Outcomes in Urban Uttar Pradesh, India." *Reproductive Health* 12 (4). doi:10.1186/1742-4755-12-4.

Speakman, E. M., A. Shafi, E. Sondorp, N. Atta, and N. Howard. 2014. "Development of the Community Midwifery Education Initiative and its Influence on Women's Health and Empowerment in Afghanistan: A Case Study." *BMC Women's Health* 14 (1): 111.

Storey, D., M. Boulay, Y. Karki, K. Heckert, and D. M. Karmacha. 1999. "Impact of the Integrated Radio Communication Project in Nepal, 1994–1997." *Journal of Health Communication* 4 (4): 27–94. doi:10.1080/108107399126823.

Stover, J., and J. Ross. 2010. "How Increased Contraceptive Use has Reduced Maternal Mortality." *Maternal and Child Health Journal* 14 (5): 687–95. http://www.healthpolicyinitiative.com/Publications/Documents/668_1_TMIH_FINAL_12_19_08.pdf.

Sutcliffe, K., J. Caird, J. Kavanagh, R. Rees, K. Oliver, K. Dickson, J. Woodman, E. Barnett-Paige, and J. Thomas. 2013. "Comparing Midwife-led and Doctor-led Maternity Care: A Systematic Review of Reviews." *Journal of Advanced Nursing* 68 (11): 2376–86. http://search.proquest.com/professional/docview/993820377?accountid=41588.

Tey, N. P., and S. Lai. 2013. "Correlates of and Barriers to the Utilization of Health Services for Delivery in South Asia and Sub-Saharan Africa." *The Scientific World Journal* 423403. doi:10.1155/2013/423403.

Thaddeus, S., and D. Maine. 1994. "Too Far to Walk: Maternal Mortality in Context." *Social Science and Medicine* 38 (8): 1091–110.

Thapa, S., S. K. Sharma, and N. Khatiwada. 2014. "Women's Knowledge of Abortion Law and Availability of Services in Nepal." *Journal of Biosocial Science* 46: 266–77.

Thomsen, S., D. T. Hoa, M. Målqvist, L. Sanneving, D. Saxena, S. Tana, B. Yuan, and P. Byass. 2011. "Promoting Equity to Achieve Maternal and Child Health." *Reproductive Health Matters* 19 (38): 176–82.

Torgay, T., T. Dorji, D. Pelzom, and R. V. Gibbons. 2011. "Progress and Delivery of Health Care in Bhutan, the Land of the Thunder Dragon and Gross National Happiness." *Tropical Medicine and International Health* 16 (6): 731–36. doi:10.111/j.1365-3156 .2011.02760.x.

Tripathy, P., N. Nair, S. Barnett, R. Mahapatra, J. Borghi, S. Rath, R. Gope, D. Mahto, R. Sinha, R. Lakshminarayana, V. Patel, C. Pagel, A. Prost, and A. Costello. 2010. "Effect of a Participatory Intervention with Women's Groups on Birth Outcomes and Maternal Depression in Jharkhand and Orissa, India: A Cluster-randomised Controlled Trial." *The Lancet* 375 (9721): 1182–92.

Turkmani, S., and F. Gohar. 2015. "Community Based Skilled Birth Attendants Programme in Bangladesh; Intervention towards Improving Maternal Health." *Journal of Asian Midwives* 1 (2): 17–29.

UNESCO (United Nations Educational, Scientific, and Cultural Organization). 2014. *Institute for Statistics*. New York: United Nations. http://stats.uis.unesco.org/unesco /TableViewer/document.aspx?ReportId=121&IF_Language=eng&BR_Country=500.

UN Population Fund. 2009. "Bolivia: Training Midwives to Treat Indigenous Mothers with Respect." May 3. http://www.friendsofunfpa.org/netcommunity/page.aspx?pid=862.

UNICEF, State of the World's Children 2009: *Maternal and Newborn Health. Figure 1.7*. http://www.unicef.org/sowc09/docs/SOWC09-Figure-1.7-EN.pdf.

UN (United Nations). 2015a. "Population and Vital Statistics Report." *Statistical Papers* LXVII (Series A). http://unstats.un.org/unsd/demographic/products/vitstats/Sets /Series_A_2015.pdf.

———. 2015b. *Draft Outcome Document of the United Nations Summit for the Adoption of the Post-2015 Development Agenda*. New York, USA: United Nations. http://www.un .org/ga/search/view_doc.asp?symbol=A/69/L.85&Lang=E.

———. 2015c. *Outcome Document of the Third International Conference on Financing for Development: Addis Ababa Action Agenda*. Addis Ababa, Ethiopia: United Nations. http://www.un.org/ga/search/view_doc.asp?symbol=A/CONF.227/L.1.

United Nations Secretariat Division for the Advancement of Women. 2008. "The Role of Men and Boys in Achieving Gender Equality." Women 2000 and Beyond: Published to Promote the Goals of the Beijing Declaration and the Platform for Action, United Nations, New York, December 2008.

USAID. 2007. *An Analytical Report on National Survey of Female Community Health Volunteers of Nepal*. Washington, DC: USAID. https://www.dhsprogram.com/pubs /pdf/FR181/FCHV_Nepal2007.pdf.

———. 2009. *Rwanda Twubakane Decentralization Programme & USAID. Good Governance and Health: Assessing Progress in Rwanda*. Washington DC: USAID.

———. 2011. "Training Midwives to Care for the Mothers of South Sudan." May 19. http://reliefweb.int/report/sudan/training-midwives-care-mothers-south-sudan.

———. 2012. "The Community Midwives Program in Pakistan" Research and Development Solutions Policy Briefs Series No. 20. http://www.resdev.org/files/policy_brief/20/20.pdf.

———. 2013. *DELIVER PROJECT: In Pakistan, Evidence-Based Modeling Suggests Improved Maternal and Child Health Through Increased Access to Family Planning Commodities.* http://deliver.jsi.com/dlvr_content/resources/allpubs/logisticsbriefs/PakiEvidBaseMode.pdf.

Van Lerberghe, W., Z. Matthews, E. Achadi, C. Ancona, J. Campbell, A. Channon, L. de Bernis, V. De Brouwere, V. Fauveau, H. Fogstad, M. Koblinsky, J. Liljestrand, A. Mechbal, S. F. Murray, T. Rathavay, H. Rehr, F. Richard, P. ten Hoope-Bender, and S. Turkmani. 2014. "Country Experience with Strengthening of Health Systems and Deployment of Midwives in Countries with High Maternal Mortality." *The Lancet* 384: 1215–25.

van Lonkhuijzen L., J. Stekelenburg, and J. van Roosmalen. 2012. "Maternity Waiting Facilities for Improving Maternal and Neonatal Outcome in Low-resource Countries." *Cochrane Database of Systematic Reviews* (10): CD006759. http://onlinelibrary.wiley.com/enhanced/doi/10.1002/14651858.CD006759.pub3.

Varkey, L. C., A. Mishra, and M. E. Khan. 2008. *Creating the Conditions for Scale-Up of the Men in Maternity Intervention in India.* Washington, DC: USAID.

Victora, C. G., E. M. Aquino, M. do Carmo Leal, C. A. Monteiro, F. C. Barros, and C. L. Szwarcwald. 2011. "Maternal and Child Health in Brazil: Progress and Challenges." *The Lancet* 377: 1863–76.

Vieira, C., A. Portela, T. Miller, E. Coast, T. Leone, and C. Marston. 2012. "Increasing the Use of Skilled Health Personnel where Traditional Birth Attendants were Providers of Childbirth Care: A Systematic Review." *PLoS One* 7 (10): e47946. http://search.proquest.com/professional/docview/1229501268?accountid=41588.

Vijaykumar, S. 2008. "Communicating Safe Motherhood: Strategic Messaging in a Globalized World." *Marriage and Family Review* 44 (2–3). doi:10.1080/01494920802177378.

Vlassoff, M., A. Hossain, I. Maddow-Zimet, S. Singh, and H. U. Bhuiyan. 2012. *Menstrual Regulation and Post-abortion Care in Bangladesh: Factors Associated with Access to and Quality of Services.* New York: Guttmacher Institute.

Vora, K. S., D. V. Mavalankar, K. V. Ramani, M. Upadhyaya, B. Sharma, S. Iyengar, V. Gupta, and K. Iyengar. 2009. "Maternal Health Situation in India: A Case Study." *Journal of Health Population and Nutrition* 27 (2): 184–201. doi:10.3329/jhpn.v27i2.3363.

Wagstaff, A., and M. Claeson. 2004. *The Millennium Development Goals for Health: Rising to the Challenges.* Washington, DC: The World Bank.

Wakefield, M. A., M. Loken, and R. C. Hornik. 2010. "Use of Mass Media Campaigns to Change Health Behaviour." *The Lancet* 376 (9748): 1261–71. doi:10.1016/S0140-6736(10)60809-4.

Wang, H., R. K. Juyal, S. A. Miner, and E. Fischer. 2012. *Performance-Based Payment System for ASHAs in India: What does International Experience Tell Us?* Bethesda, MD: The Vistaar Project, IntraHealth International Inc., Abt Associates Inc.

Westoff, C. F., and D. Koffman. 2011. "The Association of Television and Radio with Reproductive Behaviour." *Population and Development Review* 37 (4): 749–59.

Whitworth, M., and T. Dowswell. 2009. "Routine Pre-pregnancy Health Promotion for Improving Pregnancy Outcomes." *Cochrane Database of Systematic Reviews* (4):

CD007536. http://onlinelibrary.wiley.com/enhanced/doi/10.1002/14651858.CD007536.pub2.

WHO (World Health Organization). 2001. "Programming for Male Involvement in Reproductive Health." Report of the Meeting of WHO Regional Advisers in Reproductive Health WHO/PAHO, WHO, Geneva, September 5–7. https://extranet.who.int/iris/restricted/bitstream/10665/67409/1/WHO_FCH_RHR_02.3.pdf.

———. 2005. *Improving Maternal, Newborn and Child Health in the South-East Asia Region*. New Delhi: WHO.

———. 2006. *Working Together for Health*. Geneva: WHO.

———. 2007. *Everybody's Business: Strengthening Health Systems to Improve Health Outcomes. WHO's Framework for Action*. Geneva: WHO.

———. 2008. *Worldwide Prevalence of Anaemia 1993–2005: WHO Global Database on Anaemia*. Geneva: WHO. http://whqlibdoc.who.int/publications/2008/9789241596657_eng.pdf.

———. 2010a. *The World Health Report – Health Systems Financing: The Path to Universal Coverage*. Geneva: WHO.

———. 2010b. *Monitoring the Building Blocks of Health Systems: A Handbook of Indicators and Their Measurement Strategies*.

———. 2010c. *National Health Accounts Series*. http://apps.who.int/nha/database/World_Map/Index/en.

———. 2012. *Health Systems Financing: The Path to Universal Coverage Plan of Action*. Geneva, Switzerland: WHO. http://www.who.int/health_financing/Health_Systems_Financing_Plan_Action.pdf.

———. 2014. *World Health Statistics 2014*. Geneva: WHO.

———. Global Health Observatory. 2015. *Health Expenditure Ratios by Country*. http://apps.who.int/gho/data/node.main.

WHO, UNICEF, UNFPA, the World Bank, and the UN. 2014. *Trends in Maternal Mortality: 1990 to 2013*. Estimates by WHO, UNICEF, UNFPA, The World Bank, and the United Nations Population Division. Geneva: WHO.

Wilson, A., S. Hillman, M. Rosato, J. Skelton, A. Costello, J. Hussein, C. MacArthur, and A. Coomarasamy. 2013. "A Systematic Review and Thematic Synthesis of Qualitative Studies on Maternal Emergency Transport in Low- and Middle-income Countries." *International Journal of Gynaecology and Obstetrics: the official organ of the International Federation of Gynaecology and Obstetrics* 122 (3): 192–201. http://search.proquest.com/professional/docview/1372283410?accountid=41588.

Wilson, R., K. Kade, A. Weaver, A. de Lorenzi, B. Yeager, S. Patel, K. Ahmed, D. Ambruster, and J. Bergeson-Lockwood. 2012. "Medicines for Maternal Health: Key Data and Findings." Prepared for the United Nations Commission on Commodities for Women and Children's Health. UNFPA, New York, February. http://www.unfpa.org/sites/default/files/pub-pdf/Key%20Data%20and%20Findings%20Maternal%20Health%20Medicines-FINAL.pdf.

Witter, S., T. Ensor, M. Jowett, and R. Thompson. 2000. *Health Economics for Developing Countries: A Practical Guide*. Oxford, UK: Macmillan Education.

World Bank. "Some Key Statistics on Youth in South Asia"(accessed in 2015), http://go.worldbank.org/7QM6YCSW00.

World Bank (accessed in 2015). http://data.worldbank.org/about/country-and-lending-groups.

———. 2008. *Global Monitoring Report 2008: MDGs and the Environment, Agenda for Inclusive and Sustainable Development.* Washington, DC: World Bank. http://siteresources.worldbank.org/INTGLOMONREP2008/Resources/4737994-1207342962709/8944_Web_PDF.pdf.

———. 2009. *IDA at Work: Bangladesh Stipends Triple Girls Access to School.* http://go.worldbank.org/RRBXNQ0NX0.

———. 2010. *Bangladesh Health Sector Profile 2010.* Washington, DC: World Bank. http://documents.worldbank.org/curated/en/2010/01/16270661/bangladesh-health-sector-profile-2010.

———. 2013a. *World Development Indicators 2013.* Washington, DC: World Bank. doi:10.1596/978-0-8213-9824-1.

———. 2013b. "Implementation Completion and Results Report for the Bangladesh Rural Transport Improvement Project." ICR 2480, February.

———. 2014a. World Development Indicators 2014 (accessed on April 1, 2014). http://data.worldbank.org/).

———. 2014b. *The Export Opportunity.* (Fall). Washington, DC: World Bank. http://www.worldbank.org/content/dam/Worldbank/document/SAR/south-asia-economic-focus-export-opportunity.pdf.

———. 2015a. World Development Indicators 2015 (accessed on October 1, 2015). http://data.worldbank.org/).

———. 2015b. *Publication Series: Maternal and Reproductive Health in South Asia.* http://www.worldbank.org/en/topic/reproductivematernalchildhealth/publication/publication-series-maternal-reproductive-health-in-south-asia.

———. 2015c. *Business Plan: Global Financing Facility in Support of Every Woman and Every Child.* Washington, DC USA: World Bank. http://www.worldbank.org/content/dam/Worldbank/document/HDN/Health/Business%20Plan%20for%20the%20GFF,%20final.pdf.

Yargawa, J., and J. Leonardi-Bee. 2015. "Male Involvement and Maternal Health Outcomes: Systematic Review and Meta-analysis." *Journal of Epidemiology and Community Health* 0: 1–9. http://search.proquest.com/professional/docview/1657758921?accountid=41588.

You, F., K. Huo, R. Wang, D. Xu, J. Deng, Y. Wei, F. Shi, H. Liu, G. Cheng, Z. Zhang, P. Yang, T. Sun, X. Wang, B. Jacobsson, and C. Zhu. 2012. "Maternal Mortality in Henan Province, China: Changes between 1996 and 2009." *PloS One* 7: e47153.

Yuan, B., M. Malqvist, N. Trygg, X. Qian, N. Ng, and S. Thomsen. 2014. "What Interventions are Effective on Reducing Inequalities in Maternal and Child Health in Low- and Middle-income Settings? A Systematic Review." *BMC Public Health* 14: 634. http://search.proquest.com/professional/docview/1539370115?accountid=41588.

Zamawe, C., M. Banda, and A. Dube. 2015. "The Effect of Mass Media Campaign on Men's Participation in Maternal Health: A Cross-Sectoral Study in Malawi." *Reproductive Health* 12 (31). doi:10.1186/s12978-015-0020-0.

Zere, E., P. Tumusiime, O. Walker, J. Kirigia, C. Mwikisa, and T. Mbeeli. 2010. "Inequities in Utilization of Maternal Health Interventions in Namibia: Implications for Progress towards MDG 5 Targets." *International Journal for Equity in Health* 9 (16).

Environmental Benefits Statement

The World Bank Group is committed to reducing its environmental footprint. In support of this commitment, we leverage electronic publishing options and print-on-demand technology, which is located in regional hubs worldwide. Together, these initiatives enable print runs to be lowered and shipping distances decreased, resulting in reduced paper consumption, chemical use, greenhouse gas emissions, and waste.

We follow the recommended standards for paper use set by the Green Press Initiative. The majority of our books are printed on Forest Stewardship Council (FSC)–certified paper, with nearly all containing 50–100 percent recycled content. The recycled fiber in our book paper is either unbleached or bleached using totally chlorine-free (TCF), processed chlorine-free (PCF), or enhanced elemental chlorine-free (EECF) processes.

More information about the Bank's environmental philosophy can be found at http://www.worldbank.org/corporateresponsibility.

http://dx.doi.org/10.1596/978-1-4648-0963-7